THE PHILOSOPHICAL INFLUENCES OF MAO ZEDONG

CONTENTS

Foreword xi
Preface xv
Acknowledgements xxii

1 Introduction to the Philosophical Mao 1

    The Good and the Bad Mao 1
    Traditional Western, Traditional Chinese Philosophy and Mao 6
    Mao's Individual Thought versus the Official Philosophy of Mao 7
    The pre-Marxist Mao and its Continued Influence 12
    The Place of Frederick Paulsen's *A System of Ethics* in Mao's Thought 14
    Mao and Confucianism: A Preview 16
    The Influence of Philosophy on Mao's Thinking 17

2 Mao's Youthful Philosophical Development 21

    The Influence of both Western Philosophy and Chinese Philosophy 21
    Mao's Introduction to Western Philosophy and the Ideas of the West 25

3 Mao in the Margins: Mao's Philosophy of Egoism 35

    The Influence of Paulsen's *A System of Ethics* 35
    The Significance of 'Mao in the Margins' 36
    Paulsen's, *A System of Ethics* 38
    The Continuity of Mao's Thought 38
    Mao's Views on Ethics 39
    The Idea of the Great Man and the Primacy of the Will 39
    Mao Collapses Moral Instinct into the Instinct for Self-preservation 40
    Mao on Aristotle and Confucius: A Prelude 44
    Mao on Schopenhauer 45

Mao on Buddhism and Mohism 46
Mao's Individualism 47
Mao and Zhuangzi 49
Synopsizing Mao's Views of Egoism and Ethics from
    his Marginal Notes 50
The Egoism–Altruism Conundrum 50
Mao on Aesthetics and Ethics 56
Mao on Good and Evil 62
Synopsizing Mao's Views on Individualism and Society from his
    Marginal Notes 63

4 Mao's Early Philosophical Influences and Reflections 65

Confucian and Aristotelian Influences 65
The Impact of Aristotle's Ethics on Mao 66
Aristotle and Confucius 67
Mao and Mencius 68
Confucius's Idea of the Self 69
Mao's Interpretation of Confucius 70
Mao and Confucianism: Universal Love versus Familial Love 71
Confucius's Central Ethical Principle 73
Filial Piety 74
Mao and Confucianism 75
Mao and Mencius 77
Mao on Following One's Impulses 79
Mao's Key Interpretation of Mencius 80
Mao's Philosophy of Egoism and his Early Metaphysics 82
Mao's Early Metaphysics 83
The Question of Suicide 85
Mao Does Not Subscribe to Absolute Evil 85
Mao as an Existentialist 86
Mao on Happiness and Virtue 88
Mao and Nietzsche 88
The Child is the Father of the Man 92
Mao and Zhuangzi 93

For my spouse, Irèné, who has always been my muse, whose companionship, incisive intellect and fierce passion has infused this passing life with glamour and dignity and for Irene Eber, in memoriam, a dear friend, fellow scholarly partner and lifelong savant of Chinese studies.

Winter Clouds[1]

Fluttering snow weighs down the winter clouds.
All flowers have wilted.
Up in the sky cold currents flow;
On the ground warmth still breathes.
Alone, a hero drives away tigers and leopards,
The brave have no fear of bears.
The plum tree welcomes a snowy sky,
Caring nothing for the flies frozen to death.

COMPOSED ON HIS 69TH BIRTHDAY
26TH DECEMBER 1962

THE PHILOSOPHICAL INFLUENCES OF MAO ZEDONG

Notations, Reflections And Insights

ROBERT ELLIOTT ALLINSON

BLOOMSBURY ACADEMIC
LONDON • NEW YORK • OXFORD • NEW DELHI • SYDNEY

BLOOMSBURY ACADEMIC
Bloomsbury Publishing Plc
50 Bedford Square, London, WC1B 3DP, UK
1385 Broadway, New York, NY 10018, USA

BLOOMSBURY, BLOOMSBURY ACADEMIC and the Diana logo are
trademarks of Bloomsbury Publishing Plc

First published in Great Britain 2020

Copyright © Robert Elliott Allinson, 2020

Robert Elliott Allinson has asserted his right under the Copyright, Designs and
Patents Act, 1988, to be identified as Author of this work.

For legal purposes the Acknowledgements on p. xxii constitute an
extension of this copyright page.

Cover design: Eleanor Rose
Cover image: Portrait of Mao Zedong (Mao Tse-tung) (1893–1976).
© Chronicle/Alamy

All rights reserved. No part of this publication may be reproduced or
transmitted in any form or by any means, electronic or mechanical, including
photocopying, recording, or any information storage or retrieval system,
without prior permission in writing from the publishers.

Bloomsbury Publishing Plc does not have any control over, or responsibility for,
any third-party websites referred to or in this book. All internet addresses given
in this book were correct at the time of going to press. The author and publisher
regret any inconvenience caused if addresses have changed or sites have ceased
to exist, but can accept no responsibility for any such changes.

A catalogue record for this book is available from the British Library.

A catalog record for this book is available from the Library of Congress.

ISBN:	HB:	978-1-3500-5986-3
	PB:	978-1-3500-5985-6
	ePDF:	978-1-3500-5988-7
	eBook:	978-1-3500-5987-0

Typeset by Integra Software services Pvt. Ltd.
Printed and bound in Great Britain

To find out more about our authors and books visit www.bloomsbury.com
and sign up for our newsletters.

5 The Blend of the Influence of Chinese and Western Philosophy on Mao's Thought and Parallels in China's Social and Economic Development   97

   Mao on Confucianism and Paulsen's Voluntarism   97
   Mao and the *Yijing*   99
   Mao's Departure from the Classical Chinese Philosophical Tradition   103
   The Influence of Laozi's Notorious Chapter Nineteen on Mao's Cultural Revolution   104
   Mao and Hobbes   106
   Mao and Locke   107
   Mao and Marxism   108
   The Hegelian Dialectic   109
   Mao's Dialectical Thinking   110
   Flashback to the Beginnings of Mao's Thought   111
   The Confucian Revival and the Dialectic   117

6 Mao's Marxist Thought and the *Yijing*   121

   Non-antagonistic and Antagonistic Contradictions   135
   Mao on Endless Struggle   136
   The Principal and the Secondary Aspects of Contradiction   138
   Is Mao Influenced by Soviet Sources?   141
   The Superstructure and the Base: Mao's Inversion of Classical Marxism   142
   What if Other Scholars Wrote the Works Attributed to Mao?   148

7 Mao as Metaphysician and *Literatus*   151

   Mao as Metaphysician and Philosopher of Science   151
   Is Mao a Western or a Chinese Philosopher?   161
   Mao as *Literatus*   162

8 Mao's Contributions to Philosophy   169

   Mao's Philosophical Contributions to Marxism   169
   Mao's Reduction of All Laws of Dialectics to One   171
   Mao's Philosophical Contributions to Philosophy Proper   176

The Primacy of the Will 176
Mao's Deviation from Confucius 179
Mao's Notion of Continuous Struggle without Resolution 180
Theory and Practice 182
Mao and Heracleitus 185
Mao's Use of Complementary rather than Contradictory Opposites 185

Notes 189
Selected List of References 218
Index 226

FOREWORD

This is a ground-breaking work. It is Professor Allinson's great observation that both Chinese and Western philosophical traditions nourished Mao. In short, Professor Allinson takes seriously the philosophical background. His distinguished career as a comparative philosopher, including nearly three decades as a philosophy professor of both Western and Chinese philosophy at The Chinese University of Hong Kong, and his numerous books, chapters and articles on both Chinese and Western philosophy make him uniquely qualified to undertake the task of elucidating Mao's philosophical thinking.

This is a most exciting and fascinating enterprise. To consider the thought of Mao Zedong most readers point to the important role Marxist ideas had. Few are concerned with early or non-Marxist portions acquired in reading, or appropriated from teachers in his school years. Robert Elliott Allinson changes this stereotypical picture completely by introducing the reader to Mao's 'philosophical journey' as the author so aptly states it. This journey consisted in acquiring basic aspects of Chinese thought and adding to these Western philosophical ideas. Throughout this work, Professor Allinson argues that Mao's understanding of Western philosophical ideas occurred by means of Chinese philosophical assumptions. Therefore, any approach to Mao's thought must consider both the Chinese and Western strands. This is not to imply that there is a connection here to the later disastrous and tragic policies of Mao's rule. The concern of the author of this volume was to reveal the complexities of Mao's philosophical assumptions. Professor Allinson's detailed and comprehensive examination of Mao's philosophical background and training uncovers the sources of the philosophical assumptions that were to mould the thought processes of this enigmatic figure who was to exert such an immense influence on China.

That the 24-year-old Mao read a book about Western philosophers and their ideas in 1917 is not otherwise surprising. Not only was it a period of revolutionary ferment in China leading to the May Fourth Movement, it was a time of heightened intellectual interest in many aspects of Western thought. That Mao, however, wrote notes in the margins of works he read, recording his reactions to the reading, is truly remarkable. Due to these marginal notes readers today can begin to discern the Chinese philosophical background Mao brought to his reading of Western thought and, above and beyond that, how he interpreted what he read. Professor Allinson is to be congratulated for both bringing to the forefront and making a close study of Mao's typically neglected pre-Marxist works. Although the later Mao was definitely not fond of the ideas of Confucius or Confucianism, the pre-Marxist as well as occasionally even the post-Marxist Mao reveals that China's classical heritage had a role in his thought. Old literary forms should not be dispensed with and abandoned, he wrote, they must be reinterpreted and reformulated and should continue in use. Allinson's argument is that Mao's foundation of traditional thought was highly significant for it was on this basis that Mao was able to reflect on Western philosophy. Indeed, it was this background that enabled Mao's Sinicization of Marxism and thereby his unique formulation of Marxism. Professor Allinson demonstrates the influence of the *Yijing* on successive stages of Mao's thought with convincing mastery. Professor Allinson's expertise in both Chinese and Western philosophy makes this analysis possible.

Which works by Western philosophers were available to Mao in Chinese translation one hundred years ago? Here is the author's significant discovery. Mao's reading did not consist of the actual philosophical works of important Western men, but about their ideas. The work which he read and in which he made his copious marginal notes was by Friedrich Paulsen (1846–1908), who had been Professor of Moral Philosophy at the University of Berlin. In Paulsen's *A System of Ethics* (1899) Mao was able to find the ideas of Immanuel Kant (1724–1804) or Friedrich Nietzsche (1844–1900) and accept or reject them.

Mao read Paulsen's book in the Chinese translation by Cai Yuanpei (1868–1940), the noted intellectual of the early Republican period. Cai had prepared the Chinese translation from an earlier Japanese translation. The fact that Mao read a twice translated work cannot be sufficiently emphasized. Translations are unique because they are an interpretative literary form, both identical with and different from the original. Above all a translator must create a reader-oriented work and a translator must participate in the concerns of his/her own culture to do so. Mao's response is, therefore, in large measure a response to more than one interpretation. Mao's reading of Paulsen's book is the result of not only several translations, but also of several interpretations. His marginal notes have resulted from the interpretation of Chinese classical writings he had brought along to the reading of Paulsen.

We must take notice of the important issue raised by Professor Allinson in his work, Mao's background of studies in the *Yijing* or *Book of Changes*. The *Yijing*, whatever its shape or content may have been at one time, is among China's oldest written works. Without exaggeration, one might say that it contains today the wisdom of the ages. Generations of Chinese philosophers have resorted to it for ideas or have sought to resolve by its means quandaries. It is the last feature that has brought the book to Western attention for soothsaying purposes.

The basic assumption of the *Yijing* is that everything is in a constant state of change where absolutisms do not exist. Change occurs as the constant and continuous alternation between yin and yang, the two basic aspects of existence. Equivalence of these two, or their equitable harmony, is never reached because when approaching such a state, the process is reversed and begins anew.

The end of the process of change is, therefore, not the resolution of contradictions, a synthesis as it were, but its continuation and assumption of new forms. In accordance with the *Yijing*'s basic assumption, Mao Zedong, according to Professor Allinson, abandons the concept of resolving contradictions and arriving at a synthesis.

Clearly, more attention must be devoted to Chinese classical foundations of thought in order to understand better how they interact with Western thought. Foundations laid at an early age do not disappear without a trace at a later time. Professor Allinson's connecting Mao's thought with the *Yijing* [*Book of Changes*] is a new and fascinating departure. I very much like his daring conclusion of a Maoist Confucianism. It is certainly important that his work which is a *tour de force* of constructive thought, breadth and depth of scholarship reach as wide an audience as possible. It is a major contribution to Mao studies as well as a magnificent statement on behalf of East–West philosophy.

Irene Eber

Former Director and Louis Frieberg Professor Emerita of Chinese History
and Philosophy, The Louis Frieberg Center for East Asian Studies
The Hebrew University of Jerusalem
Israel

Senior Fellow Harry S. Truman
Research Institute for the Advancement of Peace
The Hebrew University of Jerusalem
Israel

PREFACE

There is, for some, a surprising figure who is of considerable consequence to Chinese thought, namely Mao Zedong. The noted scholar of Chinese intellectual history, Herlee G. Creel, includes Mao in the very title of his seminal book, *Chinese Thought from Confucius to Mao Tse Tung*.[2] The distinguished historian of China, Frederick Wakeman, Jr. devotes an entire book to the analysis of Mao's philosophy and also includes Mao's philosophy in the title of his striking work, *History and Will, Philosophical Perspectives of Mao Tse-tung's Thought*.[3] Arguably the most eminent Chinese philosopher in the United States, Wing-tsit Chan, wrote that 'Philosophy in Communist China can be summed up in one word, "Maoism."'[4] Why do scholars of this high reputation and authoritative status in the field of Chinese thought consider that Mao's philosophical thinking is of such great significance and requires this deep a level of study?

While Mao is not a philosopher in the usual sense, he formally studied philosophy in college and as a result of his studies, he theorized and wrote philosophical essays. His actions were based upon his theoretical analyses and conclusions. His ideas played an extraordinary role in influencing the history of China in the twentieth century. Mao cast a larger-than-life imprint on the present century and millions of his fellow country persons, and was one of the most significant leaders of the twentieth century. Now that there has been an extensive revival of Confucianism in present-day China, it is time to re-examine the thought of the man who banned this thinking and ushered in a period of anti-intellectualism in the dark period of China's history known as the Cultural Revolution.[5] This volume is designed to demonstrate to the English-reading public that Mao's ideas were not only political, but that he had an early interest in philosophy that was to remain influential for his thinking over the course of his lifetime.

A true scholar has no axe to grind. One should not confine one's reading of Mao to his later, Marxist writings. One should read Mao's early writings because they reflect his early thinking, a thinking that preceded any wish or need to propagate political aims. By examining his early works, we see into the child's mind of Mao; we see the pure Mao. We can see how Mao both amalgamated and withdrew from traditional Confucianism. We can see how Confucianism, after Mao, was ushered in again. We can see how Mao's mind was formed prior to any real exposure to Marxism. This is access to the pure (non-Marxist) Mao. This is access to the Chinese mind as it is also exposed to Western intellectual influences.

That social and economic development in China in turn followed the dialectical twists and turns of Mao's thought process, is fascinating. Was it pure coincidence that there was such a parallel development? It would be difficult to sort out an answer to this question. However, it is not so important. What is important is that by studying the course of Mao's thought development, we can gain a particularly special insight into how and why China developed in the twentieth and into the twenty-first century. We can see how Confucianism, Daoism and Hegelianism are all valuable elements in understanding China's social and economic development.

It does not matter if Mao were conscious of his influence on Chinese history or if this concatenation with history were merely empirically coincidental. What is important is that Chinese history can be understood by studying relevant Chinese philosophy. In this case, Chinese philosophy is already permeated by Western influences. This is of no moment. It is not a story of Chinese philosophy versus Western philosophy. It is a story of the value of the analysis of philosophical development to the understanding of the stages of the growth and/or decline of a culture and a civilization. Mao's mind, when examined in its early, pure stages, through the process of its development into his mature thought is a prism through which we can see and understand the enigma that is China.

Ariadne's Thread: The Contrapuntal Structure of the Volume

The main theme of this volume is to show the influence of both Chinese and Western philosophy on Mao's philosophical development and to share with the reader Mao's own philosophical reflections which reveal the penetrating influence of his philosophical education. A second theme of this work is the analysis of the social and political changes in China with special regard to the rise of Confucianism in contemporary China and in what way parallels with the early Mao's interpretation of Confucianism can be noted. The order of the chapters and discussions within the chapters reflect a yin-yang movement between these two concerns. The principal aspect of this contradiction, to utilize Mao's famous contribution to Marxist thought, is the study of the thought development of Mao Zedong; the secondary aspect of the contradiction is the observation of the reflection of Mao's contradictory thought in the contradictions that form the dynamism of contemporary Chinese society.

The order of the chapters and the inner content of the chapters reflect the development of two themes similar to contrapuntal movements in a musical composition. The first chapter introduces Mao as a philosopher; the second chapter flashes back to the early philosophical development of Mao; the third chapter delves into the making of Mao into a pre-Marxist philosopher and his commentaries on the book of philosophy that was to exert such enormous influence over his later philosophical development; the fourth chapter analyses the influence of both Eastern and Western philosophers on Mao's early thinking; the fifth chapter explores the blend of Eastern and Western philosophy that characterizes Mao's unique philosophy while at the same time noting the parallels in China's social and political development. The sixth chapter returns to more pure philosophical discussions and focuses on the Mao's contributions to Marxist philosophy and the nature of the influences of the *Yijing* on Mao's thinking. The seventh chapter connects the early, middle and later philosophical Mao by weaving back and forth between theoretical discussions of Confucianism, Hegelianism and Marxism and the discussion of the relationship of Mao's thought to changes that were to take place in China after his passing. The seventh chapter includes a pure philosophical investigation of Mao's speculations about the nature of the universe and displays both the connection of Mao's mature thought to his early philosophizing and the creativity and curiosity that characterized Mao's philosophical thinking. The seventh chapter discusses Mao's artistic and literary gifts and shows how the later Mao continues his study of the Chinese Classics. The seventh chapter brings the two themes of the volume together by specifying the role of these classics in influencing Mao's political philosophy. The eighth chapter recounts Mao's philosophical contributions and innovations both to Marxist philosophy and to philosophy proper.

A Synopsis of the Content of each of the Chapters of this Work

Chapter One, Introduction to the Philosophical Mao, presents Mao as a philosopher. This chapter concerns itself with the distinctions between the classifications of Mao from the official Marxist standpoint from the individual philosophy of Mao. The reader, who prefers to immediately immerse herself or himself in the individual philosophy of Mao, may initially skip over this chapter and commence reading this volume with Chapter Two.

Chapter One sharply distinguishes Mao as a philosopher from Mao as a politician. This distinction is based upon the distinction between philosophy proper and ideology. Philosophy proper does not have an axe to grind. Its analysis does not contain the intention of serving the cause of propaganda. Ideology, on the other hand, advocates a position and takes a definite political stand.

Chapter Two, Mao's Youthful Philosophical Development, sets the stage for what is to follow. Mao's philosophical foundation is made up of both Western and Chinese sources. This chapter discusses the syllabi of the philosophy courses in which he was a student that cover both Chinese and Western philosophers and thus seed his mind with a comparative philosophical outlook. We can see how this openness to integrative philosophical thinking creates Mao's philosophical thinking throughout his life and adumbrates the breakthrough meeting with Nixon that marks the culmination of Mao's East–West thinking.

Chapter Three, Mao in the Margins, is key to understanding the young Mao's pre-Marxist philosophical thinking. The chapter title alludes to Mao's writing in the margins of one of the most influential texts on Mao's thinking, the nineteenth-century German philosopher, Friedrich Paulsen's *A System of Ethics*. Mao's writing in the margins not only reflects his agreements and disagreements with Paulsen's philosophical points, but reveals early on Mao's philosophical talent for his own constructive thought. What is more is that in these marginal notes Mao shows his capacity both for close reading of a philosophical text and the fact that he does not simply accept the philosophical points raised, but shows a capacity for a keen critical reflection upon them. What is especially interesting about these marginal writings of Mao is that from these notes one can see the beginnings of Mao's Philosophy of Egoism that is to play such a large role in his thinking for the rest of his philosophical life.

Chapter Four, Mao's Early Philosophical Influences and Reflections, describes how Mao interpolates the thought of the philosophers who exercised such a powerful influence on his philosophical development. We see how his special interpretations of Confucius and Mencius provide the philosophical foundations for his concept of the Self and his concept of the Great Man. It is in this chapter that we see how Mao presents his own unique solution to the Egoism–Altruism conundrum and elaborates his own approach to Ethics.

Chapter Five, The Blend of the Influence of Chinese and Western philosophy on Mao's Thought and Parallels in China's Social and Economic

Development, both reflects Mao's philosophical thinking and sounds the theme of parallel social and economic developments in China. This chapter shows the connections between Mao's early philosophical thinking and his later Marxism. It shows that Mao's thinking is highly influenced by the *Yijing* and that his dialectical thinking possesses more in common with the dialectic of the *Yijing* than it does with the dialectic found in Hegelian and Marxist sources. This chapter weaves point and counterpoint together by turning to the *Yijing* to provide an explanation of the changes in China that were to take place both during and after Mao's reign. It proposes that, in the end, Mao deviates from the values of traditional Chinese philosophy and presents his own unique philosophical standpoint.

Chapter Six, Mao's Marxist Thought and the *Yijing*, subjects Mao's philosophical thinking during his Marxist period to close examination. Questions are raised such as the relation between theory and practice, whether Mao's Marxism was anticipated in Soviet sources or whether Mao contributed something new to Marxist thought that was not present in Soviet sources, antagonistic and non-antagonistic contradictions, the relationship between the Superstructure and the Base, the Unity of Opposites, the Negation of Negation, Principal and Secondary Aspects of Contradiction and Mao's Inversion of Classical Marxism. There are close discussions of Mao's principal Marxist writings and comparisons and contrasts made with Hegel, Engels and Marx. The parallels of Mao's thought with the *Yijing* are discussed in depth.

Chapter Seven, Mao as Metaphysician and *Literatus*, is a chapter that connects the two themes of the volume: Mao's early, middle and late periods of philosophical development with interpretations of the changes that were taking place in China. It expounds Mao's metaphysical speculations, demonstrating their continued connection with the philosophical speculations of his youth and a creativity that transcends solely Marxist issues and concerns. Surprising evidence of Mao's intense curiosity about co-temporary discoveries in physics and dialogue with famous physicists that he invites to dialogues with him about scientific topics in co-temporary physics is brought forth. This chapter makes it clear that Mao's philosophical interests are not to be confined to political philosophy. It reflects the wide scope of Mao's thinking which reflects the direction of thought of the traditional philosopher, Chinese or Western. It explores the theme of Mao as *literatus*, revealing evidence of Mao's artistic and literary prowess and relates how even in his later years he continued to show his long-standing interest in Chinese classics. This chapter illustrates how Mao applies the classical education of his youth to address global political problems. In this respect, this chapter brings together the twin themes of this volume: the exploration into Mao's early philosophical education and its parallel with social and political events in China. This chapter demonstrates how his knowledge of the classics influenced his political philosophy.

Chapter Eight, Mao's Contributions to Philosophy, investigates what constitutes Mao's unique philosophical discoveries whether to Marxist philosophy or to philosophy proper. It covers the debates over whether Mao's contributions to Marxist philosophy were original or derivative from Soviet sources. This chapter summarizes Mao's philosophical discoveries and earmarks Mao's stature as a philosopher.

ACKNOWLEDGEMENTS

To my wife, Irèné, of many devoted years, I owe this book. In addition to her brilliant commentary on my thinking, it is only due to her unfailing encouragement that I embarked upon this project to distil the essence of both traditional Western and Chinese philosophies on the mind of Mao. In order to make this present work completely transparent to the reader not familiar with the Chinese language, insofar as it is feasible, I have attempted to keep to sources published in the English language, including those written by Chinese language scholars. To my original teachers of Mandarin, Miss Zhou of Southern Illinois University, Carbondale, and to Loretta Pan of Columbia University, I must offer my gratitude, for without these early inspirations, I doubt very much that my mind would have been led to make further explorations. To the memory of the historian Ping-chai Kuo, who introduced me to Chinese culture and civilization in his course on Chinese civilization, in the Southern Illinois University's honours curriculum, I am forever grateful. To my dedicated students of early Chinese philosophy and Western philosophy at The Chinese University of Hong Kong of many years, I owe the appreciation of bringing to classes both their Chinese cultural heritage and their knowledge of co-temporary Chinese education in the Chinese classics. To my colleagues during my long tenure as professor in the Department of Philosophy at Chinese University, I owe much to their stimulating conversations on fine points of Chinese philosophy. Here, I must pay tribute to the memories of Liu Shu-hsien, Lao Yung-wei and D. C. Lau for their many years of friendship and collegial interchange. I will always treasure Lao Yung-wei who after one of our dialogues remarked to me that 'you have made a significant contribution to Chinese philosophy'. I want to express my deep appreciation to my colleague, the John Harvard Fellow, K. C. Lam, for the unwavering friendship he has shown to me over the years. I am grateful for the inspiration and support of Sir Joseph Needham and to the Society of Anglo-Chinese Understanding for their kind willingness to allow me to reproduce the epochal photograph of Mao and Kissinger in Mao's office. It would be amiss not to express my gratitude to Chung-ying Cheng for the sterling quality of his friendship and unfailing support of my study of Chinese philosophy over many years. It would be equally amiss not to express my appreciation for the great friendship and constant support of Robert Neville and the inspiration his love for Chinese philosophy continues to have on my own dedication to traditional Chinese philosophy. I owe a debt of continuing gratitude to Tu Weiming for his inspiring encouragement and support of my study of Chinese philosophy over these many years. Irene Eber's lively encouragement and ongoing, stimulating conversations in her home have been a source of deep inspiration. The Chinese scholars who gave strong support to my dedication to Chinese philosophy over my career are too numerous to mention, but I cannot close without paying tribute to the memory of Anthony Yu whose never-failing support was always a source of inspiration, to Mark Elvin for his unforgettable support while I was at St. Antony's College at Oxford University, to the memory of Benjamin Schwartz for his wise conversations, to the memory of Tang Yijie, who was kind enough to invite me to Peking University to offer lectures and with my wife to his home, to Donald Leslie, who shared his wisdom and showed his hospitality to my wife and me when I visited Australian National University, to the memories of Charles Fu, Tony Cua and Li kek Tong who gave me their very strong and persistent support over all these years. When, after Tong's passing, Tong's daughter came to me and asked me if I would keep his personal books of the Chinese classics including Confucius and Mencius, I came to realize what an enormous debt I had to repay to Chinese philosophy. This book is but a small down payment on such a debt and it is to the spirit of Chinese philosophy that this book is offered as a token. I cannot close without a tribute to the memory of those faculty members of the Department of Philosophy at Fudan University who accompanied my wife and I to the airport when I was to return to Hong Kong in 1988 after being Visiting Professor to Fudan and said goodbye to us, their cheeks glistening with tears. One philosopher had spent virtually all of his monthly salary to purchase a pair of Shanghainese opera shoes for my wife when he learned that she loved Chinese opera. To all of these inspiring figures, whatever truths contained in this book are to be dedicated; whatever errors are to be found are of my own making. It needs to be emphasized that books are not a sole effort and require a supportive staff and encouragement. I especially want to thank Colleen Coulter of Bloomsbury Publishing for her enthusiastic support of this book project from its inception and Gosha Domagala from the library of Soka University of America for her constant readiness to help with my research needs. I want also to thank my students in my courses in Chinese philosophy and Comparative East–West philosophy at Soka University of America whose keen interest and stimulating questions are a source of continued inspiration.

1

Introduction to the Philosophical Mao

The Good and the Bad Mao

In this approach to Mao's thinking, the method is to attempt to discover the philosophical dimensions to his thought. *My purpose is not to focus on the political ideology or actions of Mao. My purpose is to focus on the philosophical rather than the political thought of Mao.* Views of the good Mao and the bad Mao have been based on evaluating his political thought in terms of its allegiance to or divergence from Marxism and/or the good that Mao brought to China versus the harm that he wreaked. There is no intention on my part to demonstrate that in the end, on balance, the good that Mao accomplished for China overweighs the evil, or the other way around.[1] Accounts vary on this issue. Nick Knight writes that according to the official Chinese government account in its 1981 'Resolution': if we judge his activities as a whole, his contributions to the Chinese revolution far outweigh his mistakes. His merits are primary and his errors secondary.[2]

Arthur Waldron reports that John K. Fairbank, upon returning from a visit to China in 1972, stated that 'The Maoist revolution is on the whole the best thing that has happened to the Chinese people in centuries.'[3]

On the other hand, accounts abound that detail the human suffering and death toll that occurred as a result of Mao's policies. It is an open question how much of this was a result of Mao's initiative and how much was caused by excesses of local and regional leaders.[4]

In their Introduction to *Was Mao Really a Monster*, Gregor Benton and Lin Chun quote the historian Maurice Meisner, who wrote in 1999: 'Despite all the horrors and crimes that accompanied the revolution … few events in world history have done more to better the lives of more people.' Meisner refers to China's subsequent economic development as 'one of the greatest achievements of the twentieth century.'[5]

Lee Feigon also concludes with a favourable opinion of Mao on the whole:

Mao enriched the lives of the Chinese people.[6]

And,

… no one can deny that Mao was a great leader who transformed China. … his [Mao's] own name will inspire discussion for years to come, and his influence – largely positive – will be felt in China for generations.[7]

Even Walder writes that despite severe problems under the surface:

In addition to these genuine accomplishments [infant mortality rates decreased from 175 per thousand births in 1953 to 45 per thousand in 1976, life expectancy at birth which was only 40 years in 1953, had risen to 64 years] which survived to the end of the Mao era, aggregate measures of China's gross domestic product (GNP) were also impressive. Gross output of China's industry and agriculture grew in nominal terms almost tenfold during the Mao era; industrial output grew twice as fast.[8]

The 70–30 view – ironically coinciding with Mao's appraisal of Stalin – 70 per cent good and 30 per cent bad, is interpreted by John Bryan Starr to mean that '[Mao] is viewed as 100 per cent right for 70 per cent of his career, and close to 100 per cent wrong for the last 30 per cent.'[9] It is important to bear in mind that these calculations are evaluations of Mao's political thought and its effects, and not of his philosophical thought proper.[10]

The line between the philosophical and the political is sometimes difficult to draw, but it is not impossible. For example, Andrew Walder attributes Mao's political decisions to his fixed ideas concerning the need for violence in revolution, the following of the Stalinist Party History, *The Short Course*, etc. These tactical political decisions and their justifications need to be distinguished from Mao's strategic objectives, and the metaphysics and epistemology which underscored his philosophy of change.

As for his errors, Stuart Schram writes near the end of his work *The Thought of Mao Tse-Tung*:

> It cannot be disputed that Mao's two major policy innovations of his later years, which were also the two major innovations in his thought, the Great Leap Forward and The Cultural Revolution, were ill-conceived and led to disastrous consequences.[11]

It could be argued that these two disastrous policies were not related to philosophical thinking, but to agricultural theory and public policy planning. However, it has been argued that even Mao's Great Leap Forward policies were influenced by Mao's concepts of physics, if not philosophy.[12]

Lee's views resemble those of Schram:

> As I have made clear, Mao must be held responsible not only for the disaster of the Great Leap but also for many of the innocent, cruelly tortured victims of the Cultural Revolution. It is not much consolation to the victims of his campaigns that Mao, unlike Stalin, never went over the lists of people to be imprisoned or executed and was probably largely unaware of most of the egregious assaults of the Cultural Revolution. Mao also fell short in his

personal life. He was, as Frederick Teiwes has put it, 'a randy old bastard who abused his authority' to have sex with a great many women.[13]

Dikötter goes further in his analysis: Insensitive to human loss, he nonchalantly handed down killing quotas in the many campaigns that were designed to cow the population.[14]

Suspending judgment, pending evidence for the validity of this claim that is made by Dikötter, it could be conjectured that beneath whatever excesses that ensued from Mao's policy decisions lay an overweening trust in his own willful decision making and a view of himself as a Great Man, values that echo Mao's early reading of Paulsen's *System of Ethics*. This underlying willfulness, in my own view, a blend of his early Western philosophical exposure to Paulsen and Mao's own personality, is for Schram, the most important negative factor of Mao's legacy.[15] A reflective illustration of this is to be found in Bill Willmott's story of his brother's visit to China in 2005 and his brother's question of an old man he met in Chengdu. When he asked him what he thought of Mao, the old man's reply was, '*Ren buhao. Sixiang hao*' (Man not good. Thoughts good).[16]

Stuart Schram concludes his work *The Thought of Mao Tse-Tung* with a question: Was Mao a Prometheus or a Faust, 'attempting the impossible for the sake of humanity, or a despot of unbridled ambition, drunk with his own power and his own cleverness? Even today, the final verdict, both on the man and his thought, must still remain open.'[17]

In an earlier book, Schram elaborates on the polar opposites that make the choice of good or bad both a staggering and an unethical assessment:

> How does one weigh, for example, the good fortune of hundreds of millions of peasants in getting land against the execution, in the course of land reform and the 'Campaign against Counter-Revolutionaries', or in other contexts, of millions, some of whom certainly deserved to die [?!] but others of whom undoubtedly did not? How does one balance the achievements in

economic development during the first Five-Year Plan, or during the whole twenty-seven years of Mao's leadership after 1949, against the starvation that came in the wake of the Great Leap Forward, or the bloody shambles of the Cultural Revolution?[18]

For Kissinger, Mao was a man of contradiction:

Domineering and overwhelming in his influence, ruthless and aloof, poet and warrior, prophet and scourge, he unified China and launched it on a journey that nearly wrecked its civil society.[19]

Speaking of poetry, Mao is regarded by critics as a good poet, and even chose to write his poetry in one of the more sophisticated and difficult meters of the classical style. Questions have been raised as to whether others have written the poems attributed to Mao. In one case, according to an article written in the *Christian Science Monitor*, Chen Mingyuan has claimed that twelve of his poems were included in 'A Collection of Chairman Mao's Unpublished Poems' (he states that 'only those who are ignorant or who have ulterior motives will say Chairman Mao lifted his poems'). In any case, this claim is not identical to the claim that all of Mao's poetry was written by others.[20] Concerning the contradiction of Mao being the author of the Cultural Revolution and, at the same time, a fine practitioner of one of its most renowned classical arts, Fitzgerald makes the following comments. I find particularly suggestive the remarks Fitzgerald makes in the future perfect tense:

… by some strange twist of his psychology while condemning as outworn this aspect of the old culture, he nonetheless desired to be known as the last exponent of this particular form of it. No man is wholly consistent, and few can resist the enjoyment of practicing a difficult skill in which they know themselves to be very proficient. It is always possible that while he believed that these interests were not appropriate as an example in this stage of the just completed revolution, he did not want to discourage future generations, in a calmer age, from rediscovering the beauties of some aspects of the old culture, by then purely of historical or aesthetic importance.[21]

Traditional Western, Traditional Chinese Philosophy and Mao

My primary objective is to show the influence of traditional Western and traditional Chinese philosophy on the mind of Mao. There have been studies of Mao's Marxism, but very little, in comparison, of Mao's early acquaintance with both Western philosophy and classical Chinese philosophy, and of the dedication he brought to his philosophical studies. In order to illustrate Mao's philosophical journey, I shall, as a whole, attempt to focus on Mao's philosophical writings and inasmuch as is possible, not focus on his ideological writings, the purpose of which is usually to justify and persuade others to see the truth of his political actions and decisions. Although it is impossible, not to say untrue to Mao's thinking, to completely divorce Mao's philosophical thinking from his political theatre of action, the purpose of highlighting his philosophical ideas is to ensure that they are not lost in the immense complexity of the history of the social, economic and political changes that were taking place in China.[22] Stuart Schram's work, *The Thought of Mao Tse-Tung*, focuses on Mao's political thought rather than his philosophical thought *per se*, linking his philosophical thinking to his political decisions and policies. As Schram notes, his [Schram's] work focuses on mainly political concerns and not, in his words, on 'strictly philosophical issues':

> Mao's analysis of Chinese society, and the theoretical considerations he drew from it, lie on the other hand [from strictly philosophical concerns] at the centre of our concerns, and can serve as a convenient transition from philosophy to other aspects of Mao's thought.[23]

Mao's Individual Thought versus the Official Philosophy of Mao

What can we take as writing representing Mao's philosophical thought? Of course, Mao's philosophical thought changes over the course of time. Nonetheless, it is possible to point out parallels between his early and later periods of thought.[24] It does not mean that there is a seamless continuity, and the transition between his pre-Marxist and Marxist periods is marked by a distinct change. There is also the distinction scholars make between Mao's own philosophy and what is regarded as the official philosophy of Mao. Knight points out that 'one finds in the writings of the field a distinction having to be made between Mao Zedong Philosophical Thought (that is the "scientific system" which has the official seal of approval) and the philosophical thought of Mao the individual.' [25] Timothy Cheek refers to 'Mao Zedong Thought' (*Mao Zedong Sixiang*) as Mao's ideological contributions and states that it is the official ideology of the CCP today.[26] In what is to follow, we shall focus on the philosophical thought of Mao the individual. This is the opposite position of significant mainland Chinese scholars who consider that it is Mao Zedong Philosophical Thought which should be the proper object of study. Liu Rong, for example, points out that Mao Zedong Philosophical Thought (which includes the thought of Zhou Enlai, Liu Shaoqi and Zhu De) 'rectifies' errors in the thought of the early Mao. If early Chinese philosophical thought or Western traditional thought is mentioned at all, it is only in the context of exhibiting it as errors that were part of Mao's individual philosophical thought, but disappeared after Mao's conversion to Marxism. Liu Rong writes:

> … before Mao Zedong became a Marxist in 1920, he said on more than one occasion that in his early teens he believed in gods, that he worshipped Buddha; and as a youth, he put his faith in the texts of Confucius and the dualism of Kant, and advocated anarchism.[27]

Of his conversion to Marxism (there was of yet no communist party in China so that Mao was not yet a communist), Mao recounts that the books (in Chinese translation) that made the deepest mark on him in 1920 were the *Communist Manifesto, Class Struggle* by the Jewish theoretician Karl Kautsky and a *History of Socialism* by Thomas Kirkup.[28] On the other hand, according to Alexander Pantsov and Steven Levine, it was Kropotkin who had the greatest influence on Mao.[29]

It should be noted that Mao was writing about the social transformation of the masses as early as 21 July 1919, prior to his first contact with Marxism. This is evidenced by his essay, 'The Great Union of the Popular Masses, Part I.' [30]

Schram notes that in this essay Mao's notion is that the primary leadership is to be of students, not the proletariat. He also paid considerable attention to women and school teachers. It was the young, not the peasants who were Mao's movers at this time.[31]

There has been very little work of any sustained substance that has shown the developmental link between Mao's early thought and his later philosophical essays. The bulk of existing scholarship on Mao's philosophical writing focuses on his Marxist period. However, as we shall see in ensuing chapters, there is far more to Mao's philosophical development than simply his Marxist writings. Even scholars who make efforts to link the early Mao with his later period tend to view his later writing through the Marxist lens rather than taking note of how and from which pre-Marxist influences Mao formed his ideas. If they do take note of his pre-Marxist period, with notable exceptions, such as Frederick Wakeman, Stuart Schram and Maurice Meisner, they give traditional Western philosophical influences only passing reference and do not credit pre-Marxist Western philosophy as continuing to influence his philosophical development. Some do credit the influence of traditional Chinese philosophy, but still as a less important influence than Mao's exposure to Marxism. As in the case of Liu Rong, it is as if after Mao's conversion to Marxism these early ideas do not play any further role in his philosophical thinking. Schram, on the other hand, does see the influence of traditional Chinese philosophy on Mao's later writings, pointing to two of Mao's best-known theoretical contributions, contained in 'On Practice' and 'On Contradiction', as traceable before they were developed in Marxist terms, to very ancient Chinese ideas such as yin-yang dialectics and seeking truth from facts.[32] Schram points to Mao's own campaign in the 1940s for the Sinification of Marxism.[33] Most emphatically, illustrating the continuity of the influence of traditional thought on Mao's thinking, Schram writes:

> Mao truly moved, at the end of his life, from expressing Marxist ideas in a language accessible to the Chinese people to a somewhat eclectic position in which traditional values and ideas played an increasingly large part.[34]

According to Knight's account, there are three main perspectives through which Mao's thought is viewed by mainland Chinese scholars. In Knight's account, unlike Schram's account, there is no separate perspective that considers Mao's own thought.[35] The first perspective, which Knight claims to be a minority view, is to attribute Mao's philosophical thought overwhelmingly to be of Marxist origin. Knight singles out Liu Rong as representing this perspective. Knight points out that in Liu Rong's book, *A Commentary on the Philosophical Thought of Mao Zedong*, 'there is virtually no reference to traditional Chinese philosophy and its influence on Mao.'[36] It should be added that there is also virtually no reference to traditional Western philosophy save as an illustration of the youthful ideas of Mao, which he abandoned.

The second perspective, which Knight describes as the dominant school of Mao interpretation, does acknowledge some influence of traditional Chinese philosophy (although not traditional, non-Marxist Western philosophy) together with influence from Chinese and Soviet Marxist writers. According to Knight, this school holds:

> … that the origins of Mao's philosophical thought are to be found in both Marxist philosophy and Chinese traditional philosophy. In terms of

the weighting of influence between these two intellectual traditions, the emphasis is placed overwhelmingly on Marxism. Consequentially, Mao was first and foremost a Marxist; his methodology, standpoint and world view were constituted of dialectical and historical materialism, and in this respect Mao owes a considerable intellectual debt to the Soviet and Chinese Marxist philosophical writings of the 1930s which elaborated the philosophical laws and categories of Marxism in a concise and accessible form.[37]

The interest of this second school of Maoist studies is in viewing Mao as a Marxist and, thus, their attention is drawn to his Marxist writings and comparisons with the Soviet and Chinese Marxism. There is an acknowledgement of Mao's debt to the concepts of yin and yang from the *Yijing* and in the *Daodejing*, but these dialectical influences only serve to facilitate Mao's Marxism. According to this school:

> In particular, the concepts of *yin* and *yang* which appeared in the *Yi Jing* and were subsequently elaborated in the *Dao de Jing* created an intellectual predisposition to view the world as constituted of opposites – life and death, large and small, strength and weakness, difficulty and facility ...[38]

However:

> ... early Chinese dialectics was not based on a scientific foundation, was simplistic, and often mixed together materialism and idealism and dialectics and metaphysics; it could not, therefore, be incorporated into modern Chinese Marxism without undergoing a process of critical scrutiny and selection, in which elements incompatible with dialectical materialism were sifted out and rejected.[39]

It is clear from this perspective that early traditional Chinese philosophical elements needed to be sifted through and refined in order to make them compatible with Marxism. Chinese traditional philosophy was utilized to service Marxist ideas, perhaps as a primitive anticipation with idealistic and materialistic elements that needed to be extirpated. There is no mention made of the possible influence of pre-Marxist, traditional Western philosophy.

Zhang Wenru would appear to belong to this second school when he writes:

> Mao Zedong's philosophical thought does not derive from a continuation and transformation of China's own philosophical inheritance, but derives from the study of Marxist-Leninism; its direct theoretical source is Marxist philosophy, and it is the continuation and development of Marxist philosophy in China …[40]

Zhang Wenru sharply distinguishes between Mao's own philosophical thought and the official version:

> Comrade Mao said: 'We should sum up our history from Confucius to Sun Yat-sen and take over this valuable legacy'. … To critically continue China's ancient philosophical legacy is to continue and develop all rational and progressive thought from China's traditional philosophy, and at the same time to thoroughly eliminate its negative, backward and rotten elements.[41]

All in all, this second perspective on Mao's thought, which Knight considers to be the dominant perspective, is that Chinese philosophy, in its undeveloped and confused form, was rectified by Mao's Marxism and that Chinese philosophy's contribution was to offer an Eastern condiment that flavoured Marxism:

> It was the employment and incorporation of these aspects of traditional Chinese philosophy and culture which provided Mao's philosophical thought and his Marxism generally with a distinctly Chinese flavor. … His achievement was to draw critically on the dialectical and materialistic themes already present in often undeveloped and confused form within

traditional Chinese philosophy. Nevertheless, the basic categories, concepts and principles which characterized Mao's philosophical thought were Marxist, and these formed the foundation which provided the standpoint and method from which the Chinese tradition could be evaluated.[42]

The third school of interpretation of Maoist thought, regarded by Knight as a minority point of view, does see both Marxist and Chinese philosophical traditions as contributing to Mao's thought, but emphasizes the influence on Mao of Soviet and Chinese Marxism. Traditional pre-Marxist Western philosophy is not recognized as a significant contribution. Mao's intellectual debt is clearly stated to be to Marxism.

The pre-Marxist Mao and its Continued Influence

This present volume treads a different and unique path. It focuses on the pre-Marxist writings of Mao and presents Mao as a unique philosophical thinker, drawing upon his early exposure to both Chinese traditional philosophy and Western traditional philosophy. Mao's Marxism was also of a unique style, utilizing concepts from the traditional *Book of Changes* or the *Yijing* to give to Marxism a content that departs both from Engels and the Soviet model. It argues that there is a development of Mao's thought that takes its rise from its earliest stages and is sustained while following a dialectical pattern in which his idealist and later, materialist tendencies trade places in respective positions of predominance and subservience in true yin-yang fashion.

Mao's impact on China was enormous, and his philosophical study was a major factor in forming the decisions that he made and that were to influence the course of history in the century in which he lived. While it is impossible to make an examination of Mao's thought without referring to his theatre of action and the politics of China, the intent of this volume is to distil the essence of Mao's thinking in order to study how the intellectual history of Mao contributed to the history of contemporary China.

The present author has had the privilege of being an eyewitness to history. I lived through the aftermath of the Cultural Revolution period in Hong Kong, from 1977 to the early years of this present century, as a tenured Full Professor and a member of the Graduate Panel in the Department of Philosophy of The Chinese University of Hong Kong. For over two decades, I was the sole Western philosopher in the Department, a Department consisting for several decades of all Chinese males (in double digit numbers). All departmental meetings were conducted exclusively in Mandarin. The present author also served as a full member of the University Senate, as a member of the Assembly of Fellows and as a member of the Board of Trustees for Shaw College – one of the four Colleges of the University fashioned after the Oxford system. During this period, the present author was one of the first Americans able to travel and be in China as a Visiting Professor to Peking University and Fudan University's respective Departments of Philosophy among others in the People's Republic of China (PRC). The present author participated in spirited debates and discussions with Chinese colleagues and political figures during the aftermath of the Cultural Revolution. Vignettes of lived historical encounters with evidence experienced first hand, both in Hong Kong and in the PRC, inform and enrich this re-examination of Mao and his philosophical development.

Although there has been much study of Mao as a Marxist thinker, this volume is not intended to focus only on Mao as a Marxist. Although there is no question that Marx and Marxist thought were greatly influential for Mao, there were other philosophers who possessed an impact on his thinking and who were significantly influential in forming Mao's philosophy. It is to these philosophical influences and the role they played in shaping Mao's Marxism that this volume is mainly dedicated to examining. Whether Mao interpreted these philosophical teachings correctly is an issue of considerable importance.

However Mao understood or misunderstood the philosophers that he studied, there is no question that he was influenced by philosophers other than Marx and Chinese and Soviet Marxists.

Mao was influenced by both traditional Chinese and traditional Western philosophers, perhaps in equal measure. He was influenced by Confucius, Laozi, Mencius, Aristotle, Hegel, Schopenhauer, Nietzsche, Marx and by his understanding of Zhuangzi. This is the story to be told in the ensuing pages. Of special interest is how Mao's understanding of Marxism was influenced by his previous study of both Chinese and Western philosophy. It is difficult, if not impossible, to assess properly Mao's understanding and interpretation of Western and Chinese philosophy without familiarity with the philosophies of both traditions. The reason for this is that Mao himself was conversant with the philosophies of both traditions, because his philosophical education consisted largely in the studies of the philosophies of both traditions. If one is familiar only with Marxist philosophy or only Chinese philosophy, it presents an obstacle to understanding how Mao interprets these traditions and how Mao's own philosophical development depends upon his understanding of these traditions. In order to know whether Mao properly interpreted or misinterpreted the Chinese and Western philosophies that formed the foundation of his own philosophical development, one must possess a substantial foundation in both of these philosophical traditions.

The Place of Frederick Paulsen's *A System of Ethics* in Mao's Thought

The key to unlocking Mao's early philosophical thought that was to have such a great influence on his later Marxist thought is the examination of the notes in the margins of Friedrich Paulsen's *A System of Ethics*, that Mao made while a young student of Philosophy. In this work, that Mao comprehensively commented upon in the margins to the work he read, the history of Western philosophy is systematically examined from the ancient Greek period to nineteenth century German philosophy. Mao brings to bear both his own Western and Chinese philosophical background to delve into Paulsen's analysis of the Western tradition. Mao is not a passive learner, accepting Paulsen's exposition of Western philosophy or Paulsen's development of his own philosophical position. Mao both absorbs Paulsen's historical and philosophical writing and adds to it his own philosophical observations and conclusions. Mao is an active learner and frequently utilizes Paulsen's expositions as a stimulus to his own creative, philosophical observations and conclusions.

The years 2017–2018 marked the hundredth anniversary of Mao's 1917–1918 seminal marginal notes in Friedrich Paulsen's *A System of Ethics*. As such, it is a fitting occasion for a re-examination of Mao's thought through the mirror of these notes which can, for the first time, systematically trace the influence of Mao's reflections on Paulsen for the course of his future thought development.

With the entrance of China on the world stage and its increasing movement to the centre of that stage, coupled with the continuing signs of a resurgence of Confucianism in China, it is, therefore, of relevant interest to examine the early pre-Marxist philosophical development of Mao to see how it sets the stage for Mao's later Marxist period and how China may draw guidance from studying the philosophical basis of Mao's thinking for the understanding of its own historical development. Mao's early philosophical development draws much from both Mao's interpretation of the Western tradition and Mao's interpolation of the classical Chinese philosophical tradition. It is from a study of this pre-Marxist stage of Mao's thinking that China may have the most to benefit. For, in the most formative period of Mao's intellectual development, Mao's thought was influenced by pre-Marxist Chinese and Western thinkers in a way that shaped his later political career. Even during his Marxist period, this early influential development did not disappear, though it may have appeared to have been dormant for many years. It is the thesis of the arguments to come that Mao developed his thinking in concert with and in contrast to the philosophical influences to which he was exposed, as he understood them. It is especially useful to examine some of the major influences in some detail to spot both how Mao's early thinking provides inspiration for his later intellectual development and how, in addition to his understanding of Marxism, his understanding of both Western and Chinese philosophical traditions influenced China's direction. Indeed, Mao's understanding of Marxism would not have been the same as it was had he not first studied non-Marxist philosophy.

Mao and Confucianism: A Preview

If one follows these arguments and notices on what basis Mao develops his philosophy of Egoism, much of value can be learned for guidance to China's current intellectual development. A close attention to Mao's early interpretations of both Western and Chinese philosophy will cast much light on the path to China's current intellectual renaissance of Confucianism, on the one hand, and its valuation of Mao's thinking on the other.

Mao's early philosophical development shows signs of being influenced by both Western and Chinese models. In China's current economic development, it appears that it has been influenced by a Western, capitalist model, one that is opposed to a Marxist model, which emphasizes social equality. On the other hand, China has introduced a movement to recapture its own Confucian heritage, a heritage that placed ethics above the pursuit of profit.[43] This uneasy marriage has led to China's pivot to strong leadership to balance the conflict between ethics and profit. In this sense, China's turn already resembles a return to Mao. This conflictual relationship between ethics and profit is actually at the heart of Mao's early philosophical development and is characterized by his philosophy of Egoism which attempts to bring together the marriage partners of ethics and profit of his pre-Marxist days. By looking closely at the roots of Mao's early philosophical studies, we can see how his interpretations of both classical and nineteenth-century Western philosophy as well as his understanding of classical, Chinese, Confucian and Daoist philosophy have shaped China's intellectual course and steered it into its present course of direction.

The Influence of Philosophy on Mao's Thinking

What lesson is to be learned? It is hoped that one lesson to be learned is that one should not underestimate the influence of philosophy. To adapt John Maynard Keynes's famous quip: 'Practical men who believe themselves to be exempt from any intellectual influence, are usually the slaves of some defunct philosopher.' This adaptation is more accurate than one might think since the thinker that Keynes probably had in mind was Adam Smith, a professor of Moral Philosophy. Economics as a special discipline had not yet been founded and Smith, while a philosopher, is now considered the Father of Economics.

While only relatively few people have actually read the texts of philosophers, the influence of their ideas has filtered down through other sources to influence the proverbial 'Everyman'. Mao actually studied the works of serious philosophers, and he studied them in some depth. In his case, the influence was not indirect; it was very direct and very extensive. He studied philosophy, both in university and in intensive and extensive periods of self-study. He actually married Yang Kaihui, the daughter of his philosophy professor, Yang Changji, and was a frequent guest at the home of Professor Yang Changji.[44]

It is better to be explicitly aware of the philosophy that influences and informs one's decisions than it is to think that one is totally free from philosophical influences. Mao's actions and decisions were based on philosophy, whether good or bad philosophy, philosophy well understood or philosophy misunderstood. And, the philosophy that formed the framework for his decisions was not simply the philosophy of Marxism. In any case, it is important to understand accurately the philosophies that influence one's decisions and one's life in general. In this regard, this volume is an object lesson in how early philosophical influences can have a formative impact on one's later thinking processes.

In Mao's case, because of the giant lever of his position of political power, his early training and exposure to philosophy were to have tremendous consequences. An iconic example is the misunderstanding or even, in the case of Mao's possibly correct understanding of how a reading of Laozi's infamous Chapter 19 of the *Daodejing*, can have disastrous consequences. While it can well be argued that Laozi did not mean for this passage to be taken in the sense that seems parallel with the Cultural Revolution, it can nonetheless be argued that it is not surprising that Mao could have been influenced by a literal interpretation of this passage.

Consider the parallel between this chilling passage from Chapter 19 of the *Daodejing* and Mao's anti-intellectual campaign of the Cultural Revolution:

'Exterminate the sage, discard the wise, and the people will benefit a hundredfold.'

While this case of the far-reaching influence of early education in the classical, Chinese philosophical canon is possibly the most dramatic example how philosophy can possess disastrous effects on the course of human events, an understanding of Mao's understanding of the Ur-philosophies that shaped his formative intellectual development can go far to enhance our understanding of the tremendous changes in China that influenced the course of history in the past century and continue to influence global history in the present century.

In the course of this volume, the intention is to put forth five major theses that have been relatively unexplored: (i) that Mao's philosophical development and his subsequent political career was powerfully influenced by his early training in both Western and Chinese philosophy; (ii) that the pre-Marxist philosophy that formed the essence of Mao's formative years was to influence his later writings and his philosophical development in equal measure to his later exposure to Marxism; (iii) that Mao's thought, in the end, was a break with both traditional Chinese philosophy and Western philosophy, and went beyond doctrinaire Marxism; (iv) that Mao would not have been surprised either by the rise of capitalism[45] in China today, compared to Mao's time or the renaissance of Confucianism; (v) that though the hope for China's future lies in the direction of its revival of classical Confucianism, a correction of Mao's interpretation of classical Confucianism will conduce greatly to China's ethical development. Classical Confucianism brings with it a set of ethical values that can counteract the materialistic dimensions that appear to currently dominate the contemporary Chinese value system. The argument of this volume is that clarifying and disentangling Mao's conflation of Confucianism with Egoism may redirect Confucianism in present-day China back to its classical roots that are not entangled with Egoism.

What follows represents the first concentrated and extensive study to address the first available full-version of Mao's marginal notes to Paulsen's *A System of Ethics* – the first full-length monograph that demonstrates the continuing influence of Mao's pre-Marxist philosophy on his later Marxist thought and politics; the first full-length monograph that spells out, in detail, the possible influence of both traditional Chinese philosophy and traditional Western philosophy on the formation of Mao's philosophical thinking. In this respect, this study constitutes three firsts.

It is hoped that by showing the breadth and depth of Mao's exposure to philosophical reflections upon and interpretations of both Chinese and Western philosophy, one may develop a greater understanding of the mind of Mao. This volume is offered in the spirit of being a mixture of historical events and an interpolation of the influence of Mao's early philosophical education upon his later philosophical development, a philosophical history, so to speak. Unique to this volume is a detailed account of Mao's interpretations of both Confucius and Mencius, and his vision of the Great Man, itself a mixture of his interpretation of Mencius, and the idea of the Great Man inherited from his early exposure to Western history. Unique to this volume is an extended philosophical analysis of Mao's integration of will and conscience, a philosophical conflation that may have precipitated both the scope of his political vision and the unbridled extent of his political excesses. In short, it is intended as an inner journey into the mind of Mao, into his philosophical journey. It is also hoped that this volume will prove to be a contribution to the art of philosophical history, that is, the study of the connection between philosophical schooling, philosophical interpretation and its far-reaching influence on one's future thought, future conceptualizations and future decision making.

2

Mao's Youthful Philosophical Development

The Influence of both Western Philosophy and Chinese Philosophy

Mao's interest in Western thought was clearly evident from his earliest years. According to the historian Maurice Meisner:

'In 1909 the 15 year old Mao was determined to attend a middle school (the Dongshan Higher Primary School) where the Western new learning was part of the curriculum … At the Higher Primary School, Mao Zedong entered the world of China's traditional gentry elite. Less than 1 per cent of the boys and none of the girls were afforded a middle school education in early twentieth-century China. … Mao recalled … "I had never before seen … sons of landlords wearing expensive clothes … many of the richer students despised me because I was wearing my ragged coat and trousers"'.[1] One can already glean a sense of how Mao would link education with upper class origin.

According to the noted historian of China, Herrlee G. Creel, 'Robert Payne states that the thinking of Mao Tse-tung has been strongly influenced by Confucianism, but he also quotes Mao as having said, "I hated Confucius from the age of eight".[2] It is enormously interesting to consider how Mao's early reaction to Confucius may have played a role in his famous, later repudiation of Confucius. Mao had a love–hate relationship with Confucianism, but there is no doubt that the Chinese Classics played a pivotal role in his intellectual development. Rebecca Karl writes that Mao was acquainted with Confucian texts: 'He cited Confucian texts from memory, sometimes hurling Confucian sayings at his father during their arguments.'[3] It is not as well known that Western studies also played a crucial role in his intellectual development. In 1965, Mao wrote, 'I have studied Confucius, the Four Books, and the Five Classics. I studied them for six years and really believed in Confucius. Later on I spent seven years in a bourgeois school learning everything they had to teach – natural sciences, social sciences and even some education.'[4] In the May Fourth movement in Beijing during the Spring of 1919, Mao was to leave Beijing to visit Confucius's grave in Shandong, to visit the little town where the sage lived as a child, and to see the small stream where Confucius's disciples bathed their feet.[5]

What is not commonly known is that Mao's practice was guided by his intense, extended and meticulous early philosophical studies and self-constructed philosophical principles. *What is even less commonly known is that Mao's philosophical principles which were to guide him through his momentous political career were already set in motion in his early thought long before he became familiar with Karl Marx.* Thus, it is of enormous importance to become acquainted with Mao's early philosophical development. Not the least compelling reason for this is the consideration that the ideas to which one is exposed at an early age tend to make an indelible, deep and lasting impression on one's mind, because the undeveloped mind is more open to and less resistant to its first impressions. The mind of youth is receptive and impressionable. The ideas that it forms sink deep into one's consciousness or even, as Freud teaches, one's pre-consciousness. Freud focuses on the impressions one forms in early childhood. In like manner, one is susceptible to intellectual influences in young adulthood as well. For Mao, in much of what follows, I argue that his exposure to both traditional Chinese thought and Western philosophical thought was to play an enormous role in his subsequent philosophical development. For the moment, we may make a comment concerning the relation of Mao's Confucian heritage with current developments of Confucianism in China.

In contemporary Chinese intellectual history, there is a focused Confucian revival. Consider the number of Confucius Institutes that have been established worldwide. It is important to decipher Mao's Confucian heritage in order to see exactly where his thought took its rise from Confucianism and in what respects his thought departed from Confucianism. It is vital to take note that Mao's early thought, in his own mind, built upon Confucian foundations. It is another matter altogether that Mao may have misconstrued the genuine Confucian tradition upon which he developed his ideas. What is clear, however, is that Mao's ideas would not have developed in the direction that they did had he not first attempted to construct them on Confucian foundations.

It is unimaginable how Mao could have changed the face of China without his coming into contact with the philosophy of Marx and succeeded in adapting it to apply to the Chinese mind and the policies of the People's Republic that he founded. That this was possible was in no small way due to the fact that Mao's mind had already been preparing itself with a philosophical foundation based on an assimilation of, a reaction to and an adaptation of both Western and Chinese philosophical ideas. Mao was not an illiterate peasant. He even spent some time as a school teacher. He was exposed to classical Chinese thought. On his own, he read Chinese novels. According to Jerome Ch' en, at the age of seven, Mao was already reading *The Monkey*, *The Water Margin* and *The Romance of the Three Kingdoms*.[6] In his later years, in 1961, Mao would compose a poem 'Watching the Opera: The Monkey King Thrice Fights the Skeleton Spirit,' following Chapter 27 of *The Monkey*. According to Ch' en, Mao utilizes the characters to stand for political entities. For example, the Monkey stands for Marxist-Leninism and the Skeleton Spirit symbolizes revisionism.[7]

Mao chose to expose himself to Western thought. He did not have to do that. What he did with both Western and Chinese thought was atypical. He blended them together in his own inimical way. His thought processes, over a long period, had an incredible influence on millions of people in the world. He put his thought to practical purposes. The result of this was to change the face of China.

I want to commence to enter into a philosophical dialogue with the early Mao and examine how Mao used both Western and Chinese sources to develop his own way of thinking. It is of interest to take note of how Mao was both influenced by and yet deviated from the sources that he cites as supportive of his own way of thinking. It is of special interest to take note of how Mao's thought was initially so influenced by Confucianism. Regardless of how the later Mao reacted against Confucianism, there is no doubt that the early foundations of Mao's thinking were strongly moulded by a Confucian model. Understanding how Mao's thinking deviated from this model goes far to explain both how Mao's thought was influenced by the Confucian tradition and how his understanding of the Confucian tradition configured his later thought, even while proclaiming Marxism, and played no small role in his rise to power. If we are to place a label on the early philosophy of Mao which was to prefigure his later thinking, it would not be amiss to refer to it as Mao's philosophy of Egoism. We must take care not to confuse Mao's Egoism with that of Yang Zhu, whose Egoism was purely selfish.

While Mao is not known primarily as a thinker or a philosopher, the influence of his thinking, put into practice by his political power, was without parallel in China in the past thousand years. What was also unique about Mao was his willingness to grapple with the ideas of the West. In the words of Stuart Schram: 'Mao … boldly grappled with the political and intellectual challenge of the West as no Chinese ruler before him has done.'[8] It is time, now, to turn to Mao's exposure to Western Philosophy.

Mao's Introduction to Western Philosophy and the Ideas of the West

Mao entered First Teachers Training School, the Hunan Provincial Fourth Normal School in Changsha, for Mao was preparing for teaching. Mao was later to do some teaching in history for senior students in evening classes at a Teacher's Training School. During his education at the First Teachers Training School, the Head of the Philosophy department, Yang Changji, became Mao's philosophy professor and introduced Mao to the nineteenth-century German Idealist philosopher, Friedrich Paulsen.[9] Mao became Yang's favourite student. Yang was to rank Mao as the third best among the thousands of students he had taught at Changsha. According to Mao's self-account, Yang gave him the mark of 100 for an essay Mao had written on ethics.[10] Changji's daughter, Kaihui, became Mao's first wife.[11] What is important to take note of is that Yang had studied abroad for ten years in Japan, Scotland and Germany.[12] Yang, who was later to take up a Chair at Peking University, had personally experienced much Western exposure and, according to some scholars, had taken his Ph. D. in Philosophy at Edinburgh (though I have found no evidence for this interesting latter claim). It is revelatory to consider that Mao's primary philosophy professor was a philosopher who had spent ten years studying philosophy in the West (and Japan)! Mao probably had more background in Western thinking taught inside his native China than any Chinese leader before or after him. The other leader who was to change the face of China, Sun Yixian (Sun Yat-sen), the first President of China's Republic, received most of his Western education in Honolulu and Hong Kong. When one considers the degree to which the young Mao was educated in Western thinking, and especially by a philosopher trained in the West, it is as if the stereotypical blindfold that Mao was an illiterate peasant or a Chinese leader ignorant of Western culture and Western ideas is suddenly removed from one's eyes and one begins to perceive Mao in an entirely new light.

In addition, Yang also admired Song Confucianism and his nickname was 'Confucius'. It is of interest to consider these facts in light of Mao's later renouncement of Confucianism. Mao's teacher, of whom he was the favourite student, was a philosopher who already was familiar with both Chinese and Western philosophy. According to Ch' en, Yang was drawn to thinkers such as Kant, Spencer and Rousseau on the Western side and Neo-Confucianism on the Chinese side, particularly the pragmatism of Wang Fu-chih.[13] Such a coupling of intellectual skills from the different civilizations of the East and the West is rare, even by today's standards. With such a teacher, it is not surprising that Mao proceeded to integrate both Western and Chinese philosophy into his own philosophical thinking.

Yang introduced Mao to the magazine *La Jeunesse, New Youth (Hsin-ch'ing-nien)*, whereupon, according to the historian Terrill, Mao avidly read every edition and even copied portions of articles into his school notebooks.[14] According to Wakeman, 'Mao devoured every issue of *New Youth*.'[15] Of *New Youth*, the historian Maurice Meisner writes:

It is difficult to overestimate the importance of the intellectuals who coalesced around *New Youth* for their writings molded the beliefs of a whole generation of young students who were to achieve political prominence after the May Fourth incident of 1919 and who were to become leaders of the modern Chinese revolution. Among their *avid* readers and followers was the *youthful Mao Zedong, who was influenced profoundly by New Youth* – and whose first published writing (an essay stressing the importance of 'physical culture') appeared in that periodical in 1917. One of the *enduring influences that New Youth conveyed to the young Mao and* his contemporaries was the notion that a complete cultural and moral transformation was the primary prerequisite for meaningful social reform and political action. ... *What they demanded was the total annihilation of all the values, traditions, and customs of the past and their replacement by a wholly new culture based on the Western democratic and scientific models they so admired. ... Another striking feature of the New Youth intellectuals ... was an extraordinary faith in the power of ideas to change social reality ...*[16]

Was the young Mao a Chinese Daniel doing both the writing and then reading the writing on the Chinese wall? Meisner continues:

> In new forms and under vastly different historical circumstances, the problems and tensions that were generated by the pre-Marxist Cultural Revolution of 1915–1919 were again to appear in the Maoist-inspired Cultural Revolution of the 1960s. ... A young Mao Zedong was the intellectual product of the first Cultural revolution, and an aging Mao was the political promoter of the second.[17]

Meisner confirms how Mao's reading of *New Youth* prefigures and inspires his Cultural Revolution that was to change the face of China. Meisner's grasp of the continuity in Mao's thinking and the influence of his early pre-Marxist period on the rest of his intellectual and political career as well as on the social and political history of China is notable. What must engage our attention next is the *content* of *New Youth* that so shaped the mind of Mao. It is one thing to emphasize the influence of the magazine *New Youth*. It is even more revealing to take a closer look at what kind of articles were included in *New Youth*.

The abbreviated version of the table of contents of the fourth issue (15 December 1915) provides an idea of the content and scope of Mao's reading and the possible influences on his thinking:

1 A portion of Oscar Wilde's *An Ideal Husband*.
2 Detailed news and commentaries on international and internal situations.
3 An account of Marshal Hindenburg's life and role in the war on the eastern front.

4   'Femininity and Science': an article by a Japanese scholar.

5   An essay on 'The Fundamental Distinction in the Thinking of Eastern and Western Peoples,' contrasting the Western sense of individuality, respect for law, with its Eastern opposites: familialism, traditionalism, anti-legalism.

6   An article arguing that movements like the French Revolution or South America's emancipation from Spain had created more security in the end, and the shortsighted Chinese resistance to these movements would only perpetuate enslavement and insecurity.

7   An article arguing that a nation is not the final resting place of human life, which retrieved theories of German political scientists like Bluntschli and Holtzendorff.

8   An article on the History of Art and Literature in Modern Europe focusing on Tolstoy.

9   A translation of an editorial from a London newspaper.

10 [Most significant in my opinion] A philosophical essay on Schopenhauer's Self-Will.[18]

Such a wide reading of Western sources represents an education in Western thinking that can be favourably compared in its exposure to Western thinkers to the background of the Chinese University undergraduate students I was teaching for nearly three decades in Hong Kong, in the years following Mao's death. When one couples this with the Western philosophical training that Mao received under Yang as well as his own intensive self-studies, one realizes that the young Mao was more Westernized in his training, perhaps more than some students who were educated in a Western colony (at that time) decades after his death. Indeed, when one considers the highly specialized education students typically receive in the West today, such a broad generalized, intellectual background including exposure to German, French and American

History, International Studies, British Journalism, Japanese Cultural Criticism, British Theatre, German Philosophy, Modern European Art and Literature, Latin American Studies, German Political Science and even Comparative Philosophy, a branch of philosophy rarely studied even in today's Western universities, is to say that it is unusual even by today's standards is a vast understatement. The myth of Mao as an illiterate peasant untrained in Western thinking until he came under the spell of Marxism is completely dissolved.

When Mao graduated from Teachers College after concentrating on Moral Philosophy and Journalism, and Yang left to take up a coveted Chair in Philosophy at Peking University, Mao was to follow him and join the Philosophy Society and the Journalism Society. In Mao's own account related to Edgar Snow, he joined the Philosophy Society and the Journalism Society in order to be able to attend classes at the University.[19] At the age of 26, as an unregistered student at Peking University, he would audit and raise questions in classes.

Sir Joseph Needham points out that at the time Mao was a young librarian at Peking University, figures such as Bertrand Russell, R. H. Tawney and John Dewey were lecturing in Beijing and it is possible that Mao picked up some ideas from what was going around and being talked about at that time.[20] According to Tian, Mao attended one lecture by Dewey, titled 'Three Contemporary Philosophers,' delivered at Peking University in 1920. Tian also writes that Mao was an active participant in the preparation for Dewey and Bertrand Russell's visits to Hunan in 1920 and even was a stenographer at symposia given by Dewey and Russell.[21]

During 1917–1918, the period during which Mao is making his marginal notes is the time, according to Schram, that marks the high point of Mao's absorption of Western thought and during this time, both from his own self-education reading program in the Hunan provincial library for more than six months, as a student, from his reading of the Chinese edition of Paulsen, and from the lectures of his teacher, Yang Changji, Mao was familiar with [in

Chinese translation] 'Aristotle; Bentham; Darwin's *Origin of the Species;* Fichte; Goethe; Hobbes; Kant; T. H. Huxley's *Evolution and Ethics;* Leibniz; John Stuart Mill's *A Study of Ethics,* his *Logic* and his famous *On Liberty;* Montesquieu's *De l'esprit des lois;* Nietzsche; Plato; Rousseau's *Du contrat social;* Schopenhauer; Adam Smith's *The Wealth of Nations;* Spencer's *The Study of Sociology,* his *The Principles of Ethics,* and Spinoza.'[22]

Mao ranked first of those who passed the entrance examinations to the First Provincial Middle School, though he withdrew after half a year because of the rigid curriculum and antiquated regulations and undertook his own self-study period.[23] When one contemplates that the youthful Mao possessed the determination and persistence to conduct a six-month self-study period in such a difficult subject as philosophy, one begins to realize what a strong love that Mao possessed for philosophy. Ch'en cites Mao as saying that 'the library was to him as a vegetable garden was to an ox.'[24]

In Wakeman's reconstruction of Yang's classroom, Mao began his study with the Stoics, continued with the hedonism of Aristippus and Epicurus, and followed this by studying the selfish individualism [Wakeman's description] of Hobbes, Machiavelli and Nietzsche. Afterwards came Bentham, Mill, Spencer, Darwin and T. H. Huxley, followed by a study of Aristotle, Kant, Fichte, Hegel, F. H. Bradley and T. H. Green.[25] Snow includes the philosophers already mentioned in his account.[26]

Mao's biographer, Ross Terrill, relates the story of Mao's first contact with the book, *Great Heroes of the World.* 'He borrowed it from his classmate Emi Xiao and penciled numerous circles and dots next to paragraphs on Napoleon, Washington, Peter the Great, Gladstone, Lincoln, Catherine the Great, Rousseau and Montesquieu'.[27] Mao was steeped in Western politics from reading Hobbes, Montesquieu, Machiavelli, Rousseau and accounts of both the respective French and the American revolutions. His classmate Xiao San was actually nicknamed Emi after the title character of Rousseau's immortal *Émile.* One can only imagine the effect of reading about Lincoln, Washington,

Napoleon and Catherine the Great on a young and malleable mind. According to Terrill's account, Mao read aloud to his fellow schoolmates this sentence about George Washington: 'Victory and independence only came to the U.S.A. after eight long bitter years of fighting under Washington.'[28] How could this not have been an inspiration for Mao's long revolutionary struggles in China? Who would have imagined that Mao's role model was none other than that same role model for every American schoolboy – the most iconographic figure of American history, George Washington.

When one contemplates that the formative influences on the young Mao included such diverse Western thinkers as Oscar Wilde and Schopenhauer, and an essay actually titled 'The Fundamental Distinction in the Thinking of Eastern and Western Peoples,' one begins to realize just how sophisticated Mao's education was in the areas of Western and comparative thought. Mao's Western education was not simply from textbooks written by non-Western scholars who were one or two steps removed from the original sources. He studied from original texts as we shall see, in the subsequent chapter, in particular from the German Idealist Paulsen's *A System of Ethics*. According to many accounts, Mao did not master foreign languages though he tried his hand at learning French and English.[29] The works he read were in Chinese translations (no different than Western students who read Plato and Kant in English translations). He was steeped in both the content of the ideas of the West, in comparison to the ideas of the East, and, in the methodology of Western thinking, that is, in analysis and argument. His studies of Western thinkers were not limited to standard figures such as Aristotle and Kant. He studied the notoriously difficult Spinoza, of whom it is said that Kant himself found difficult. He studied not only the iconographic figure of Hegel, but the more esoteric philosophy of F. H. Bradley. At the same time, he was steeped in traditional Chinese Classics and in the classical method of studying those classics, that is, through rote memorization. He was thus familiar with both Western and Eastern pedagogies of learning and could benefit from the advantages peculiar to each way of thinking. Mao's rise to power was no blind power play. His vision for the Chinese people was neither unguided by Western ideas nor by ideas from classical, Chinese education.

Conservatively speaking, this scope of knowledge and Mao's intellectual appropriation of it is comparable to that of a talented, well-read undergraduate major in philosophy at the end of her or his studies in that rare liberal arts American university that would include a broad, diversified program in philosophy. In addition to all of this, Mao read of the great men of the Western world including George Washington and the American Revolution, Napoleon and the Napoleonic War in Europe, Abraham Lincoln and the fight against slavery, the Duke of Wellington, Catherine and Peter the Great of Russia, and others.[30]

Of course, Mao also knew the Chinese classical philosophers and the literary classics. Mao's valuation of the Western tradition is prominent in the following quotation from his marginal notes: 'All our nation's two thousand years of scholarship may be said to be unthinking learning.'[31] This quotation might well reveal a Nietzschean influence for it much resembles Nietzsche's own critique of German "thinking". Consider Nietzsche's comment in one of his most concise, readable and trenchant works, his *Twilight of the Idols*: 'Learning to think: in our schools one no longer has any idea of this.'[32] Either Mao was influenced by Nietzsche or Mao independently was coming to a critique of Chinese education that was parallel to the critique that Nietzsche formed of his own German education.

Mao's valuation of the Western intellectual tradition is also noted in his 1917 Foreword to Xiao Zisheng's *All in One Self-Study Notes* where Mao writes: 'The defect of our country's ancient learning lay in its disorganized and unsystematic character. … As for Western studies … The classifications are so clear that they sound like a waterfall dashing against the rocks beneath a cliff. [Here we see evidence of Mao's nascent poetic abilities]. Today, anyone who is resolved to pursue learning, and yet does not follow this principle, will not be able to attain excellence.'[33] It is evident that, from the inception of his studies of both Chinese and Western philosophy, Mao greatly valued systematic, analytic thinking. Mao's own famous, later writings show that Mao himself develops his thinking in logical, systematic arguments, unlike the early Chinese tradition that he studied. In this respect, his thinking is more influenced by the Western method of thinking than the classical, Chinese wisdom tradition that formed the basis of Chinese philosophical education. Aristotle once defined philosophy as the making of distinctions. Mao's poetic rendition of his appreciation of clear and distinct distinctions as the sounds of a waterfall dashing against the rocks below a cliff shows his admiration of Western philosophical methods. The sound of a waterfall is clear as a bell and when it falls down from a great height to hit rocks, its sound is crystallized and, at the same time, becomes more distinct in addition to being even more clear-cut. A better description in poetic paraphrase of the precision and distinctness of Western classifications would be difficult to find. The ability to capture more clarity and precision in a metaphor than is to be found in a prose paraphrase requires the combined analytic skills of someone who has absorbed Western philosophy and the skill of a poet who has quenched his thirst at both Chinese and Western literary wells.

3

Mao in the Margins: Mao's Philosophy of Egoism

The Influence of Paulsen's *A System of Ethics*

Mao's preparation for taking on the philosophy of Marx was due both to his self-studies and his schooling, especially his studies with his future father-in-law, where he was introduced to the ethics of a German professor of philosophy, Friedrich Paulsen. Mao had the habit of philosophizing in the margins of Paulsen's *A System of Ethics* and, while he has not been well known for his marginal notes, these notes of a young man of twenty-four years *foreshadow, and to a very considerable extent, govern the direction of his thought for his entire life.* It is remarkable that a German philosopher whose name was not Karl Marx was to exert such a profound influence over Mao's future thinking.

The instructive feature of his marginal notes is that they show how Mao's thinking took shape as they are a living record of his active, engaged reaction to Paulsen's thinking. His marginal notes reveal Mao's self-appropriation and marshalling of Chinese Confucian and Daoist philosophy (including even one Buddhist reference), to speak to Paulsen's points. The examination of the development of these notes is the key to understanding how he formulates his own unique synthesis of all of these influences into his own particular philosophical approach.[1] It is only important to add that for Mao, these philosophical influences were ones that he saw as influences to be put into practice in his own life and not to be left at the level of pure theory. That he did so, and how he did so, did much to influence the history of China in the twentieth century. Mao's own practice of synthesis at this early stage is inconsistent with his later theoretical denial of synthesis, but this must await further discussion. In any event, it would not be the first example of a philosopher's practice not adhering to his theory.

The Significance of 'Mao in the Margins'

'Mao in the Margins,' is of special scholarly interest to study because, according to the translator, 'This crucially important document has previously been known only on the basis of fragmentary extracts taken out of context. In 1979, the Chinese published for internal circulation an ostensibly full text, subsequently reproduced in Volume 9 of the Tokyo edition of Mao's pre-1949 works, but this version was also seriously defective in two respects: the editors had left out long passages of Mao's often virtually illegible handwritten annotation and misread others; and they did not indicate clearly the passages of Cai Yuanpei's translation of Paulsen to which his [Mao's] comments referred.'[2]

Friedrich Paulsen (1846–1908) was Professor of Moral Philosophy at Berlin and promulgated a system based on an instinct or will to live (as distinct from rational desire). It is of interest that this principle of Paulsen was strongly influential on Mao's thought throughout Mao's entire life. The edition Mao studied was translated by Cai Yuanpei into Chinese, based primarily on the Japanese version translated by Kanie Yoshimaru, *et al.*, although Cai did check his version against the German original. Cai only translated Book II into Chinese and, in most cases followed the omissions of Frank Thilly, the American who did the English translation, and made further omissions of his own. Cai titled his translation of Book II of Paulsen, *Principles of Ethics* (*Lun Li Xue Yuan Li*), just as Kanie Yoshimaru had done before him.[3]

Mao's notes in the margins provide stunning evidence of his close, comprehensive reading of and intellectual reaction to Paulsen's philosophical work. Such a careful study of a German philosopher's mature writing is remarkable in and of itself. What is notable from his marginal notes is his appropriation of his own Chinese philosophical traditions and his reaction to Western philosophers. His thinking at this time of his development, which is pre-Marxist, is of special interest because it is at such a formative time of his development that he is attempting to construct a philosophy of Egoism which both possesses links to Western and Chinese traditions while, at the same time, forging ahead to break new ground. What is noteworthy about Paulsen's book is that it is not simply a single philosopher's philosophy of ethics. Paulsen ranges over the entire history of Western philosophy of ethics from ancient Greek times through Schopenhauer, passing through discussions of Aristotle, Augustine, Hobbes, Spinoza, Leibniz and Kant. In poring over Paulsen's commentary on these thinkers, Mao immerses himself in the topics and issues that form the essence of the history of Ethics in Western philosophy. As a result, though on one level, Mao's notes in the margins are a commentary on Paulsen and a springboard to his own thinking, on another level, these notes comprise an assimilation, evaluation and reaction to Western philosophy and its approaches to Ethics as a whole.

This present chapter possesses the unique value of being, to the best of the present author's knowledge, the first account to be based upon the full version of Mao's marginal notes that contains clear indications of which of Mao's comments refer to which sections of Paulsen. Such is the special significance of the study which commences below. Mao in the margins is a remarkable display of how Western philosophy influenced his thinking. At the same time, it reflects how Mao incorporated Western philosophy into his own, individual philosophical development and integrated it with his understanding of Chinese philosophy that he brought with him to the text.

Mao's marginal notes are a showcase of how the Chinese philosophical tradition from its early stages in Confucius still figures into the Chinese intellectual tradition in the early twentieth century, in the formative thinking of one of China's most influential political figures. In addition to this, while many writings both in Chinese and other languages make passing references to Mao's marginal notes to Paulsen's *A System of Ethics*, this chapter and significant portions of the sequel represent, to the best of the author's knowledge, the first concentrated and sustained study of Mao's marginal notes to Paulsen's *A System of Ethics*, which in itself constitutes a unique contribution to the literature of Chinese intellectual thought.[4]

Paulsen's, *A System of Ethics*

In Paulsen's book of 100,000 words, Mao's notations add up to over 12,000 words. According to Li Jiu, 'In addition, each word and sentence has circles, dots, single and double underlinings, triangles, crosses and other marks of punctuation added. This is a rare thing in the history of book-reading.'[5] Mao's characters that he prints in the margins are actually located in the blank spaces at the top and the bottom of the page and between the columns of text. The small ones are of No. 7 type and one needs a magnifying glass to see them clearly. The greatest number of notations of nearly 6,000 characters occur in Chapter IV, 'The Evil, the Bad and Theodicy,' and Chapter V, 'Duty and Conscience,' of *A System of Ethics*. According to Li's tally, there are over 1,500 characters notating Chapter VI, 'Egoism and Altruism,' and 1,100 characters notating Chapter I, 'Good and Bad: Teleological and Formalistic Conceptions.'[6]

The Continuity of Mao's Thought

Mao's views through time were to undergo considerable change. While his later Marxist thought is well known, his pre-Marxist standpoint of Egoism is not nearly as well known.⁷ It is assumed that Mao sheds these early educational influences fully when he adopts his Marxist philosophy. However, what I hope to demonstrate in this chapter and throughout this volume is that his early philosophy of Egoism is never truly abandoned and comes to shape Mao's thought even in the later period when his Marxism becomes predominant.

Mao's Views on Ethics

Since Mao's marginal notes are notes to Paulsen's book, *A System of Ethics*, it is important at the outset to take note that Mao's view of ethics, as Paulsen's, is not of a theoretical subject, but of a practical subject, that is, a subject which is designed to be put to use in the life of a human being. The distinction that is utilized by both Paulsen and Mao that points to this fact is the distinction between viewing ethics as a science or as an art. For both Paulsen and Mao, to describe ethics as a science meant that it was considered a theoretical subject. To describe ethics as an art meant that it was to be considered as a subject which should be used to guide and change one's life. This is the way in which Mao strongly considered the subject of ethics and, thus, his idea of philosophy was not simply to be viewed as a theoretical subject, but to be applied as a guide to the direction of life.⁸

The Idea of the Great Man and the Primacy of the Will

An important focus of this present volume lies in elucidating Mao's arguments for the primacy of the individual, the ego and the will, which form the basis for the idea that has lasting influence on his life, the idea of the Great Man.⁹ It is this idea, whether sub-consciously or self-consciously, that was to play an enormous role in shaping Mao's self-concept. However, these reflections anticipate further discussion. We must first examine how this idea of the Great Man was formulated and how the ideas were forged that were to guide and direct the actions of the Great Man.

It is of interest to examine the unique features of this philosophy of Egoism by contrasting it with other influences on Mao and other thinkers whose ideas have been considered to be parallel to those of Mao, such as Hobbes and Nietzsche. A key feature of this present book is to demonstrate which influences, and which of Mao's understandings of Western or Confucian ideas, played a role in shaping individual aspects of Mao's thinking development.

Mao was already assimilating ideas about great men that he would synthesize with his study of Paulsen and his interpolation of Chinese philosophy. One can begin to form an idea of how Mao would attempt to synthesize the ideas of the Great Man, and the primacy of the Will that he would glean from his reading of Paulsen, with the quality of the importance of the subjective that Mao would see in Confucius, together with the ethical values of Confucianism that formed the education of his youth.

Mao Collapses Moral Instinct into the Instinct for Self-preservation

To commence our examination proper of 'Mao in the Margins', we can start with the disagreement that Mao has with Paulsen's view that there is a natural instinct towards morality and Mao's thinking that moral behaviour stems from the desire to preserve one's own life.[10] For Mao, there is no separate moral instinct. Morality is inseparable from the desire for self-preservation. While this is a strong deviation from Confucius, for whom there was a sharp separation between self-interest and morality, Mao attempts to harmonize his view with the Confucianism of Confucius and Mencius. He notes that it was the view of early Confucians that morality resided in human nature and that it was universal.¹¹ His analytical interpretation of Confucius shows the analytic and synthetic skills he is developing from his exposure to Western philosophy. He uses reasoning to attempt to demonstrate that Confucius was really committed to the notions that he, Mao, was considering. This type of thinking was not typically part of traditional Chinese philosophical education which was commonly historical, exegetical and expository and generally did not focus on analytic examination of texts. At the same time, he considers that the Western view, represented by Paulsen, that each human being is unique is important.¹² This shows Mao's tendency to attempt to take from both Eastern and Western philosophical traditions and is a precursor to his later appropriation of Marx. It is of interest both that Mao received such an East–West education and that his response to it was not to accept one and reject the other, but to attempt somehow to amalgamate the two traditions, taking what he thought were the best points from each. Again, later, as we shall discover, he professes not to approve of such syntheses in thinking, but at this early stage there is no doubt that he engages in synthetic thinking.

Mao takes strong issue with Paulsen's idea that human beings are just as concerned about the welfare of their relatives and their friends as they are about themselves. For Mao, 'It is impossible to say that any mind is purely altruistic without any idea of self-interest.'¹³ Ultimately, for the early Mao, as for the early Marx, the individual comes first.¹⁴ Mao utilizes his version of Confucian philosophy and not Paulsen's rendition of European philosophy of altruism to explain morality. For Mao, one must love the self first before extending this love to others. Is it possible that Mao took note of Oscar Wilde's famous quip: 'To love oneself is the beginning of a life-long romance'? This epigram is actually a line Oscar Wilde gives to Lord Goring in his play, 'The Ideal Husband' in his speech to Phipps. 'The Ideal Husband', we recall, was the Oscar Wilde play that was part of Mao's formative education.

The ultimate beneficiary, for Mao, at this stage of the development of his thought, is the individual, and society exists for the sake of the individual and not vice versa. Mao has a rather unique interpretation of the idea of self-interest. For Mao, it is part of our nature to help others (in greatest likelihood he is influenced by the real Confucius, here). However, Mao's understanding of this is that the helping of others is the result of the desire to fulfil one's own nature and not from an altruistic motivation *simpliciter*. 'Objective morality' is the result, for Mao, of that which is subjective.[15] This motivation, to fulfil the potential of the human being, a kind of justification of morality as self-actualization, shows more of Mao's own contribution to the Chinese philosophical tradition. Normally, Egoism is put forward as a philosophy that is contradictory to Altruism. Likewise, Altruism is put forward as a philosophy that is contradictory to Egoism. Mao's attempts to link Egoism with morality form a unique contribution. Whether or not this coupling is ultimately coherent is another issue. What is of interest is Mao's unique attempt to bring the two distinct approaches into some kind of unity.

Mao did not separate morality from our nature. His view of conscience was that conscience sprung from and was not in contradiction to our instincts. This view is in stark contradiction with Christian morality and, with respect to Western philosophy, in contradiction to Kantian ethics. Mao builds his philosophical case for conscience as not opposing our instincts in these notations:

> The desire to eat contributes to my life, sexual desire is good for my development, and both of these come from natural instincts. Since the will is based on instincts, how can the conscience, which is part of the will, be an exception? Since the conscience too originates from the instincts, it should in principle be consistent with the instincts.[16]

This is an example of Mao's original philosophizing. It is through pure philosophy that Mao is arriving at his conclusions. He is not a social scientist relying upon empirical data for his conclusions; nor is he a historian, compiling his observations from the lessons of history. Neither is this sequence of reasoning an example of the borrowed plumage of ideology, an example of dogmatizing, based on and derivative from some previous thinker. Nor is it an example of political advocacy. It is the original philosophizing of Mao found as it is in the marginal notes he writes in his own hand. While ostensibly the marginal notes he makes to Paulsen's, *A System of Ethics* could be a commentary on Paulsen, Mao goes far beyond noting his reactions to Paulsen. The marginal forum provides Mao with a venue for his own philosophizing and he goes about it with vigour and acumen.

Mao is aware that there will be objections to his alliance of the conscience with instincts. He defends the alliance in advance by arguing that the conscience only guides instincts in certain cases in which it needs to restrain the instincts in order to allow them to flourish in situations in which they do not require restraint. Such occasional restraints are not proof of an antagonism between conscience and the instincts. Rules that we learn *a posteriori* that are opposed to our instincts sometimes do interfere, but we must not confuse the application of such rules with the natural instincts with which we are born. Mao puts together this defence of the alliance between the instincts and the conscience in the following passage:

> The conscience certainly always sees our appetite for food and for sex for what they are. It is only at a particular time and place that the conscience will suggest restraining the impulses, as when the desire for food or sex becomes excessive. And then the conscience acts only to restrain or moderate the excess, certainly not to oppose or deny these desires. It is this restraint that perfects the job of the instincts. Thus, the instincts and the conscience are consistent as a matter of course, in harmony rather than in conflict. A posteriori training and habits that are rigid and excessive will lead to incidents that deny nature and instinct, and will cause the conscience, which derives from the same source as instinct, which is likewise true and

natural and real, to become warped and unnatural and false. This is the tragedy of excessive rigidity.[17]

What is striking about this passage is not only the content of the ethical theory that Mao is constructing, but also the fact that he is constructing an ethical theory utilizing systematic philosophical thinking. Mao was not only influenced by the content of the philosophies that he was studying; his mind, as evidenced from this passage, was becoming a trained, philosophical mind.

Mao sums up his reaction to the moral philosophies of Kant, Fichte, Spinoza, Bentham and Mill in this pithy comment:

> Because these all have insisted on separating natural will and the sense of duty in opposition to each other, they have failed to recognize that they are one, and the differences are only ones of degree, and of time and place.[18]

Whether or not Mao is correct in his critique of these philosophers of ethics and whether his own ethical theory is correct or philosophically coherent remains to be seen. What cannot be denied is that Mao has constructed his own ethical theory and has shown himself to be a systematic philosopher.

Mao on Aristotle and Confucius: A Prelude

In a sense, Mao's justification of morality owes more to Aristotle than it does to Confucius, though it represents a partial understanding of Aristotle. For Aristotle, one does become self-actualized through ethical behaviour and does reach happiness in that way. The difference is that self-actualization is not the motivation for ethical actions for Aristotle (or Confucius) as it is for Mao.

One could put forth an argument that the motivation for ethical actions for both Aristotle and Confucius is moral self-growth, but this still differs from Mao's concept of self-actualization. It may not even be strictly accurate to say for Aristotle and Confucius that moral self-growth is the motivation for morality, but at least this serves to illustrate a comparative dimension. A stricter delineation of Aristotle, Confucius and Mao appears in the sequel. Suffice it to say that while for Aristotle it is evident that the building of a moral character is indistinguishable from the adjuration to perform ethical acts, in Confucius it could be argued that the two enjoinders are more separable. At the very least, it could be said that the connection between ethical acts and the formation of an ethical character in Confucius is discussed in separate places.

For Aristotle, a moral character is built for the sake of performing moral acts and moral acts in turn build the moral character. For Confucius, building a moral character is also an end in itself. The systematic tie between these two adjurations is implicit.

Mao on Schopenhauer

Mao builds his philosophy of Egoism in his reactions to Western philosophy. Mao takes issue with Schopenhauer, or to be more precise, Paulsen's interpretation of Schopenhauer, that the self can take no pleasure in moral acts. For Mao, this is proof that Schopenhauer does not understand true Egoism, which allows that moral value need not originate from Altruism, but rather that Altruism is a natural outgrowth of self-love, or Egoism.[19] Strictly speaking, Altruism, or a pure selfless act, makes no sense for Mao, because the other is simply the extension of the self. All ethics is thus based on Egoism. This part of Mao's thinking is difficult to grasp, because of the subtlety of his philosophical thinking. Mao is making two distinct points. Firstly, all acts are proceeding from the self so that acts that appear to be for the other are still acts that stem from the self. Secondly, there is no clear distinction between self and other because the so-called 'others' are in reality other selves.

It would appear that the later Mao deviates from this integration of Egoism with Altruism in his commemoration of the Canadian physician, Norman Bethune, that are reflected in his 'In Memory to Norman Bethune' (21 December 1939), in which he praises selflessness. Either the later Mao moves from the position of the early Mao adopted in these passages, or this tribute to Bethune is motivated by his later, political intention to move the masses, i.e. a political motive, and does not constitute a shift in his philosophical outlook.[20]

There is always the problem of distinguishing between the writings that constitute Mao's individual philosophical foundations and motivations, and Mao's political writings. The concerns of this volume rest with the writings that reflect Mao's individual philosophical development.[21] In my view, the examples that K. T. Fann enumerates of Mao's explicit pronouncements about how we must move away from bookish philosophy and professional philosophy fall into the category of political writings.[22]

Mao on Buddhism and Mohism

In Mao's own words:

> Every act in life is for the purpose of fulfilling the individual, and all morality serves to fulfill the individual. Expressing sympathy for others, and seeking the happiness of others, are not for others, but for oneself. My heart contains this love of others, so I need to fulfill it, for if it cannot be fulfilled then there is something lacking in my life, I have not achieved my ultimate end. This is how both Sakyamuni and Mo Di achieved their ultimate ends.[23]

Ironically, the critique that is frequently brought forth against ethics is that when one performs an altruistic act, one is only doing it for one's self-interest (to feel good, for example) and therefore this diminishes the ethical value of the act or dissolves it altogether. For Mao, the very meaning of ethics is to enhance one's self-interest.

It is to be noted that Mao cites both the Buddha and Mozi (the Chinese philosopher known for his teaching of universal love) as supportive of his own ideas of individual Egoism. While neither Buddhist scholars nor Mozi justified their ideas of morality in this fashion, it is the case that Mao thought that he could and should draw upon their authority to support his concepts. It is clear from such evidence that Mao is aware of both Buddhism and Mohism and while he may misunderstand their ideas, what is important to realize is that the ideas that he forms would have not taken the shape that they take had he not come into contact with their ideas. Mao's ideas grow out of his contact with and reaction to the philosophers with whom he had come into contact. There is no doubt that it is a result of such an interaction between these philosophers and his own thinking that Mao forges his own philosophy.

Mao's Individualism

However one characterizes Mao's thinking, it is evident that however one construes his understanding of both Chinese and Western philosophers, Mao has built his own philosophy of Egoism on the foundation of a sequence of ideas based on assumptions followed by carefully constructed arguments. Mao has not simply adapted values blindly that have no basis or origin in tradition. At the same time, for Mao, moral actions must be based on one's feeling and will, or else moral actions are simply a kind of blind morality which, for Mao, has no value at all. Mao's philosophy of Egoism is a blend of philosophical argument and its expression in feeling and will. The incipient contradiction one can detect in these early formulations is that if the ultimate justification is self-actualization, and in the scheme of things, if altruism is a means to this end, then it is logically possible that altruism could be overridden should a more efficient or effective means to achieving self-actualization be discovered. This hidden problem may play a role in Mao's decisions to sacrifice human lives to achieve greater ends in his political decision making later in his life.

All values, for the early Mao, are based on individualism. This foundation in individualism clearly reflects the influence of Western thinking on Mao's mind. Mao goes so far as to say that, 'Thus, it can be said that the value of the individual is greater than that of the universe ... there is no greater crime than to suppress the individual or to violate particularity.'[24] It is fascinating to compare the early Mao with the early Marx for parallels in this respect although at this point in his philosophical development, Mao is unaware of Karl Marx.[25] It is also of note to consider how much the early Mao values individualism, setting its value above that of the universe. To hold individualism as the highest value is a prioritization of values that is particularly Western because, of all values, individualism is perhaps the most treasured value for the Western thinker and certainly the value most characteristically associated with that of the Western mind. On the other hand, Mao's later sacrifices of individuals during the Cultural Revolution could be interpreted as sacrificing the individual for the sake of society.

For the early Mao, the idea of individualism and the idea of self-realization are the same. As he states in the margins:

> The only goal of human beings is to realize the self. Self-realization means to develop fully both our physical and spiritual capabilities to the highest.[26]

As pointed out above, the danger of Egoism as an ethical foundation is that if love of others is ultimately for the actualization of oneself, then if one can actualize oneself while sacrificing others, the sacrifice of others can be justified. If it is the individual self, in the end, that is to be actualized, it is possible that others can be sacrificed in the interest of the self. While this is mitigated by the concept that one's self is actualized in the love of others, since the individual self is the ultimate arbiter of value, it is always possible that some others can be sacrificed or even all others can be sacrificed in the actualization of the self. At the very least, a stage has been set for a conflict of values and, hence, the founding of ethics which includes a melding of Altruism with Egoism is a less than coherent doctrine. Confucius entirely avoids this problem by excluding the happiness of the individual from being a motivation for moral choices. While Aristotle does include the happiness of the individual as a result of moral choice, the happiness of the individual does not form the motivation for the moral choice. These two philosophies are constructed to avoid the potential problems that ensue by founding Altruism upon a foundation of Egoism.

Mao and Zhuangzi

The danger that others might be sacrificed to achieve the goals of the individual will be seen in our later analysis of Mao's reference to the passage relating the story of the cicada catcher in the *Zhuangzi* (Stuart Schram considers Zhuangzi to be Mao's favourite philosopher).[27] While the intent of the passage in the *Zhuangzi* (to be examined below) may not be to elevate self over others, Mao's reference to the passage of the cicada catcher can be understood in this way. It is a good example of how Mao adapts the thought of classical philosophers to suit his own purposes. Whether or not Mao thought he was simply expounding the doctrines of these philosophers in the first place is an interesting and valid question.

One way out of the ethical dilemma posed by the built-in hierarchy of the philosophy of Egoism which prioritizes self over others is to locate ethical values in both the individual *and* the other. In this way, there is no clear path to the sacrifice of the other for the sake of the self. Both self and other have ultimate ethical value and neither can be sacrificed for the sake of the other. To say that society exists for the sake of the self is to take one side as possessing value and not the other. It is safer, for example, to take Aristotle's view that society exists as a necessary venue for performing ethical actions (actions that benefit others). In this view, there is value both for the individual and society even though one exists for the sake of the other. We can delve into the way in which Confucius and Aristotle address this issue in the following chapter.

Synopsizing Mao's Views of Egoism and Ethics from his Marginal Notes

It is challenging to synopsize Mao's views on Egoism and ethics for three main reasons: (i) his notes reveal a development of his views as he makes notes in the margins; (ii) it is a difficult philosophical task that Mao takes on; (iii) Mao's attempt to forge a coherent philosophical view is imperfect. It is important to take special note of (ii) so that we can realize the enormity of the task Mao takes on and to realize that the lack of perfection in his efforts is not simply because of any weakness in his philosophical thinking, but because of the intransigence this ethical problem holds for any thinker of any stature.

The Egoism–Altruism Conundrum

The problem that Mao undertakes to solve is the classical philosophical problem of reconciling, or in some respect, making sense of adjudicating between the needs of the individual and the ethical demands to sacrifice the individual for the sake of the other. This problem is not unique to Western or Chinese philosophy; it is a problem that is a problem for both Western and Chinese philosophy. It is a problem that may be said to lack a coherent solution. Philosophers, for the most part, tend to stress either the Ego versus Altruism, such as Hobbes, or Altruism over Egoistic desires such as Kant. If one stresses the individual, ethics, or concern for the other, tends to be de-emphasized.

If one tends to stress concern for the other, the status of the self tends to be thrown into jeopardy. This problem is one of the most difficult of all problems that the philosopher must confront and Mao's unique attempt to forge a unity between Egoism and Altruism exemplifies the boldness of his philosophical thinking processes. What marks Mao as a philosopher is his concerted effort to resolve the Self-Other problem. He neither evades it nor does he simply follow other thinkers by accepting a ready-made solution to the problem. He attempts to set forth his own solution to the problem. Whether or not one agrees with his solution, finds it coherent, incoherent, or based upon a misconstruction of classical philosophers, such as Confucius, one cannot argue with the fact that Mao's grappling with this problem clearly reveals philosophical thinking.

In the sequel, we shall discuss how Mao's views may also derive from an early interpretation of Confucianism. At the moment, we shall occupy ourselves with attempting to see how Mao attempts to solve the Egoism–Altruism conundrum. First of all, we should make certain that we understand the immense importance of this problem. This problem is a manifestation of the basic existential question: What is the meaning of life? That Mao saw it this way is evidenced by his early, existential philosophizing.

When we question the purpose of life, it is natural to consider whether our life should be one in which we attempt to serve our individual self-interest or whether our life should be one in which we attempt to improve the world or to serve the needs of others, especially those others in particular need. Those who choose self-interest are labelled as Egoists and those who choose to help others are labelled as Altruists. In his early studies, Mao strongly favoured a life in which the self was to be actualized to its fullest potential. However, he did not think that such a priority eliminated concern for the other.

Mao thought that those who favoured Altruism, that is, sacrificing the self in order to serve others, were wrong-headed. Because of his strong interest in manifesting his individual will, he was opposed to the idea of self-sacrifice. This was not a universal opposition as he cites examples in his marginal notes where self-sacrifice is warranted. However, even in these instances, Mao argues that these self-sacrifices are founded on the will of the individual. The individual, in these circumstances, sees that in order to fulfil her or his ultimate values, she or he must sacrifice her or his self. The sacrifice is still, in Mao's terms, the fulfilment of that individual's ultimate values, and hence, serves the mission of fulfilling that individual's will. This fusion of Altruism and Egoism, while not a commonly held or understood notion, is not *prima facie* incoherent.

Mao's concept of Egoism is a concept that includes Altruism within it. It is not a concept that pits Egoism as over against Altruism. Mao was not opposed to Altruism *per se*. Mao was opposed to sacrificing the ego for the other. While he does not provide specific argumentation for this point, he takes the position that pure Altruists, such as Schopenhauer or Kant, do not possess a true understanding of human motivation. For Mao, our motivation must be based upon the self, not upon a denial of the self. His thinking is based upon a prior notion that all our knowledge is based upon our experience.[28] Implicit in his thinking is the notion that we experience our self as motivated by self-interest. The expression of our true self must be consistent with this. Even our conscience, Mao writes, emanates from the same self as the self that wills its way through life. Here, Mao parts company with those who consider that conscience or duty is something separate and external to self. Such a viewpoint is unique and reveals Mao's creativity as a philosophical thinker. If duty were something that were external to the self, whence would it come? From God? Mao addresses this point directly with a startling conclusion:

> Some say that we must believe that the moral law comes from the command of God, for only then can it be carried out and not be despised. This is a slavish mentality. [The influence of Nietzsche can be seen here] Why should you obey God rather than obey yourself? You are God. Is there any other God other than yourself? Our study of the origin of the conscience shows that this problem also comes from ourselves, so we should obey that which comes

from ourselves. All the myriad things that exist in space and time should obey what comes from themselves, for there is nothing greater in value.[29]

Mao's declaration that you are God goes well beyond Nietzsche. He integrates this idea with his concept that obedience to one's individual self is the highest value we should hold. He integrates this concept with a metaphysical conclusion that this is true of all things that exist in the universe. Mao is not simply an Existentialist arguing for Egoism. He is a metaphysician arguing that what he claims to be true of human existence holds true for the universe as a whole.

Mao expresses his strong agreement with Paulsen when Paulsen anticipates Sartre's famous point in his 'Existentialism is a Humanism' that one should be moral irrespective of whether the Deity exists or not. When Paulsen writes, 'Whether or not there is life after death in no way changes the principles of ethics … And should there be only this life, and no life after death, the moral law should still be obeyed',[30] Mao exclaims: 'Quite true!'.

Mao did not see his Egoism as in conflict with morality.

The idea that ethics should stem from the sake of duty, as in Kant, is one that Paulsen opposed. In Paulsen's words:

> Thus in Kant's opinion, a human act has value only when the will contains a conflict of the inclinations or impulses, but one acts purely from a feeling of duty.[31]

In the margins, Mao writes:

> I would say that this kind of sense of duty can only be sought in the world of the unconscious, or in the world of the dead.[32]

Paulsen goes on to say:

> But a humanity that is good solely for the sake of duty would be dry and insipid, like so many wooden manikins.[33]

In response to this, Mao exclaims: 'Quite so!' [34]

Paulsen's attack on duty continues:

> Kant overemphasized the consciousness of duty, and Fichte was even worse. ... Moral philosophers have always considered that perfection could be attained only when all actions of the will were determined by the idea of duty. Spinoza's sage is governed wholly by the dictates of reason, and his impulses have no effect whatsoever on his behavior, and the wise man of Bentham or Mill differs little from him. They are modeled on the Stoic and Epicurean sage. In reality, reason or the idea of duty, is not necessarily this important. The impulses are the hanging weights of the clockwork of life. Reason definitely cannot replace them. Why? Reason has no motive force of its own.[35]

In response to these remarks, Mao writes: 'This is the idea that regulates me.' [36] [Seemingly Mao is referring to the key idea that reason regulates the instincts, but cannot replace them.]

Mao exclaims: 'Excellent point!'[37] [It appears that Mao is particularly struck by Paulsen's metaphor that the impulses are the hanging weights of the clockwork of life and that reason cannot replace them, because it has no motive force of its own.]

On what basis does Mao find such agreement with Paulsen? One might conjecture that Mao has recourse to a phenomenological inspection of his own motivations, and through self-inspection, arrives at the conclusion that he is motivated by impulse and not by reasoning. Such thinking of Mao is not distant to that of Freud's perspective.

In response to Paulsen's comment that Kant over-emphasized the consciousness of duty, Mao writes: 'The view of our Song Neo-Confucians is the same as Kant's.'[38]

Mao shows at this early stage of his thinking not only his familiarity with both Chinese and Western philosophy, but his ability to do comparative philosophy. This degree of versatility and breadth of thought is unique even by today's standards of professional comparative philosophy, Chinese and Western. It is clear that no love is lost between Mao and Song Neo-Confucianism. Mao applies the same critique against Neo-Confucianism that he applies against Kant.

Mao displays the same familiarity and versatility with his references to both Western and Chinese history that he does with Chinese and Western philosophy. For example, Paulsen writes about the Prussian General York, who disobeyed his king's order by signing a peace treaty with his enemy [Russia] in order to force Napoleon to withdraw from Russia, thus violating his duty to observe military obedience, in order to save his country. Of this action on the part of General York, Paulsen writes:

> Was this action still in accordance with duty, and was it permissible morally? According to the Kantian formula, certainly not. It is bad for the country for a general knowingly to act contrary to his king's order. Moreover, if pursued to its limit, at another time it might be impossible to use the universal formula to keep Prussian soldiers under command. … After having wanted to rebuke him, the Prussian king also admitted that he was right. And today, there is no historian who does not think that this action benefited Prussia. And even though this action was most disadvantageous for the French, French historians do not question it.[39]

Kant's formula, to which Paulsen refers, is the Categorical Imperative, one version of which is that one should always act as if one's action were to be a universal law of nature.

In response, Mao writes in the margins: 'The same was true of the dissolution of Parliament by Cromwell.'[40]

Mao concurs with Paulsen that General York was right to disobey his king and buttresses his agreement with an example of his own taken from his own knowledge of British history.[41] What is most striking about Mao's marginal notes is his prescient comment referring to what justifies the action of great men when the state is in an emergency and universal morality must be transcended:

This is necessarily true in the case of a revolution.[42]

Is it possible that these early reflections cast a long shadow on Mao's thinking?

Mao on Aesthetics and Ethics

Paulsen writes:

So, too the most perfect morality is to live naturally by realizing one's instincts, rather than being concerned with ethics. Both aesthetics and ethics possess no creative power. It is their job to guard against going beyond the bounds of beauty and morality. Thus, they are restrictive, not creative.[43]

Mao's reaction to these words is illuminating. In the margins he comments: I strongly support this view.[44]

Mao's insight is that our desires for morality and beauty are built in. We are moral actors and appreciators and creators of beauty [think of the cave paintings at Lascaux] many centuries prior to the construction of ethical and aesthetic theories. In Mao's words:

Beauty existed long before there was a field of aesthetics, and every human being had virtue and attained his ultimate end long before there was a study of ethics.[45]

In these words, one can almost hear the echo of Mao's early exposure to Rousseau.

In later chapters, as above, it will be noted that the merger of Altruism and Egoism is susceptible to the danger of Altruism being subsumed by Egoism. However, to be fair to Mao, we must distinguish Mao's version of Egoism from the crude view of egoism in which one only concerns oneself with the narrow boundaries of one's empirical ego. Mao's Egoism is more refined and more comprehensive.

Mao's vision of the individual, whether stemming from reading Paulsen, from his interpretation of Confucius and Mencius, or a combination of these influences, is a view in which one need not eliminate Altruism. In one passage in the margins, Mao writes in his own refutation of Hobbes:

> Since human beings have an ego, for which the self is the centre of all things and all thought, self-interest is primary for all persons. That this serves the interests of other is due to the fact that those others who belong to the same category as the self share related interests. Thus we may say that the self cannot but benefit others. The starting point of altruism is the self, and altruism is related to the self. It is impossible to say that any mind is purely altruistic without any idea of self-interest. Nothing in the world takes the other as its starting point and the self does not seek to benefit anything in the world that is totally unrelated to the self. Otherwise, such concepts as 'individual personality', 'self-discipline', and 'freedom' would be absurd. These concepts are indeed a noble egoism, an egoism of the spirit. If I open my eyes wide and say that mankind is the greater self, and say that all living things are the greater self, and then say that the universe is the greater self, does this negate self-interest? Why should self-interest be untrustworthy? Ultimately, the individual comes first. [46]

Mao's view of Egoism bears a similarity to ancient Greek ethics in which nobility of action was considered ethical.[47] Ancient Greek ethics did not rely upon *agape* or charitable love to consider others. The consideration of others grew out of an expansion of self-love. For Aristotle, for example, one accumulated private property in order to exercise the largesse of generosity.

This is not to say that Mao's noble Egoism is without problems. What is significant at this stage of analysis of Mao's thought is that Mao thought he could amalgamate Egoism and Altruism without any sacrificing of the self. One cannot help but think of one part of Hillel's famous statement, 'If I am not for myself, who will be for me?' In fact, one can find Mao expressing a similar thought:

> The theory of universal love is not altruism, for universal love includes the self, is to extend the love of self to loving all men. By basing the theory on self, it has a starting point, a criterion. If self and other are treated as having equal weight, there is no starting point, and the criterion is lost.[48]

Again, this makes sense from Hillel's point of view when in the Hebrew Bible it states that one should love the other as one's self.

Mao's Egoism is not to be confused with the notion that when one does something for someone else, one is doing these acts *only* for the pleasure it brings to the self. When Paulsen writes that the narrowest sense of duty means considering what is in the interest of others, Mao takes exception:

> I, however, think that we have a duty only to ourselves, and have no duty toward others. This duty arises naturally within my spirit, such as repaying debts, keeping promises, not stealing, not being false, and although they are things that involve other people, it is also my wish that they be done. The meaning of duty to oneself means no more than just developing fully one's own physical and spiritual powers. [Could these youthful philosophical reflections have contributed to the mature Mao's famous swim in the Yangzi River?] Helping others in need ... sacrificing oneself to save others, are no more than duty, since I desire to do them, and only then will my mind be

at rest. If I see someone in danger and do not try to rescue him, even if not doing so would not be considered wrong will I really think in my own mind that not helping him is right? The fact that I think it is not right is what makes it my duty to try to rescue him. We rescue those who are in danger to set our minds at rest, and to develop fully the capacities of our spirit.[49]

Mao is interested in encouraging human beings to fulfil each person's individual potential to the fullest. In so doing, he thinks that all human beings can flourish. Mao sees no conflict between doing what is right and feeling pleasure or, in his words, peace of mind, as the result. In this regard, Mao's ethical theory is very close to that of Aristotle.

For Mao, individualism and the complete fulfilment of one's potential are not simply existential values or values that are important for psychological health as in the humanistic psychology of Abraham Maslow. They are *ethical* values. Mao's concept of duty towards oneself is what he considers the ultimate value. If one takes the theologian Paul Tillich's definition of religious values as one's ultimate values, then Mao's valuation of duty to oneself is a religious value. I call attention to this, not to argue that Mao was religious, but only to emphasize how highly Mao valued the obligation one had to fulfilling the potential of the self. This following passage from Mao emphasizes this:

Laws are made only to forbid people to do evil, and not to encourage people to be good. ... Duty is directed toward oneself. Duty to oneself cannot be a matter of degree. Our duty should be to put the highest good into practice, that is, to develop our mental and physical capacities to the highest, and to experience life to the fullest. If I have a job to do and the ability to do that job fully, my sense of duty forbids me to slack off or fail to do it. ... Duty means more than just not doing something or other; it also means that there are some things that ought to be done. Duty is not just negative; it also has a positive meaning.[50]

He specifically contrasts his view with Hobbes's Egoism. In Paulsen's exposition of Hobbes, Paulsen writes:

> This view [the view of Hobbes] states that everyone strives for what is agreeable or useful to oneself, regardless of whether it furthers or detracts from the welfare of others. This view, formulated as a theory, is known as egoism; it is also called individualistic utilitarianism.[51]

Mao's critique of Hobbes illustrates his attempt to merge Altruism with Egoism. In Mao's merger, he does not seek to eliminate Altruism. The question, which will be taken up in later chapters, is whether Altruism can survive the merger. It is worthwhile to examine how Mao forges the merger between Egoism, as he sees it, and Altruism:

> I really feel that this explanation [the one of Hobbes above] is incomplete. Since human beings have an ego, for which the self is the centre of all things and all thought, self-interest is primary for all purposes. That this serves the interests of others is due to the fact that those others who belong to the same category of the self share related interests. Thus we say that the self cannot but benefit others. The starting point of altruism is the self, and altruism is related to the self. It is impossible to say that any mind is purely altruistic without any idea of self-interest.[52]

If one were to take the last statement in this rejoinder to Hobbes out of context, it could appear that altruistic acts were performed for the sake of self-interest. However, this reading of Mao's meaning is too simplistic. Mao's thinking is more subtle. He is saying that serving the self cannot help but help others. Whether this thinking is sound is another question. Mao seems not to recognize that there could be conflicts of interest between some selves and other selves. Nevertheless, no matter how coherent or incoherent Mao's theorizing turns out to be, his Egoism is not to be confused with the Egoism of Hobbes.

Mao clearly holds that in the Egoism–Altruism mixture, Egoism is primary. At the same time, he does not think that Egoism negates Altruism:

> If I open my eyes wide and say that mankind is the greater self, and then say that the universe is the greater self, does this negate self-interest? Why should self-interest be unworthy?[53]

For Paulsen, the will is the primary motivator of mankind. Paulsen writes:

> It may be said that the goal of my will is the common shared welfare of the individual and society, or we may say that the welfare of society includes the welfare of the individual.[54]

In Mao's notes adjoining this statement of Paulsen's, he exclaims: 'Quite true, quite true!' [55]

Mao does not foresee any problem arising from attempting to satisfy the needs of society and the needs of individuals.

Although counter-intuitive to a Christian view of ethics, Mao is a passionate advocate of ethics as part of Egoism. Indeed, his view of Egoism is that it is man's highest calling. Mao's Egoism is not simply an empirical description based on observation and historical data that human beings tend to serve their own self-interest; it is a normative value:

> Self-interests are indeed primary for human beings, but it does not stop there. It is also of our nature to extend this to helping others. This is one and the same human nature, so working for the interests of others is in my own self-interest. … I do not agree … that moral values apply only to those acts that are motivated by altruism. Morality does not necessarily depend on others. … My desire to fulfill my nature and perfect my mind is the most precious of the moral laws.[56]

The task of integrating Egoism with Altruism is no easy task. It may be that the two do not mix, like oil and water. Nevertheless, the young Mao attempts to integrate the two with the argument that Altruism is a means to Egoism and Egoism is the primary term:

> ... it is egoism that pursues life, and altruism is simply one of the methods it employs to attain one's life objectives. It goes without saying that there is absolutely no basis for pure altruism.[57]

Mao does seem to realize that there is the problem of the conflict between egoistic interests of different individuals, but still thinks the theory has merit:

> Pure egoism is also merely a theory that definitely cannot be realized in this world of multiple individual entities and diverse activities. Although it cannot be realized, although it is not a factual reality, it does still have meaning. The basic meaning of human life still lies in fulfilling the individual.[58]

This is different from Nietzsche who does not include working for the interests of others in his ethics. For Nietzsche, self-overcoming is advocated, but Nietzsche does not explicitly advocate working for others as part of one's nature.

Mao on Good and Evil

For Paulsen, absolute evil does not exist on its own, but only as a means to realizing what is good. Paulsen refers to Augustine's critique of the Persian religion of the Manichaeans in which good and evil possess equal ontological status.

In Mao's formulation, evil is not equivalent in value to good because evil only exists as a lesser good:

> Something that is evil is so because it is inferior to the good, it cannot be equal in value to the good. It is not evil by nature. ... But it cannot be said to be without value. At a particular time we may feel that it is totally without value, and not only that it has no value, but that it is very harmful. This refers just to that particular time, and in relationship to something else. This does not mean that by nature it is valueless in itself.[59]

When Paulsen points out that Spinoza and Leibniz held that the difference between good and evil lies solely in the fact that our ways of looking at things are incomplete, Mao responds: 'I agree very much with this statement.'[60]

Even the elimination of evil is not, from Mao's vantage point, an end in itself but because evil interferes with the actualization of life:

> We want to do away with evil because it is enemy to the fulfillment of life. Thus we eliminate evil in the process of fulfilling life, not just to eliminate evil.[61]

Synopsizing Mao's Views on Individualism and Society from his Marginal Notes

Mao, as usual, does not put forth a simplistic view of the relationship between individualism and society. His solution to the relationship between the individual and society bears a resemblance to the views he puts forth on the relationship between Egoism and Altruism. He strongly emphasizes that society exists for the sake of the individual and not vice versa. He arrives at this conclusion by taking note that the individual exists first, and not society. Society comes into being as an aggregate of individuals. From this fact Mao deduces that society comes into being to serve individuals and not vice versa. While one may take the position that this is not a convincing argument that society should serve the individual, it is not an argument that is wholly without merit. Regardless of whether one sides with Mao on this matter, the point is that his position is not arbitrarily chosen, but is based upon philosophical reasoning.

Of course, Mao's views on society as existing to benefit the individual are in complete accord with his notion of the primacy of the individual. However, his views of society as existing to serve individual interest are not based solely on the philosophical position of the primacy of the individual. His views of prioritizing the individual are based on a separate and independent philosophical argument, namely, that individuals pre-exist social formation. Society, therefore, must come into being to further individual benefit.

Needless to say, the difficulties with the problem of reconciling social needs with individual needs are not solved by the dictum that society exists to fulfil individual needs. Nevertheless, it cannot be denied that such a prioritization paves the way to showing respect for individual rights. One may well argue that Mao's later thought and his governance runs contrary to these youthful, philosophical values. On the other hand, one could interpolate from Mao's early views on individualism that Mao's vision for China was motivated by the thought that the society that he could bring into being was a society in which the interests of each individual could best be furthered and fulfilled. Whether the means he utilized to achieve this were justified is an entirely different matter. Whether or not Mao was correct about his vision for China and the methods he chose to use to attempt to bring the sort of society he envisioned into being, one cannot conclude that Mao had totally moved away from his youthful ideals. In contrast, it could well be argued that Mao never lost sight of these core ideals.

4

Mao's Early Philosophical Influences and Reflections

Confucian and Aristotelian Influences

How does Mao's thought relate to the Chinese and Western philosophers who have influenced his early philosophical development? We may begin with Confucian and Aristotelian influences on his thought. For Mao, the individual does actualize the self in moral action (so far, Aristotle, Confucius and Mao are in agreement). For Confucius and Aristotle, while the individual actualizes the self in moral action, moral action is mandated not for the sake of individual actualization, but because the moral action is itself correct. The individual actualization is a happy by-product of the performance of the ethical action. However, the ethical action is not performed for the sake of the individual actualization. In Confucius and Aristotle, seminal moral thinkers, the ethical act is performed because it is the right action to perform and for no other reason.[1] It is only because the act is performed, because it is right to perform such an act (such a criterion bypasses the dichotomy between Egoism and Altruism for it is not for self or for other) that the individual can realize the self.

The Impact of Aristotle's Ethics on Mao

While the connection, for Confucius, between right action and self-realization is not as direct as it is to be found in Aristotle, it is nevertheless there because right action is an essential part of human nature. This is unlike morality in Kant where right action is something separate from human nature. Mao's view comes closer to Aristotle's than to Confucius's because in Aristotle, one's happiness derives from one's moral actions and in Confucius, the performance of moral acts has nothing to do with happiness. In this respect, the morality of Confucius resembles that of Kant. For Confucius and Kant, specific moral acts cannot be performed for the sake of personal happiness. This is the same for Aristotle though in Aristotle's philosophy, the case is more blurred because ultimately one does obtain happiness by performing ethical actions. Kant would be farther apart since any satisfaction of natural inclination would be a mark of a departure from morality.

It is eye opening to consider that Mao's thought on this issue may be more deeply influenced by one of the most influential thinkers of the West than by one of the most influential thinkers of his own native China. Mao's view is not identical to that of Aristotle, because morality for Aristotle (as it is for Confucius) is mandated on the basis of its rightness, not on the basis of its functioning as a fulfilment of human nature. It does fulfil human nature for Aristotle, but that is not the reason why it should be practised. This subtle distinction is sometimes lost on those commentators of Aristotle who consider Aristotle to be a virtue ethicist with a eudemonistic justification.[2] Of course, some of these distinctions may be moot because Aristotle, as Confucius, is not as concerned with the determination of the rightness or wrongness of particular acts as he is in the development of moral character. To describe Aristotle and Confucius as virtue ethicists is accurate if one considers that virtue ethics includes the provision that the end goal is to develop a settled moral character, not simply to develop discrete virtues.

Aristotle and Confucius

One may describe Aristotle as a virtue ethicist if one takes into account that for Aristotle, the formation of a moral character is developed by and for the sake of performing noble actions. While Confucius does not frame his argument in this manner, the meaning is equivalent: If one possesses a moral character, one will naturally perform moral acts. This does not take away from the fact that the development of a moral character is, for Confucius, a separate moral goal in itself. It could be argued that the *raison d'être* for developing a moral character is to perform moral actions or to refrain from immoral ones. The distinction between agent morality and act morality is moot.

For Aristotle, the performance of noble actions is the means by which one develops one's moral character. One recalls Aristotle's famous saying, 'One becomes just by performing just acts.'[3] Confucius does not emphasize this aspect as much, but they both agree moral actions are chosen on the basis of their rightness. The main difference between Confucius and Aristotle is that morality for Aristotle produces happiness, and this result becomes part of Aristotle's argument that the performance of moral acts constitutes the way to happiness (not that they should be performed for that reason).[4] However, for Aristotle, if human beings desire happiness, this is the way in which happiness (for most people) is achieved. Confucius does not make this argument. This is one of the most essential and distinguishing features of the ethics of Confucianism and the ethics of the Greek tradition.

The philosophers, Aristotle and Confucius, both agree that moral actions can produce happiness. Aristotle goes so far as to say that 'the man who does not rejoice in noble acts is not even good.'[5] The case of Confucius and Mencius is obscured by the fact that according to my late, distinguished colleague, D. C. Lau, who was my dear colleague for nearly thirty years, and for many years I would regularly invite to lecture in my classes on Chinese philosophy: 'Both Confucius and Mencius repeatedly use the phrase "delighting in the

Way." Once more this emphasizes the sheer naturalness of morality. Delight and joy are usually experienced when a man pursues a natural activity unimpeded.'[6] However, from many personal, philosophical conversations with D. C. Lau, I vividly recall that from D. C. Lau's point of view, what Confucius meant here was that moral choice was not for the sake of self-interest, though its accomplishment could bring happiness. Here, Aristotle and Confucius are not far apart.

In a sense, Mao's thought is similar to Confucius insofar as Confucius does place great value on the moral growth of the individual. However, Mao has not understood Confucius rightly. For Confucius, while he did value the individual, what he valued was the actual moral growth of the individual, not the development of the individual or individuality *simpliciter*. Confucius was keenly aware that individuals differed from each other and, as a result, the same treatment could not be applied to all equally alike. But, for the most part, he restricted this concept of different treatment to pedagogical circumstances.

Mao and Mencius

In Mao's earlier studies, he appears to display a closer understanding of the teachings of Confucius and Mencius. He writes in his classroom notes made when he was a student in the Fourth Normal School in Changsha in a summary of a lecture by his teacher, Yang Changji on self-cultivation: 'Mencius said, "Some parts of the body are noble, and some ignoble; some great, and some small … He who nourishes the little belonging to him is a little man, and he who nourishes the great is a great man. … The individual self is the physical self; the universal self is the spiritual self"'.[7] These notes do not have the authoritative weight as do his marginal notes to Paulsen, because they are notes taken in the classroom rather than his own reflections and comments, and hence, must be regarded as belonging more to his teacher than to himself.

In 1967, Mao would famously repudiate the doctrine of self-cultivation in his cleansing of Liu Shaoqi. Mao did not slight Chinese studies. He writes in his 1915 *Letter to Xiao Zisheng* [his senior schoolmate], ' … general knowledge of Chinese studies is most crucial for our people. It has been said in the past that if one wants to know one of the classics, one must first know all of the classics.'[8] In the Cultural Revolution of Mao, all of this was to change and this change marked what was perceived of as the temporary demise of Chinese traditional thought.

Aristotle also was keenly aware of individual differences. But, for Aristotle, these differences were relevant only in so far as they required a different application of the identical universal value. The middle way of eating would be different in the case of a giant or a Sumo wrestler and that of a dwarf. Each would need to respect and to observe the form of the middle way, but the application of the middle way would differ between them. The application of the idea of individuality for Aristotle and Confucius did not reach the extreme it did for the early Mao.

Despite Mao's reference to early Chinese philosophers, his Egoism differs from Confucianism, proper. What makes Mao's partial appropriation of Confucianism seem like Confucianism proper is his reference to the beginning of love of others in the love of self which is first extended to family and then beyond, universally.

Confucius's Idea of the Self

For Confucius, the starting point is not self-love, but rather self-sincerity. This is a very notable difference. In the *Great Learning*, one of the Confucian classics, where the idea of self, family and then society is elaborated, the passage reads: 'Wishing to order well their States, [the ancients] first regulated their families. Wishing to regulate their families, they first cultivated their persons. Wishing to cultivate their persons, they first rectified their hearts. Wishing to rectify their hearts, they first sought to be sincere in their thoughts.' The emphasis here is on self-rectification which precedes self-cultivation and sincerity which precedes self-rectification, not on self-love, which appears to be Mao's starting point.[9]

The motivation here is the ultimate order of the state. This ultimate motivation differs from Mao, for whom the ultimate justification is the realization of the individual. It must be remembered that the *Great Learning* is most probably the work of the grandson of Confucius and not Confucius himself and, hence, represents an interpolation of Confucius. Confucius's *Analects*, comprising questions and answers between Confucius and his students, are considered to be the most reliable source of Confucius's own thinking. In the *Analects*, moral choices are to be made, as they are in Kant, because it is right to make such choices, not because they redound to the good of society. In this sense, Confucius, as Kant, is a deontologist. Moral choice making, both for Aristotle and Confucius, builds character, but moral choices are not made simply in order to build character.

Mao's Interpretation of Confucius

Mao's beginning with self has a different meaning for Mao than it has for Confucius. Mao writes, 'I think that the theories of our Confucian scholars are based on egoism, as ... can be seen in "He who first cultivates himself may afterwards bring peace to the world."'[10] This is Mao's unique interpretation of the famous passage in the *Great Learning*. In the *Great Learning*, the starting point is self-rectification through a very sincere self-reflection. It is not solely self-cultivation, because one must first rectify or purify the self. Otherwise, the self that would be cultivated, as it is for Mao, would be the ego-driven self.[11]

This is a point that must be emphasized. According to Schram, Mao would quote the passage from the *Analects*, 'What the superior man seeks is in himself.'[12] However, it is very important to take note of what the self means in Mao and what the reference to the self means in Confucius. It is true that in both, the counsel is to seek one's own counsel and not turn to others. However, for Confucius, the self to which one is called is the moral self, the self that is discovered by sincere reflection and self-rectification. For example, consider the close connection Confucius makes between overcoming the self and observing the rites and the importance he attributes to overcoming the self.[13] For Mao, it is the Ego. This difference is dramatic. This adaptation of Mao is illustrative. It is illustrative of the point that Mao would probably not have arrived at the ideas that he did had he not both known Confucianism and attempted to integrate it into his own way of thinking. In other words, without Confucianism, we would not have had the Mao that we had. This characteristic, of imbibing from classical philosophy and literature and applying and adapting it to his own way of thinking, was to stay with Mao for the remainder of his life.

Mao and Confucianism: Universal Love versus Familial Love

There is, of course, the conflict between those who consider that Confucius's extension of love from the family to others still favours family members while Mozi's doctrine of universal love does not privilege family members. This conflict is to a very large extent a pseudo-conflict, because the care that Confucius prescribes for all human beings (and implies belongs to human nature itself) is the relevant topic for Ethics. The only conflict that could come into being is if one had to make a choice between helping a family member or helping a stranger. This is a matter of special circumstance, not of general ethics. In the interpolation of the present author, in this case, familial love takes precedence because of the strength, importance and priority of the felt love and loyalty to the family member, and does not fall under the category of treating others ethically. Mencius makes this clear when he writes, '[A gentleman] is attached to his parents, but is merely benevolent towards the people....'[14] There could be a conflict between family love and universal morality. *But, there is only a conflict when special circumstances arise.* Confucius seems to go further than Mencius in extending love beyond one's family when he states that 'A young man ... should love the multitude at large ... '[15]

Confucius presents no example of a case of a conflict between family love and universal morality. His statements concerning care for others are unrestricted. For example, consider his principle, 'Do not do to others what you do not want others to do to you.'[16] This principle is unrestricted. There is no qualification attached to it privileging family members above other human beings. Indeed, if we were naturally disposed to be good, as the thought of Confucius would strongly appear to suggest, how could this natural moral disposition be restricted to family members?[17] Of course, there is also the famous passage where it is said that 'All within the Four Seas are his [the superior man's] brothers.'[18] This statement is as clear a case of an unrestricted ethical principle as can be found in any ethical system.

The oft-cited counterexample is the singular case when Confucius does not think well of the son who gives evidence against his father for stealing a sheep.[19] Confucius's view of the case reflects his good sense (similar to the classic case of the value of lying when the Gestapo is inquiring if one had a Jewish person in one's cellar), that honesty, in this case, was ludicrous and missed the crucial point of ethics. In this interpretation, this is the real point of the story, which does not constitute support for the theory of the primacy of consanguineous love or filial piety in Confucius. Indeed, Confucius refers to a moral quality of straightness or rectitude as a description of examples of sons covering up for their fathers and vice versa and does not refer to filial piety as the rationale. In fact, it is not clear that the act of fathers covering up for their sons would fall strictly under the category of filial piety. Confucius's point seems to be that it is in accordance with rectitude that sons cover up for their fathers and fathers cover up for their sons. He is not putting forth this example as a support to the conclusion that familial love is superior to universal love.

However, even if one considers this anecdote to constitute a case of a lack of filial piety on the part of the son who does not conceal the act of stealing of his father, it would then constitute a case of legality wrongly taking precedence over felt family love and loyalty, not a case of filial piety or consanguineous love taking precedence over care or concern about or for others who are not family members. Circumstances could arise in which there is a conflict between care for one's family and care for others, but Confucius does not seem to offer a clear-cut case of such an example, which suggests that such an issue does not constitute the fundamental problem or issue of ethics. The cornerstone for ethics is whether one should be ethical or not and on the fundamentals of this issue, Confucius does not deviate.

Confucius's Central Ethical Principle

When Confucius states his central ethical principle, he states it as a universal proscription. When Confucius is asked if there is a single saying that one can act upon all day and every day, his answer is not familial loyalty, but the refrain, 'Never do to others what you would not like them to do to you'.[20] Hillel gave the identical answer, couched in the identical negative sentential form, when he was asked to condense the teaching of the Torah into what he could say when standing on one foot.[21]

Filial Piety

Filial piety is not mentioned when Confucius is asked what is the single saying one can act upon all day, every day. It follows then that it does not form part of Confucius' central ethical principle. In addition, when Confucius refers to the single thread that binds all his teachings together, it is not filial piety that is identified as the single thread.[22] Filial piety, while mentioned by Confucius, is not central to his ethics. One must read very carefully through the passages in Book II in which Confucius explains the instances of filial piety with which one should never fail to comply. He makes it clear that he is referring to a filial piety that includes observing the rites, not causing anxiety, and showing reverence. *These are rules specific to relating to parents (both mother and father), not general moral formulae.*[23] It is Mencius, not Confucius, who in one passage, reduces universal morality to filial piety.[24] On the other hand, Mencius's famous example of how compassion and alarm are aroused in all human beings when one witnesses a child about to fall into a well makes no provision that the child must be a family member. If a universal feeling of compassion is to be aroused when any child, not a member of one's family, faces harm or death, this implies that the feeling of compassion is a universal one, and possesses no reference to familial preference.[25] If familial love possessed primacy, Mencius should have qualified this example to read that if the child were a family member, the feeling of alarm and compassion aroused would take priority over a child who was of no family relation. Mencius does not in any way make this qualification. It seems from this point that Mencius did not consider that in urgent ethically relevant situations, e.g. when it comes to observing if one's feelings of compassion were aroused when a human child was in danger, the matter of familial love does not factor into the equation.

Mao's interpretation of Confucianism on the issue of universal love is reflected in this excerpt from the eulogy he writes for his mother, whom he deeply loved:

> The highest of my mother's virtues was her universal love.
> She was kind to all human beings, whether closely or distantly related.
> Her compassion and kindness moved the hearts of everyone.
> The power of her love came from true sincerity.
> She never lied or was deceitful.[26]

It is possible that the tendency to equate Confucius's idea of a universal morality with filial piety stems from three main influences. Firstly, the mention of filial piety occurs early (in Books I and II) of the *Analects* though it is scarcely mentioned thereafter. Secondly, it is not considered that views concerning filial piety found in the *Book of Filial Piety* (composed during the third century BCE) that are attributed to Confucius are written long after he lived. Thirdly, there is the influence of Mencius, though here again Mencius may well be misconstrued especially when one considers his most famous ethical anecdote, the case of one observing a child about to fall into a well discussed above and again in the sequel. As pointed out above, Mencius does not ask if the child is a family member or not. The alarm and compassion in one's heart that he states will arise is not qualified as to arise only in the case of danger to family members.

Mao and Confucianism

Mao's incorporation of Confucianism includes one very interesting non-Confucian element that we have alluded to above. For Mao, caring for others, being part of human nature, is a mode of developing the potential of the human being. For Confucius, caring for others is a mode of developing the moral growth of the human being, not the overall potential of the human being. For Confucius, the extension of care for one's family members to society in general is a mode of moral development, not a mode of the actualization of all the potential, including non-ethical potential of a human being.

Confucius does not explicitly argue, as does Aristotle, that moral actions constitute the road to moral growth, but his position famously implies it. In a notable passage, he writes that by the time that he has reached the age of seventy, 'I followed my heart's desire without overstepping the line.'[27] One's moral choices coincide with what one wants to do. In this sense, Confucius has the same position as Aristotle. For Aristotle, moral choices create a moral character.

Confucius cites cases where one must make a moral choice. He points out, for example, that in a conflict between what is right and what is profitable, one should choose what it right.[28] While Confucius does not provide the logic of an argument that such moral choices are character building, in the context of the entire *Analects*, the overall effect of such moral actions would appear to conduce to moral self-growth. The differences between Confucius and Aristotle here might simply be due to the fact that Aristotle's presentation reflects a need to provide a greater overall logical coherence to his point of view while Confucius prefers to emphasize moral instruction. This could be a pedagogical difference in that while Confucius's points are put in the context of a question and answer format with students, Aristotle's points are found in lecture notes taken by students.

What is unique to Mao is that caring for others, for the early Mao, is a mode of developing human potential *per se*. Mao, unlike Confucius, commences with Egoism, with self-love. In contrast, Confucius commences with self-sincerity and then proceeds to family. Mao starts rather with self-love and then moves to the family. His starting point is different from that of Confucius. The family love for both Mao and Confucius is extended to society in general. Such an extension, for Mao, then further builds the Ego. For Confucius, the extension of family love to society in general is, in part, purely natural. After all, we are all members of the same human family. In part, it is derived from first experiencing love in the family and then extending that love to society in general. The extension to society is an ethical extension. We experience love first in the family: that is its epistemological origin. It does not follow that it is restricted to its first experience.

The self as starting point is different for Confucius and Mao. Consider the famous passage that occurs several times in Confucius, 'Do not do to others what you do not want others to do to you.'[29] Here, Confucius uses the self as a basis for understanding how it is and why it is that one should not harm others. In this sense, Confucius uses the self as a starting base. However, this is not the same as considering self-love to be the origin of ethics. The difference is that one does not use the self as a point of self-gain, but only as an illustration that just as one would not like to be hurt, one should not hurt others. For Confucius, the self with which one begins is the moral self, that is, the self that has already been cultivated, not the pure Ego. The idea of self functions differently in Confucius and in Mao, and this difference, as we shall see below, makes all the difference.

Mao and Mencius

In Mencius, one is not a human being unless one has a spontaneous altruistic inclination. This altruistic inclination has no self-benefit for Mencius. He makes it plain in his example of the spontaneous feeling of feeling compassion for the child about to fall in the well that this is for no purpose of gaining reputation.[30] This is one step further than Mao. For Mao, Altruism is an expression of the natural self. Counter-intuitively, Altruism for Mao has an egoistic origin.

For Mao, if we feel no compassion, we are not fully human. This aspect of Mao is in close alignment both to Confucius and to Mencius. The desire to save the child from death is not altruistic for Confucius, Mencius or for Mao. In this sense, Mao is part of the Chinese philosophical tradition and not the Western philosophical tradition, which, for the most part, sees morality as something separate and usually contradictory to human nature (Aristotle is a major exception here, but Aristotle is a pre-Christian philosopher). The difference between Mao and the Chinese tradition must be noted. For Confucius and Mencius, Altruism is part of human nature, but it is not part of the egoistic self and it does not benefit the egoistic self. If the urge to save the child from death does not arise, for Mencius that is a matter of wrongful conditioning. One is not fully human, for Mencius, unless one spontaneously feels compassion and alarm upon observing the danger of a child about to fall into a well. This seems to fit Mao's model of Altruism as part of human nature, but for Mencius there is no egoistic fulfilment from the spontaneous feeling arising of compassion and alarm. This is a difference, however moot it might appear on the surface, and it can make a large difference.

The central difference between Mao and Mencius (I choose Mencius to simplify the argument) is that for Mencius there is no egoistic benefit here. For Mencius, the self is defined as a moral self. It is the moral self that is expressed in ethical motivation, not the egoistic self. For Mencius there is no Altruism as something that is *ab extra*; the moral self (the proper human self) is naturally altruistic. The two views, those of Mencius and Mao, would almost seem to coincide. The difference is in the *almost*.

Is the difference between Mao and Mencius only semantic? Is the difference between Mao and Mencius a difference that makes a difference? The problem, for Mao, is that if egoism includes Altruism within itself and is its ultimate justification, then Altruism can be perceived as subordinate to Egoism or, if you like, a means to accomplishing the end of egoistic satisfaction and fulfilment. While Mao does not say this in his early response to Paulsen, the logic of his justification of morality as the means to developing the egoistic self is vulnerable to this weakness. For Mencius, the ego can never become a priority over the moral self or one loses one's humanity. This is the same, though less explicit, for Confucius. Moral actions always take priority over personal benefit. For Mao, since egoism and morality merge, with egoism put forth as the ultimate reason for and justification of morality, there is a danger that morality could become submerged under egoism. Instead of putting forth the argument that Mao's later excesses, in both his rise to power and when he becomes established in power, are proof that he was not a philosopher, one could put forward the argument that the problem was precisely that Mao was a philosopher, but that Mao's philosophy was not well founded.

Mao on Following One's Impulses

It should be noted that Mao's prioritization on following one's instincts is not a total negation of the contribution of intellectual knowledge. Mao's thought is subtle. For Mao, one can also add to one's understanding with knowledge that is gained from the mind. In his own words:

> ... it is false to say that knowledge has no influence on the mind, for knowledge definitely has a great influence on the human mind. The human mind is moved half by feeling impulses and the conscience, and half by newly obtained knowledge. The progress of the human race, its revolutions, its spirit of reform, depend entirely on being guided in its actions by new knowledge.[31]

This passage is an eerie foreshadowing of the later Mao's inversion of the priority of the superstructure in classical Marxism to be discussed below. Could it be that Mao's alterations of traditional Marxism to come were due to these early pre-Marxist speculations? Even mentioning revolutions in this context seems a premonition of the role Mao is to play in the future.

Mao is no blind follower of Paulsen. His own view is more theoretically laden than Paulsen's voluntarism and he points out his disagreement with Paulsen in this regard. Mao is of the opinion that it is philosophy itself, particularly moral philosophy, that forms the basis of one's decisions and consequent actions. He writes in the margins:

> When through moral philosophy we come to know the content of the conscience, this gives us even greater courage to follow the dictates of the conscience. ... the view that clarifying something logically and psychologically necessarily destroys the true nature of the moral process is wrong. And Paulsen's view that even those who understand logic and psychology do not rely on them in their actions, but rather on their original impulses, their feelings, and conscience, is also not the best of theories.[32]

For Mao, one does not simply act on the basis of instincts, but refines one's actions through reflection upon them. This is a more complete theory than that of Paulsen's and appears a very mature theory for so youthful a thinker. This passage is important because it corrects the impression that Mao is a simple voluntarist. It also points to a subtle relationship between theory and practice that anticipates Mao's later discourses on this subject as we shall see below.

Mao's Key Interpretation of Mencius

Mao develops his ideas of the Great Man, already prefigured in his studies of George Washington and Napoleon, in conjunction with his key interpretation of Mencius, to reach the conclusion most relevant for the development of the thinking that would characterize both his thinking and his behaviour for the rest of his life:

> The truly great person develops the original nature with which Nature endowed him, and expands upon the best, the greatest of the capacities of his original nature. This is what makes him great. Everything that comes from outside his original nature, such as restraints and restrictions, is cast aside by the great motive power that is contained within his original

nature …. The great actions of the hero are his own, are the expression of his motive power, lofty and cleansing, relying on no precedent. His force is like that of a powerful wind arising from a deep gorge, like the irresistible sexual desire for one's lover … All obstacles dissolve before him … Because he cannot be stopped or eliminated, he is the strongest, the most powerful. This is true also of the spirit of the great man and the spirit of the sage. For Paulsen, the great man is not one who acts according to a sense of duty that would temper and restrain the vitality of the impulses of his feelings. How true, how true! (Note: I see this as quite similar to the view that Mencius puts forward in the two chapters: 'Haoran zhi qi' and 'Da Zhangfu'.)[33]

In these cases, Mao plainly adapts Mencius to suit his purposes. While Mencius does indeed answer that he is 'skillful in nourishing my vast, flowing passion-nature [*haoran zhi qi*],' his meaning is quite different (nourishing with integrity, and, as seen below, a qualified nourishing at that). In the words of D. C. Lau, 'for Mencius, genuine courage … can only be sustained by the sense of being morally in the right.'[34] And, Mencius's reference to the great man is also of a very different meaning (great in terms of morality). For Mencius, passion-nature is subordinate to will. In a key passage, Mencius writes:

> There must be the *constant* practice *of this righteousness*, but without the object *of thereby nourishing the passion-nature*. Let not the mind forget *its work*, but let there be no assisting the growth *of that nature*.[35]

And again,

> … when he obtains his desire for office, to practice his principles for the good of the people; and when that desire is disappointed, to practice them alone; to be above the power of riches and honors … these characteristics constitute the great man.[36]

Once more, would Mao have arrived at his idea of the Great Man without contact with both Western philosophy and Chinese philosophy? While his idea of the Great Man obviously differs from that of Mencius, it was first in Mencius (and Western thinkers) that Mao finds the idea of the Great Man. Mao's thinking is nourished in the Western and Chinese philosophical tradition. While what he grows in that soil may differ widely from his distinguished predecessors, there is little doubt that without such an intellectual soil, Mao's intellectual development might have been markedly different.

Mao builds upon his pre-existent platform his own original philosophy of Egoism. While it is strongly influenced by his reading of Paulsen, Mao's literary gifts and philosophical imagination integrate Paulsen's voluntarism with his own philosophical construction of The Great Man or the Hero. In Mao's literary description quoted above:

> [The moral judgment] comes solely from his own judgment [that of the truly great person], not in obedience to an external moral law, or to what is called here a sense of duty. The great actions of the hero are his own, are the expression of his motive power, lofty and cleansing, relying on no precedent. His force is like that of a powerful wind arising from a deep gorge, like the irresistible sexual desire for one's lover, a force that will not stop, that cannot be stopped.[37]

Mao's Philosophy of Egoism and his Early Metaphysics

In the end, Mao's thought is more his own than that of anyone else. He reads and interprets others, but with an intent to construct his own incipient theory of Egoism, which includes the development of the individual, the natural will and the sense of pleasure one takes in one's nature. In one of his marginal notations to Paulsen, Mao shows that he will not give up the natural will and natural pleasure:

Why is conflict with the natural will a necessary characteristic of the fulfillment of duty? ... When one already has a sense of pleasure, why get rid of it? This is an extreme kind of altruism. The abstract moral philosophers who are troubled by this, like Schopenhauer when he says that only an altruistic act has moral value, do not understand true egoism.[38]

For Mao, as we have seen, there is no conflict between will and duty. This is a most unusual view. The closest parallel to Mao's thought, as we shall see below, is the thought of Nietzsche who held that virtue was the result of happiness and self-realization. The difference, however, is that for Nietzsche, as we shall see below, the self is to be transcended which is never the case for Mao.

Mao's Early Metaphysics

At the same time that Mao extols the power of natural will, he agrees with Paulsen with the fact that human beings are subject to laws of nature. Paulsen writes: 'The Greek philosophers for the most part clearly believed that human beings are part of the natural universe, and thus that they are subject to the universal rules that govern the natural world.'

Mao's note in the margins is 'I agree with this view.' Mao adds, 'That human beings are subject to natural law is compatible with my view.'[39]

Mao struggles, in the margins, with reconciling being determined by laws of nature and possessing a will that is free. It is here that his philosophical creativity shows itself. At first, he writes: 'I still suspect that human beings are powerless from beginning to end.' Then, he reflects: 'After writing the above, I got another idea, as follows: Although we are defined by Nature, we are also part of Nature. Thus Nature has the power to define us, and we have the power to define Nature. Although our power is small, it cannot be said to have no effect. Nature without us would be incomplete.'[40]

It is evident from his marginal notes that Mao was not simply passively absorbing the ideas he was reading, but he was approaching his reading with a critical and analytic mind, more similar to the study habits of one who had studied analytic philosophy. He was reflecting upon the texts he was reading; he was dialoguing with texts and coming up with creative solutions to points which he found to be problematic.

In the end, the young Mao's philosophical solutions show precociousness. The idea of both creating and being constituted by nature is indeed a very sophisticated one. It does succeed in solving the dilemma of possessing a free will and, at the same time, being subject to nature's laws. This dimension of Mao's thinking, found in the margins, shows links with ancient Chinese philosophy and, at the same time, notwithstanding some differences with Spinoza's concept of freedom, may reflect the influence of Spinoza's metaphysics. In any case, it reveals itself as one of the most philosophically unique, coherent and worthwhile facets of Mao's thinking. It seems that the best of Mao's thinking is brought out in the attempt to resolve conflict. We can see this tendency emerging in some of his most famous writings. This is ironic when one considers that the later thought of Mao is tied to the idea of continuous conflict. In any case, we may safely say that conflict seems to bring out the best in Mao just as he argues that man is inherently never content in the Great Harmony. At first, it seems that the inherent restlessness to which Mao refers may reflect more of an Hegelian influence rather than the gentler modality of change indicated by the ancient Chinese philosophy of the *Yijing*. This inherent restlessness and the inevitability of change adumbrate his later theory of continuous contradiction which supersedes Hegel in that the *nisus* of the change is not the formation of a synthesis, but rather a continuous negating. On the other hand, when one considers that Hexagram 11, Peace, is followed by Hexagram 12, Stagnation, Mao's idea of continuous contradiction may reflect the influences of the *Yijing*.

The Question of Suicide

Mao's thinking is also well developed when it comes to his analysis of suicide, different levels of happiness and different levels of goodness. He disagrees with Paulsen's view that negative suicide (suicide because one can no longer tolerate life) is not self-preservative. This capacity to disagree with what one is reading while characteristic of a Western philosopher in the making, is unusual for the typical, traditional Chinese student of philosophy. Mao brings to bear Western analytic tools of reasoning when dialoguing with philosophical texts.

For Mao, the would-be suicide who finds life too much for him to bear any longer is still self-preserving and is egoistic (what Mao regards as positive). Mao melds this view with his view that there are different levels of happiness and that the superior man and the petty man both pursue happiness and only differ with regard to what they conceive their happiness to be. Here, Mao shows his philosophical finesse in utilizing classical Chinese classifications (the great man and the petty minded man), to frame a discussion of happiness that strongly reminds one of the first book of Aristotle's *Nichomachean Ethics* in which Aristotle writes that all men seek happiness, but differ in their concept of what constitutes happiness.

Mao Does Not Subscribe to Absolute Evil

Mao does not consider that there is any absolute evil, but only varying degrees of goodness. In this thinking, he reveals a Platonic influence. Mao gives the example of a traitor to his country who is still acting out of a concept of what is good, though others may condemn him. All of this thinking is reflected in the notes that he makes in the margins.[41] How Mao behaved as a leader is another question altogether and may be a function of the old adage of Lord Acton,

'Power corrupts and absolute power corrupts absolutely.'[42] Or, it might reflect that all of his cogitations on ethics were ultimately to be superseded by his strong agreement with Paulsen's comment, 'So, too, the most perfect morality is to live naturally by realizing one's instincts, rather than by being concerned with ethics.' Mao's future actions as a leader may well have been motivated by this philosophical principle. While it may be difficult to consider that one can achieve a perfect morality by realizing instincts, one can be motivated by a belief system even if that belief system is not coherent or valid. The key point, which we shall discuss in the sequel, is what kind of instincts are being realized. For Confucius and Mencius, the instincts, if that is the correct word, require self-cultivation. This is the element missing in Mao's philosophy and what can gain the most by rectification. How important it is to take great care when constructing one's philosophical foundations. No matter how elaborately we may build our philosophical edifice upon those foundations, if the foundations are faulty, the entire philosophical edifice built upon those foundations is in danger of collapse. It is well worth our while to examine Mao's early thoughts to discover cracks in those foundations, cracks that might ultimately lead to collapse. For a philosophical construction, no matter how high it reaches and how many stories it contains, is only as good as its foundations.

Mao as an Existentialist

At times, Mao's notes in the margins expand into virtually complete essays that reflect unusually deep philosophical questioning and even rise to a philosophical eloquence. His reflections on death form a good example:

> From the realm of life it is an enormous change for human beings suddenly to enter the realm of death. ... Where is the vast universe heading? This truly is enough to evoke a sense of sadness and pain in life. However, I

do not see it this way. Human beings are born with a sense of curiosity. How can it be different in this case? Are we not delighted with all kinds of rare things that we seldom encounter? Death too is a rare thing that I have never experienced in my entire life. Why should it alone not delight me? Whether it is painful or not, and even if it is, this pain will indeed be a wonderland. Even though the future is dark and unknowable, is not this dark and unknown world also a wonderland? ... When a storm rolls over the ocean, with waves crisscrossing in all directions, those aboard ship are drawn to marvel at its magnificence. Why should the great waves of life and death alone not evoke a sense of their magnificence?[43]

These reflections reveal both a literary and a philosophical mind. Here, Mao leaves Paulsen far behind. Are these cogitations not precocious for a young man of twenty-four years? Mao's youthful reflections upon death put us in the mind of a very poetic Socrates whose famed, agnostic attitude towards whether death was something good or bad led him not to fear it. In any case, it is perfectly obvious that Mao was capable of creating original, poetic and startling philosophical viewpoints. His comparison of those facing death with passengers on a ship observing waves criss-crossing in both directions and being aesthetically caught by this magnificence in the face of the imminent fate of death is an arresting metaphor. His view that if we are curious in life why should this curiosity leave us in the face of death is as uplifting as it is rational. Mao's optimism is a precursor of the existentialism of Sartre who eloquently argues early in his essay, 'Existentialism is a Humanism', that existentialism is not pessimism. Even pain can be a wonderland for Mao and the unknown, which for many thinkers is what we most fear, becomes for Mao instead, a wonderland to delight the palette of natural, human curiosity. Such cogitations as these leave even exceed Epicurus's famous philosophizing about death. If philosophy is to be defined as thinking profoundly, then there is no question that Mao possesses a philosophical mind.[44]

Mao on Happiness and Virtue

Mao is particularly struck with Chapter VII of Paulsen's, *System of Ethics*, entitled Virtue and Happiness. His general remark that he makes in the margins is, 'This chapter is extremely well done.'[45] In this chapter, Paulsen argues for the unity of happiness and virtue. Paulsen writes:

> He who acts virtuously takes only virtue as his goal, and if external happiness eludes him, and his senses suffer hardship, nevertheless his virtuous conduct brings him spiritual happiness. Spinoza said that the reward of virtue is not happiness, but virtue. This is true.[46]

To this, Mao writes in the margins, 'Excellent.'

We may gather from Mao's exclamation that Mao takes a position closer to that of Socrates than that of Aristotle. Aristotle thought that happiness did require some material fulfilment and that, unlike Socrates, one could not be happy in a prison. Mao takes the position of Paulsen/Spinoza that spiritual happiness is possible from virtue alone. This is a position that is shared by Confucius as well as we shall see in the sequel. It could form part of the thinking that would lie behind Mao's later formulation of the Cultural Revolution.

Mao and Nietzsche

What about Nietzsche? Are Mao's ideas closer to those of Nietzsche? There is a surface similarity that cloaks a deeper difference. For Nietzsche, human nature should aim for happiness, not morality. This is a position that differs from Mao's since for Nietzsche, morality is not part of developing human nature, whereas for Mao morality is part of human nature.

It might be said that Nietzsche's philosophy, as it is expressed in his multifarious writings, is not entirely coherent. He does argue for the primacy of instinct over principle. He champions individualism over herd morality. At the same time, he points to the transcendence of the ego as the ultimate goal. How does one achieve transcendence of the ego via Egoism? Perhaps, Egoism is not the appropriate description of Nietzsche's philosophy in the first place. Nietzsche easily deserves the title of being the most misunderstood Western philosopher either by his Western or his Eastern readers.

While Nietzsche's philosophy is famous for its going beyond good and evil, what is forgotten is that for Nietzsche, it is love that is beyond good and evil. Consider the little known epigram 153 from *Beyond Good & Evil*, 'Whatever is done from love always occurs beyond good and evil.' [47] Nietzsche's philosophy is not the *overthrowing* of all values; it is the *reversal* of all values. In a famous passage in the *Twilight of the Idols*, Nietzsche writes that what he is doing is *reformulating* not *abandoning* values. Nietzsche was not a nihilist. Nietzsche's reformulation may be summarized as the following: Hitherto, moralists have stated that one must be good and that is the way to be happy (Aristotle is a prime example). For Nietzsche, the formula is reversed. One must become happy and then one will naturally be good. Goodness never disappears from the picture. It is only that the way goodness is achieved is revised. Morality is the result of a healthy, instinctual self-actualization. To reiterate, this is the reversal of all values; it is not the abandonment of all values. In the famous passage in the *Twilight of the Idols*, Nietzsche writes:

> The most general formula on which every religion and morality is founded is: 'Do this and that, refrain from this and that – then you will be happy! [think of Aristotle here] Otherwise ... ' Every morality, every religion, *is* this imperative; I call it the great original sin of reason, *the immortal unreason*. In my mouth, this formula is changed into its opposite – first example of my 'revaluation of all values': a well-turned-out human being, 'a happy one',

must perform certain actions and shrinks instinctively from other actions … In a formula his virtue is the *effect* of his happiness.⁴⁸

On the surface, Nietzsche's Egoism (if it is even right to use this term to describe Nietzsche) does resemble Mao's Egoism. The difference is that for Mao, Egoism is maintained; for Nietzsche, Egoism is transcended. Egoism, for Nietzsche, only exists as a stage on the way to ethics. One may quarrel with Nietzsche that one cannot simultaneously argue on the behalf of a healthy expression of instincts and the transcendence of the ego, but this is a general problem with Nietzschean philosophy. Its resolution could consist in understanding that it is only after a transcendence of the ego that there can be a healthy expression of instincts.

Nietzsche has his own way of weaving morality back into human behaviour. Harmful behaviour, for Nietzsche, is a direct consequence of unhappiness. Only unhappy people hurt other people (or themselves). If one strives for self-fulfilment and reaches happiness, one will have no motive for hurting other people (or oneself). The happy human being overflows. She or he cannot help but give to others from the overflowing characteristic of happiness. Morality for Nietzsche is the necessary effect of achieving self-actualization. Self-actualization for Nietzsche, unlike Mao, requires self-transcendence. One finds that Sartre makes exactly this same point at the end of his essay, 'Existentialism is a Humanism'.

Egoism for Nietzsche is not the ultimate goal, as it is for Mao. Egoism only exists in order to achieve transcendence. Transcendence of the Ego is, for Nietzsche, the goal of humanity. The Ego exists to be transcended. The will to power for Nietzsche is not the will to power over others. The will to power, for Nietzsche, is the will to overcome oneself. Self-transcendence, self-overcoming is the goal of the Overman.

Nietzsche's philosophy is more of a self-transcendent philosophy than an egoistic philosophy. There are phases in the development of Nietzsche's philosophy. The lion occupies phase two. The lion stands for egoism, the Nay-saying. Consider Zarathustra's Speeches on the Three Metamorphoses:

> 'Thou shalt' is the name of the great dragon. But the spirit of the lion says, 'I will'. ... My brothers, why is there a need in the spirit for the lion? ... To create values – that even the lion cannot do; but the creation of freedom for oneself for new creation – that is within the power of the lion. The creation of freedom for oneself and a sacred 'No' even to duty – for that, my brothers the lion is needed.[49]

This is the second phase. The first stage, the stage of the camel, stands for how one begins, by carrying the heavy burden of false values on one's back. The lion is the second phase. The lion can say no to following duty. It is only after this key second phase that the third phase can be ushered in: the metamorphosis of the child, which stands for the foundation of new values, the Yea-saying.

> But say, my brothers, what can the child do that even the lion could not do? Why must the preying lion still become a child? The child is innocence and forgetting, a new beginning, a game, a self-propelled wheel, a first movement, a sacred 'Yes'. [50]

For Mao, the Ego, the lion, is supreme. For Nietzsche, the Ego exists to be overcome. On the other hand, for Nietzsche, one needs a strong will to accomplish this overcoming (the lion). Nietzsche's 'Egoism' is only a phase of his philosophy to be superseded in the end. For Mao, Egoism is sustained to the end. In this respect, it is more difficult for Mao's philosophy to remain ethical than it is for Nietzsche's.

For Nietzsche, the primacy of healthy instinct is a means to overthrow the yoke of false morality before proceeding to the work of self-transcendence.[51] The distinction here is that in self-actualization, for Nietzsche, the Overman is the man who is able to overcome his ego. In his masterful commentary on Nietzsche, Kaufmann makes this clear:

> The *Ubermensch* at any rate cannot be dissociated from the conception of *Uberwindung*, of overcoming. Man is something that should be overcome – and the man who has overcome himself has become an overman.[52]

Mao's Egoism runs into a similar, though not identical problem. For Mao, Egoism may conflict with the demands of morality (though it is not supposed to) and when it does, Egoism is the default. This is almost the opposite problem with Nietzsche's Egoism. For Nietzsche, if there is a case in which it appears that healthy instincts run counter to self-transcendence, clearly, self-overcoming takes priority. For Mao, the healthy instinct may run counter to morality. When it does, natural instinct takes priority.

The primacy of the will is evidenced even in the early life of Mao when, as a child, he goes against his father's wishes to apprentice Mao to a rice shop and instead attends the Higher Primary School which had introduced Western studies. It is interesting that Mao finds in his reading of Paulsen the philosophy of the primacy of the will that has already characterized his personality. This, in turn, takes on special meaning when we consider that in Mao's notes in the margins, he emphasizes that moral principles take their rise from what is already existent. It seems that Mao is talking about himself and he has found a philosophy that perfectly matches his own existence. Is it the case that Mao's philosophy has arisen out of his own temperament?

The Child is the Father of the Man

Terrill tells the story about the ten-year-old Mao as a schoolboy being asked by his teacher to stand when reciting the maxims from classical Chinese Confucianism, Mao said to his teacher, 'If you can hear me well while I sit down, … why should I stand up to recite?' Mao then dragged his stool to his teacher's desk and refused to stand. When the teacher pulled at Mao to get him to stand up, Mao freed himself from his teacher's grasp and marched out of the school.[53] There is a remarkable parallel between Mao's own personality as a child and the later philosophy of Egoism that he develops.

It can also be argued that Mao's sense of justice was with him from an early age. Part of his enmity against his father may have emanated from the fact that his father had amassed a fair degree of wealth from capitalistic enterprises. In his autobiographical account given to Edgar Snow, Mao relates of his father:

> The old man continued to amass wealth or what was considered to be a great fortune in that little village [where Mao grew up]. ... he bought many mortgages on other people's land. His capital grew to two or three thousand Chinese dollars [an impressive sum in those days according to Snow].[54]

Mao's early sense of justice is also indicated in his reaction to the punishment (beheading) paid out to some rebels who were protesting against a famine in Changsha:

In Snow's recounting of Mao's narrative:

> I never forgot it. I felt that ... the rebels were ordinary people like my own family and I deeply resented the injustice of the treatment given to them.[55]

Mao and Zhuangzi

How does one sum up this quixotic figure? In the end, Mao's philosophy of an Egoism that includes Altruism (though it does not recognize Altruism as something separate from Egoism) is unique. It differs even from the idea of Zhuangzi that Mao references, the idea of Zhuangzi that some might take as the expression of Egoism. Mao quotes from the notorious passage from the inauthentic Chapter Nineteen of the *Zhuangzi* which is the story of the cicada catcher and the cicada's wings. The focus of the catcher on the cicada's wings as the secret of his success can be interpreted as focusing on one's own needs and not on the needs of society. This, however, is to misunderstand the story. The story is not a story for the purpose of justifying Egoism. It is a story which shows the importance of not being attached to the result (the capture of the cicada), but only being focused on what is immediately in front of one; i.e. its wings. It may be likened to not taking one's eye off the golf ball or the tennis ball when one is hitting the ball. It is a story emphasizing how one achieves success. It is ethically neutral as such a story could be told of how one achieves prowess as a robber. This story has nothing to do with justifying Egoism. The story in the *Zhuangzi* to which Mao refers can be summarized in this way. Confucius, who is frequently used as a character in stories found in the *Zhuangzi*, comes across a hunchback (abnormal figures are also frequently used as characters in the *Zhuangzi*), who is very adeptly catching cicadas on a sticky pole. When Confucius asks him the secret to this success, this is the relevant part of his reply:

> No matter how huge heaven and earth, or how numerous the ten thousand things, I'm aware of nothing but cicada wings. Not wavering, not tipping, not letting any of the other ten thousand things take the place of those cicada wings – how can I help but succeed?[56]

The main point of this story is the focus on the task at hand. There is little here to do with Egoism. It could be applied to a surgeon in the act of brain surgery. The one sentence that lends itself to an interpretation that this is an anecdote designed to promote Egoism is the sentence that reads, 'Not wavering, not tipping, not letting any of the other ten thousand things take the place of those cicada wings.' However, in light of the sentence that follows ('How can I help but succeed?'), the function this former sentence serves is to illustrate that one must not focus on results or extraneous things when one is focused completely, totally on the task. The sentence serves to illustrate that this is the secret of success – not caring about results, about anything else, not even the whole world – not letting anything distract one from staying fully engaged with the task at hand. If it were simply a preference for one's desires over the welfare of the world (the Egoism of Yang Zhu), the entire context of the story told, the success of a cicada catcher, would not be the point of the story.

Again, Mao has interpreted Zhuangzi to fit his purposes. Mao's purpose is to emphasize the value of Egoism. From the above analysis, this would not appear to be Zhuangzi's point. With regard to the success of the revolution, it would not matter in any case since all that matters is the success of the revolution. However, in this case, Mao is interested in finding a justification in a classical Chinese text to justify Egoism. It is a moot question of whether Mao read this voluntarism into Zhuangzi or whether he honestly thought that he found evidence for it there. The crucial point is that Mao constructed his way of thinking upon his understanding and creative adaptation of the Chinese Classics and had he not studied them, we would not have had the thinking of Mao Zedong we do. We would have a very different Mao.

5

The Blend of the Influence of Chinese and Western Philosophy on Mao's Thought and Parallels in China's Social and Economic Development

Mao on Confucianism and Paulsen's Voluntarism

In this chapter, I shall endeavour to show the influence of the blend of Chinese and Western philosophical perspectives on Mao's thought and the parallels that can be found in China's social and economic development. To review what has been established so far, Mao's view of the role and the importance of the Ego while supported by Mao by references to Confucius differs in important respects from Confucius's philosophical arguments. These differences signpost the way in which Mao utilized his rendition of the Chinese philosophical tradition to guide his personal rise to power. While it could be argued that it was Mao's deviation from the Chinese Confucian tradition that actually enabled his rise to power, it would be difficult to maintain that Mao's deviation from the Chinese Confucian tradition would have been possible if Mao had not first steeped himself both in that tradition and in the philosophy of Paulsen. It was Mao's amalgamation of Chinese Confucianism and Paulsen's voluntarism that paved the way, not only for Mao's thought, but also for Mao's personal development. While most commentators refer to Mao's voluntarism as resulting from Neo Kantian or Neo-Hegelian influences, T. H. Green pointed to most frequently as an example of the latter, it seems to me that the idea of the will in Schopenhauer would be a more likely influence. Mao would take this idea of will in a very different direction. For Paulsen, and for the more historically important example of Schopenhauer, the will lies at the basis of our behaviour and not reason. This anticipates Nietzsche and, with the replacement of the primacy of the will by the unconscious, can account for Freud's later insights into rationalizations as defence mechanisms. Reading Paulsen, it seems, was the most important initiation of Mao into the elevation of the will as a key determinant of behaviour. When one considers the description of Mao's early adolescent behaviour in disobeying his father and his teacher as related above, it is not surprising Mao, in the main, was so taken with Paulsen's voluntarism. It was as if Mao had found a philosophy that perfectly suited his temperament and sensibility.

On the other hand, while Mao later reviled Confucianism, he could not and did not want to reject his Chinese roots. It is realistically difficult, if not impossible, to eradicate totally the influences of early childhood education and psycho-social development in any culture. The young Mao thought, rightly or wrongly, that he could incorporate the ethical vision of Confucianism into his own philosophy. As we have seen, his version of Confucianism differs from the teachings of Confucius and Mencius. What is important is that the early Mao presents his ideas as renditions of Confucius and Mencius. The influence of Confucianism is never entirely absent from his thinking foundations.

It is of considerable interest to note that ultimately, at this phase of development of his thinking, Mao elevates the importance of individuality over that of any social good. In other words, society exists for the sake of the individual. At the same time, he argues that the primacy of the individual does not conflict with social welfare.

Mao interpolates Mencius to argue that acts of altruism ultimately originate from oneself and not from a concern for others. This, however, has been shown to be an inaccurate adaptation of Mencius. It has been shown above that Mencius's altruism is definitely based on a concern for the other and exempts entirely from self-interest.

While Mao's thinking at this stage of this thought has been compared to that of Nietzsche's, it has been shown above that this parallel, while including similar elements, is also inaccurate. In the end, Nietzsche's Overman transcends the self while Mao's Egoism emphasizes the primacy of the self. All in all, this commentary on Mao in the margins reflects that ultimately Mao's own thought is, as he would have liked, individualistic and idiosyncratic. It is time to consider another influence, perhaps the most important influence on Mao's thinking, that of the *Yijing*.

Mao and the *Yijing*

It is of special interest to note that, in the end, it is Mao's understanding of classical Chinese philosophy, notably that of the *Yijing*, the *Book of Changes*, that probably most characterizes Mao's thinking. It is a return to this dimension of Mao's thought that may provide continuing insight into the ethics and profit dilemma that marks not only Chinese society but global society today.

Mao's rise to power is a microcosm of the fate of human nature, attempting to realize an ideal that represents a better world for humankind, while at the same time, attempting to enjoy the privileges and pleasures that attend power and falling prey to the temptations and excesses that accompany the acquisition of such power. Mao represents a unique mixture between Plato's philosopher king and Plato's tyrant of the *Republic*. If one applies the ancient Chinese philosophy of the *Yijing* to attempt to sort out the problems raised by this alliance, it may afford some insight into both what was correct and what was missing in Mao's vision for China.

As we have shown above, Mao begins his studies with an understanding that ethics is part of human nature and is not something separate from human nature and human happiness. This is a beginning set in motion by his study of Confucius, Mencius, Aristotle and German Idealism. In his study of German Idealism, he reacts by stressing the need for the assertion of the Ego, of the self, and sees no conflict between this assertion and the ultimate ethical goals that can be reached. This reaction to German Idealism marks his divergence from both the classical Greek tradition and the classical Chinese tradition of philosophy which both made a clear distinction between the Ego and ethical ideals. It is this philosophy of Egoism that marks out the distinctive character of Mao's thought and remains with him before and during his Marxist period.

What is added to this mixture is that Mao is also influenced by an early exposure to the philosophy of the *Yijing*. In his understanding of the *Yijing*, he sees no conflict between early Western and early Chinese philosophy. In his later thought, it is the philosophy of the *Yijing* that adds the ingredient of Mao's unique contribution to dialectical philosophy and offers an explanation of China at the crossroads of economic progress and yet, simultaneously, embarking upon a continuation of the classical, ethical values of Confucianism. In terms of the dialectical movement of the *Yijing*, China's extraordinary economic progress has outrun her ancient, Confucian ethical values. The explanation from the standpoint of the *Yijing* would assume the following form: When the *yi* reaches an extreme, it must change into its opposite. This is what is meant by the dialectical movement of the *yi*. In the first hexagram, for example, when the yang is at its most extreme, it must change into the second hexagram, which is the most extreme yin. The difference with Hegelian dialectics is that the opposites in Hegel are not characterized by yin and yang, which are complementary and are not (and should not be construed as) antagonistic. The interaction between yin and yang is the principle of change. The movement of the yin and the yang is one of reversal. In contrast, the movement of the Hegelian dialectic is that of an upward spiral.

Mao had played a huge role in opening the way to economic progress by placing the ancient, Confucian values in abeyance. This enabled Deng Xiaoping to open the way to Chinese market socialism. However, in terms of the expansion and contraction movement of the *Yijing*, the pendulum had swung too far in the capitalist direction, and the movement to resuscitate Confucianism has become a mark of the times. The problem that ensued was that, with the rise of Confucianism, the contradiction between the ethical values of Confucianism and the egoistic goals of capitalism, has come sharply into focus. As long as Confucianism lingered in the background, the conflict did not exist. However, with the rise of an explicit avowal of Confucian values, the conflict became evident.

With Mao's special contribution to dialectical philosophy, influenced by his understanding of the *Yijing*, the notion of the primary and the secondary aspect of the contradiction, which shall be discussed below, allows us to understand the dialectical tension between the ethical goals of Confucianism and the egoistic goals of capitalism. Mao's thought becomes both the instigator of the existence of the problem and an augury of the approach to a solution to the problem. To re-interpret Mao's appropriation of classical, Confucian thinking in order to attempt to approach a solution to the current dilemma, it is necessary to excise the egoistic dimension of Mao's thinking, brought into existence as a rebellion against his exposure to Spinoza, Kant, Fichte and Schopenhauer, from the ethical dimension of Confucianism and Aristotelianism. With ethics restored to its separate place in both classical Chinese and classical Greek thought, there is room for a more ethical analysis of capitalism, or in its Chinese version, SCC (Socialism with Chinese characteristics).[1]

Mao's employment of the cyclical movement of the *Yijing* as a model for dialectical development allows for the return to classical, Confucian values.[2] That there exists a struggle between those ethical values and an unbridled capitalism is also envisaged in Mao's departure from the classical, Chinese value of harmony in favour of a notion of constant struggle. That there is no final resolution to this problem is what can be gathered from being guided by Mao's notion of a constant struggle rather than an ultimate attainment of a satisfying harmony. The struggle, however, can be tempered by a greater attention to the ethical side of Confucianism, which is more noticeable once the egoistic interpretation of Confucianism is set aside. Mao's embrace of dialectics, especially his understanding of the dialectical philosophy of the ancient, Chinese philosophy of the *Yijing*, a philosophy that predated Confucius, is the key to understanding the situation of China today and an argument for maintaining its ties to the classical, Chinese contribution to an ethical world. The philosophical understanding of the dynamics of the *Yijing* is not to be confused with the advocacy of a Marxist ideology or any ideology. The *Yijing* is politically neutral. It is a universal explanation of change and applicable to all events and not only political events. For example, at the metaphysical level, the *yi* can also be understood to explain Bohr's concept of complementarity in physics. Bohr's theory of complementarity is an application of the general, metaphysical nature of the *yi*.[3] The *yi* possesses a dialectical nature in that while every change is in search of balance, no state achieved can ever remain in balance. This is why the book itself is called the *Book* or the *Classic* of *Changes*. The first Hexagram, The Creative, is too yang, too masculine. It lacks and needs its feminine partner. That is why it must change into its feminine half. It cannot remain in a state of pure yang.

If we apply the dynamics, so described above to the current development of Confucian thought in China, the time is ripe for the ethical side of Confucianism to assume, in Mao's language, the principal side of the contradiction, while the capitalist side of the tide of economic development, does not disappear, as it did under Marxism, but rather becomes, for the time being, the secondary aspect of the contradiction.[4] This explanation could be confused with a political agenda, but this is purely a matter of the surface coincidence of historical circumstances. Hegel, for example, argued that the Cunning of Reason (*Die List der Vernunft*) operated in the fashion that a self-interested motivation could result in an outcome that did not form part of its initial motivation. In his famous example, the desire to find a source of wealth through sailing westwards from Europe unintentionally resulted in the founding of a new nation, namely, America. Hegel did not have a vested interest in promoting American nationalism. He was simply pointing out how, according to his theory of dialectic, unintended results occurred. In this case of Mao's thought, the example of Chinese development is an illustration of the workings of the *yi* and not a justification of Mao's politics.

Mao's Departure from the Classical Chinese Philosophical Tradition

There is one area which marks Mao's most striking departure from the Chinese philosophical tradition that informed his early education. That area concerns his deviation from the traditional Chinese valuation of the Great Harmony. Instead, *prior to his exposure to Marxism*, Mao seems to be influenced by the dialectical view put forth by Paulsen. Paulsen writes:

> The forms of historical life are nothing other than the forces of the struggle between good and evil that develop with the times.[5]

However, Mao's notations in the margins alongside Paulsen's text go far beyond Paulsen and suggest a view that while resembling deviates from a strict Hegelian view which provides for the negation of the negation, or, synthesis, and anticipates and foreshadows Mao's unique, later view in which opposites continue to collide indefinitely:

... a long period of peace, pure peace without any disorder of any kind, would be unbearable to human life, and it would be inevitable that the peace would give rise to waves. Could human life stand the Great Harmony? I am sure that once we entered a reign of Great Harmony waves of competition and friction would inevitably break forth that would disrupt the reign of Great Harmony. It is for this reason that the conception of a society in which the sage is exterminated and the wise discarded, and the people of one state grow old and die without having had any dealings with those of another, put forward by Laozi and Zhuangzi, remains but an ideal society and nothing more. ... When we read history, we always praise the era of the Warring States [how Hegelian this sounds!] ... It is the times when things are constantly changing, and numerous men of talent are emerging, that people like to read about. When they come to periods of peace, they are bored and put the book aside. It is not that we like chaos, but simply that the reign of peace cannot last long, is unendurable to human beings, and that human nature is delighted by sudden change.[6]

With this passage, Mao emerges from the cocoon of Western and Chinese philosophy with his own unique formulation. In doing so, Mao makes use of the Chinese tradition and, in this case, takes one passage literally to a chilling conclusion: the passage which refers to the extermination of the sage and the discarding of the wise. Do we not see premonitions here of the Cultural Revolution that Mao initiated?

The Influence of Laozi's Notorious Chapter Nineteen on Mao's Cultural Revolution

Both passages Mao cites are from Laozi and not from Zhuangzi. The notorious passage from the *Daodejing* that Mao cites: 'Exterminate the sage, discard the wise, and the people will benefit a hundredfold,' is from

Chapter 19. It sounds eerily prescient of the Cultural Revolution Mao would engineer in the 1960s.

The passage from Laozi is indeed one that has vexed numerous scholars over time. One could consider that the passage should be taken in the context that it follows Chapter 18 in which the point is made that it is only when the Great Way has fallen into disuse that cleverness, benevolence, filial relations and loyalty emerge. Could it be that such prescriptions arise in the wake of the loss of the *Dao*? In the wake of the loss of the *Dao*, both ethics (benevolence) and, its corollary, a lack of ethics, arise. However, this is not said by Laozi and is purely speculative. While this interpretation would find some support from the later Chapter 38, Chapter 19, nevertheless, remains a troubling and problematic chapter. It might well be that Mao's interpretation of Chinese philosophy, in this case, is an accurate one. Consider these injunctions from Mao:

> Let us drive opera singers, poets, playwrights and men of letters out of the cities, and drive all of them into the countryside.[7]

In any case, Mao's interpretation of the passage suits his purposes, and it would be too much of a coincidence to consider that the practices of the Cultural Revolution were not influenced at all by this reading of Laozi. When one reads the lines, 'exterminate the sage,' and 'discard the wise,' one cannot help but think of the Cultural Revolution. The passage possesses direct reference to the art of ruling the people. In the Cultural Revolution, intellectuals were downgraded and humiliated. It is difficult to not think that Mao was following Laozi in terms of relating to intellectuals.[8]

The passage, 'Though adjoining states are within sight of one another, and the sound of dogs barking and cocks crowing in one state can be heard in another, yet the people of one state will grow old and die without having had any dealings with those of another,' is from Chapter 80 of the *Daodejing*. Why Mao attributed these passages to Zhuangzi as well is not known.

In any case, it can be argued that Mao's campaign against intellectualism, core to the Cultural Revolution, was built on his early understanding of his reading of Chapter 19 of the *Daodejing*, and thus demonstrated the continuing influence of the Chinese Classics on Mao's thinking. It cannot be gainsaid that Mao's actions in the Cultural Revolution were in strict accord with the literal understanding of Chapter 19 of the *Daodejing*. Mao's practice is probably the most chilling fulfilment in Chinese history of the ideas expressed in Chapter 19. It would be difficult to find a more epochal example of classical philosophy put into practice in the history of either Western or Chinese philosophy.[9]

The greatest deviation of Mao's marginal notes from the mainstream of Chinese thought lies in his valuation of disharmony over the value of social harmony. In the end, Mao is not Confucius, Mencius, Zhuangzi or Nietzsche. He is simply Mao. He has been influenced, at least in this early writing, by his contact with both Chinese and Western philosophy. This feature, in itself, is a remarkable fact. His appropriation of these philosophies into his own egoistic philosophy reflects his own unique, syncretic thinking.

Mao and Hobbes

Mao's Egoism may be problematic and perhaps this is the reason, by and large, great philosophers have not chosen Egoism as their ultimate philosophies. If they have, as in the case of Hobbes, there is a safeguard for the conflicts that arise from Egoism. For Hobbes, there is an absolute ruler who will restrain the egoistic desires of some individuals. This is a necessity for Hobbes and, in fact, constitutes his justification for absolutism. Life, for Hobbes, in a state of nature, in his famous phrase, is the war of every man against every man. The life of man, according to Hobbes's equally famous pithy statement, is nasty, solitary, brutish and short. The absolute ruler for Hobbes protects man against the ravages of his fellow men. While, ironically, Mao could have utilized Hobbes's justification for his own later absolutism, he does not have the view that Hobbes asserts, that Egoism is destructive and must be held in check by the absolute ruler. In this respect, the political philosophy of Hobbes is more consistent and coherent than that of Mao's, though not for that reason more desirable.

Mao and Locke

For the early Mao, Hobbes's justification for an absolute ruler is not available, since for Mao there is no indication, as there is for Hobbes, that there is something wrong with egoistic desires or that egoistic desires will necessarily conduce to social strife. For Mao, egoism and social harmony are not in conflict. Locke's political philosophy escapes this dilemma because, according to Locke, man in a state of nature is naturally good and, therefore, conflicts will not arise. Locke de-emphasizes the ego and this is his way of solving the problem of conflict. This description of man as good by nature makes Locke's case for a government weaker than Hobbes's case, though, not for that reason less desirable. For Locke, if man is good in a state of nature and conflicts do not arise, why do we need the state at all? This is why Hobbes's justification for the state is on stronger philosophical grounds. It does not mean that Hobbes's justification is valid; it only means that it is more logically grounded.

Mao has the problem of keeping and exalting the idea of egoism and at the same time considering that egoistic desires will not lead to social conflict. The maintenance of the value of egoistic desires and not considering the possibility of conflict between competing egoistic desires signals the key weakness in Mao's political philosophy.

Mao and Marxism

In the end, it would appear, the primary weakness of neglecting the possibility of conflicting egoistic desires created difficulties for such a philosophy as Mao's Egoism. Later, in its Marxist form, particularly in the case of the Cultural Revolution, it could be argued that Mao's Egoism played a role in initiating such disastrous social experiments. Here, in the present analysis, Mao's Egoism, in its incipient pre-Marxist stage, one can already detect the seeds of the later conflicts to which it might give rise. Given Mao's views on harmony, that in striking contrast to the Chinese tradition, harmony does not represent an ideal state for humanity, perhaps Mao would not have been surprised that the system he put into place was soon to be replaced by another, which possessed many of the features of its opposite.

On the one hand, it could be said that Mao brought Marxist ideas into being through a revolution that overthrew the class structure and replaced it with the first seeds of communism. This alteration was a fulfilment of Marx's prophetic dialectic. In terms of broad philosophical categories, both Russia and the People's Republic of China (PRC) have been turning into their virtual economic opposites, though market socialism fuelled by the market system of both state and private capitalism is by no means identical to private capitalism.

While it could be said from a broad philosophical understanding that the transition from communism to capitalism in China contradicts the order of Marxist progression which classically argued that communism would inevitably emerge from capitalism and not vice versa, such a transition would not be incongruent with the notion of the dialectic that characterized the later thought of Mao in which conflict was inevitable and no opposite could stay in place forever. For the sake of explaining the movement of the dialectic and excluding the stage of dictatorship in which there was no industrial proletariat proper, the dialectic has been such that it changes from communism (not, of course, in Marx's strict sense) into a form of capitalism or market socialism (SCC).[10] While a socialist market economy can be argued to be different from capitalism proper, there is no doubt that such an economy must compete globally with capitalist economies in the competitive marketplace.

While such an order of the change of social systems from socialism to a market economy is not in keeping with a pure view of Marx, such a dialectic, and a change to opposites is in keeping with the ancient Chinese philosophy of the *Yijing* where nothing is static and every event is in the process of changing into its opposite. In this sense, the case of the history of China answers the old Hegelian question of which was the ultimate end-goal of the Hegelian dialectic, Hegel's philosophy, or the process of the dialectic itself.[11] The answer in this case is clear: It is the process of dialectic that is the end goal and this certainly corresponds to Mao's early philosophy which valued struggle and change over the attainment of harmony. In this sense, the case of China itself is the fulfilment of Mao's early philosophy.

The Hegelian Dialectic

The dialectic of Marxism follows the Hegelian model. In Hegel, there are three stages, the thesis, the antithesis and the synthesis. The last stage, that of the synthesis, itself comprises three phases, the process of which is captured by the German verb, *aufheben*. This third stage partially negates what exists prior to it, namely, the contradiction between the thesis and the antithesis. It resolves the contradiction between the thesis and the antithesis (at least temporarily) by cancelling out the contradiction. It cancels out the contradiction through initiating a third stage which, in part, synthesizes what is present in both of the sides of the thesis and antithesis by creating a new product that contains elements of each of the preceding stages and also contains a new dimension (not captured by the term 'synthesis'). The cancellation is not a complete cancellation since it still retains some elements of each of the prior stages: This containment is captured by one of the meanings of the verb '*aufheben*', sublation. The third meaning of the verb '*aufheben*' is transcendence. The third stage, which is the production of a new entity, that did not exist before, constitutes a transcendence of what did exist previously.

Mao's Dialectical Thinking

The above characteristics form part of Hegelian dialectic and its Marxist version, but do not entirely encompass Mao's dialectical thinking, which bears a greater resemblance to the dialectic in the *Yijing*.[12] The case of the consonance of the *Yijing* with Mao's idea of a dialectic is not the same as the dialectic in Marxism. In this sense, Mao's philosophy is more in accord with ancient Chinese philosophy than it is with Marxism proper. The four characteristics, which are to be found in the *Yijing*, that do not form part of Hegelian or Marxist dialectic, are (i) the return of the cycle back to its starting point; (ii) the constant movement back again from where it had previously progressed; (iii) the incorporation at any stage of the movement between the two sides of a portion, in greater or lesser degree, of each of the sides; (iv) the notion that any portion of the cycle constitutes a temporary, harmonious resolution of the two elements that, at the same time, contains a seed of unrest which propels the constant development of the cycle. The harmonious resolution is an element that Mao does not incorporate. Mao does not follow the *Yijing* strictly any more than he follows Hegelian dialectic strictly. According to Schram, at one point Mao argues that dialectical theory does not follow a cyclical pattern.[13] Mao's own thought and practice, however, may not adhere to dialectics. Schram states that in the view of Yang Ch' ao, '[Mao] thought the end result of the whole process was a return to the *initial* affirmation, rather than a progression to a new and higher level.'[14] This view would suggest that Mao's thought modelled the pattern of changes of the *Yijing*. On the other hand, at one point Mao appears to combine the Hegelian movement to a higher level with the *Yijing* notion of cyclical change:

> ... cognition always moves in cycles and ... each cycle advances human knowledge a step higher and so makes it more and more profound.[15]

And yet, we find Mao asserting the contrary. According to Schram:

> In April 1957, Mao remarked: 'Dialectics is not a cyclical theory'.[16]

Mao's thought undergoes constant change. However, the former formulation attempts to capture both the old and the new simultaneously. In its merger of ancient Chinese philosophy with Hegelian dialectic, it embraces the differences between classical Chinese philosophy and Hegelian dialectic in a complementary whole that is characteristic of the pattern of changes in the *Yijing*. Is this formulation a harbinger of Mao's contribution to the philosophy of change?

Flashback to the Beginnings of Mao's Thought

To recapitulate Mao's development of thought, he begins with his study of the ancient Chinese classics and the thought of Confucius. Obviously, neither Hegel nor Marx initiated their respective thought processes from this starting point. The starting point of Mao's philosophy is Confucianism, albeit in Mao's inimitable version, though a case could also be made that the beginnings of Mao's philosophical thinking are indicated in his marginal notes to Paulsen. However, since Mao's exposure to and study of Confucius predated his reading of Paulsen, it would be more accurate to say that his philosophical beginnings should be traced to Confucianism.

Mao's dialectical thinking, considered by some Marxist thinkers to be influenced by Marxist dialectic, actually shows a strong parallel to the movement of the *Yijing*. Since the movement of the *Yijing* is a back-and-forth movement between the two sides of the complementary contradiction, when Confucianism is replaced, in the middle stage of Mao's thinking, with Marxism, in accordance with the *Yijing*, the late stage of Mao's thinking should reflect a return to Confucianism (Mao's ego-driven version). China's social and political development precedes the explicit stage of the Confucian return when Marxism is supplanted by an ego-driven profit incentive, i.e. Deng Xiaoping's encouragement to pursue wealth. The current explicit Confucian return in China parallels Mao's ego-driven version of Confucianism. If one considers the superstructure leading the base, the possibility for the next direction of social development could be towards a non-ego-based Confucianism. In this analysis, the case of the social changes that have characterized the past century leading up the present moment, follow the development of the *Yijing*, rather than a strict Marxist dialectic. From the preceding philosophical analysis, the social development of present-day China, guided by its attempt to merge Confucianism with individual pursuit of wealth appears to parallel and return to Mao's early merger of individualism with Confucianism. It could be argued that this development borrows from a Hegelian model as well since the new merger of Confucianism and profit seeking contains a new element of profit seeking which differs from early Mao's ego-driven Confucianism. Such an Hegelian analysis would also suit Mao's thinking since it would reveal an East–West philosophical influence that was present in his early philosophical development.

It is not surprising then, that China, in its present stage of development, should be returning to some form of Confucianism. In this analysis, the materialism of Deng Xiaoping was the economic counterpart of Mao's

Philosophy of Egoism. The return to Confucianism is a return with a new Maoist element: Mao's unique version of Confucianism, which includes the assertion of the ego. This element is the ingredient in Mao's thought which characterized his early philosophy and which now may be considered to characterize China today. The social and philosophical development of China today could be considered to be an implicit return to the early philosophical thought of Mao. China's explicit form of Confucianism as its guidepost is now fuelled with the content of the pursuit of profit as the place filler for Mao's emphasis on ego assertion. These remarks are not polemically intended as a defence of the Chinese version of what has been called 'market socialism'. They simply form a philosophical analysis of how it is possible that the return of Confucianism to China today can be interpreted as the complementary movement of the *yi* to Deng Xiaoping's advocacy of the pursuit of wealth which was in turn a complementary response to the breakdown of the pure Marxist model. Mao's Philosophy of Egoism, acting as it were, as the yang force, would be conducive to the development of a materialistic motivation for action. This yang movement could, in turn, serve as preparation for the movement to the yin, that is, the ethical and non-ego side of classical Confucianism. All of this is not to provide a justifying ideology for the system of Chinese rulership. The movement of the *yi* is apolitical. It is only in the thinking of Marx that such philosophical explanations assume ideological characteristics. The potential for the movement of China to turn towards pure, classical Confucianism is simply a function of the movement of the *yi*. This is a politically neutral explanation for social and political development in China, for the most part, in terms of the yin-yang movement of the *Yijing*.

It can be argued that the above analysis, that asserts the development of Mao's thought and its mirror in the social development of China, is an argument on behalf of demonstrating that the *Yijing* rather than Hegelian dialectic is the model which best explains both Mao's thought development and the development of China's social changes. It is important to remember that the return to Confucianism in China is not a return to pure Confucianism any more than Mao's starting point of Confucianism was a beginning in pure Confucianism. The Confucian revival in China is marked by its merger with socialist market (SCC) values, with its merger, in short, with egoism. This new Confucianism represents an innovative product and, in this sense, represents an alteration that is not in accord with the *Yijing*, which is the return to the beginning, but is more in accord with Hegelianism, which is not so much a return as it is an evolution to a new entity. In China, the answer is that it is both. Since one may consider that from a philosophical perspective, the social development of China parallels Mao's thought development, the social return in China is marked by a return to Mao's version of Confucius, which is a Confucianism fuelled by egoism. It is a return in the sense of the *Yijing*, in the respect that it is a return to the beginning. It is a return in the Hegelian sense in that it is not so much a return as it is a new beginning characterized by a marriage between Confucianism and egoism. While this merger was present in Mao's early thought, it is a new element in China's social development.

Mao took a large step in uncovering the real teachings of Confucius in contrast to the conventional readings of Confucius as conservative, adhering to tradition, acting obedient to authority and countenancing the rigid adherence to the obligatory performance of social roles. Schram points this out:

> Mao alluded with approval to various attitudes defined by tags from the Confucian classics, such as Confucius' practice of going about and 'inquiring into everything', his attitude of 'not feeling ashamed to ask and learn from people below', and the recommendation from the Mencius, 'When speaking to the mighty, look on them with contempt'.[17]

Mao's allusions show a great understanding of the tradition of independent thinking present in the genuine Confucius and the genuine Confucian tradition.[18] This is a step forward. Can this scholarly finger in the dyke stem the seeming rising tide of unimpeded capitalism? This is the $64,000 question. We are in the midst of a Cultural Revolution of a different kind. While it may not be as horrific and harmful as the first Cultural Revolution, it may be far more difficult to find ways in which one can extricate oneself from it. Žižek puts the problem this way:

> What are the violent outbursts of a Red Guard caught in the Cultural Revolution compared to the true Cultural Revolution, the permanent dissolution of all life-forms by capitalist reproduction? Today, the tragedy of the Great Leap Forward is repeating as the comedy of the rapid capitalist Great Leap Forward into modernization, with the old slogan 'an iron foundry in every village' reemerging as 'a skyscraper on every street'.[19]

It could be argued that this is an oversimplification of China's system of SCC. However, Confucianism has its work cut out for it to try to catch up with runaway capitalism on a worldwide scale. This problem is not only China's problem. It is America's problem and it is a global problem. What we can hope for is that China utilizes its deep intellectual well of resources to draw upon. And the quixotic figure of Mao has played a unique instrumental role both in turning China away from these resources, and with his own inventive ideas of the use of contradictions, provided pointers that can explain and justify the return to these resources.

In China's development of SCC in which State and private ownership combine, the philosophical question is, what part will egoism and Confucianism play in this mixture? The ethical flaws in China, such as greed, can be traced to the elevation of egoism. At the same time, its economic development can also be traced to the elevation of egoism. Such an elevation, in turn, gives rise to the resuscitation of Confucianism. In the present stage, by retaining Confucianism as an element in its value structure, China has created for itself a safety valve. With a pure market system, with no value system, with no ethical underpinnings, China's development would be unstable. It would lack direction and the guidance of the simple profit motive, which I have argued in my other works, is not a user-friendly Pole star.[20]

In the early days of the aftermath of the Cultural Revolution, before the inception of the profit motive, the lack of any other motivations for action became evident. When the present author was a Visiting Professor to Gweilin Normal University in 1984, giving lectures in the same room that Gary Snyder was reading from his poetry and Allen Ginsberg was reading *Howl* (substituting the *China Daily* for the *New York Times* when he came to the relevant line), we afterwards waited in a restaurant for service while waiters stood by the walls, possessing no motive to serve customers as tips were forbidden. Blue Mao jackets and trousers were the universal uniform for males and females alike. Equality and uniformity ruled aesthetics.

By 1988, returning as a Visiting Professor to Peking University and Fudan University, I was lecturing in the Edgar Snow House to which students of philosophy flocked to hear the Western professor lecture on Existentialism and Phenomenology. They had no books of Sartre and other Western philosophers and plied me with many requests to send them books. Outside, people would come up to my wife and delicately pat her hair, marvelling at the texture and colour of her hair. One day, when she rode a bicycle on the streets of Hangzhou, a Chinese bicyclist was so astonished to see a Westerner that she literally drove right into her. They both fell off their bicycles and laughed.

In contrast, in Shanghai, the ubiquitous Mao outfits were replaced by colourful and fashionable Western style clothing. In this rather short span of years, capitalism, a capitalism without values, was beginning to rear its voracious head. One day, while a Visiting Professor at Fudan University in Shanghai, a sudden downpour impelled me to find a taxi, at that time a three-wheeler resembling a golf cart. When my Charon quoted the price, I protested that it was four times higher than the usual rate. His reply was simply, 'Ni yao buyao?' (Do you want it or not?) The point was, as he understood capitalism, that when supply was short and demand high, you automatically raised your price for a maximum profit. This gave me the first inkling that the adoption of capitalism without the linkage to any ethical value could create social inequities.

For this reason, the resurgence of Confucianism, even in its less than its original, classical philosophical form, seems to the author to be a positive step. Of course, there are other motives that can be assigned to the recent rehabilitation of Confucianism. It has been often asserted that the Confucian revival serves to propagandize market socialism. Whether or not that is true, it does not speak to the point that retaining Confucianism, in whatever form, legitimizes Confucianism in addition to legitimizing Chinese social and economic development. Once the texts of Confucianism are legitimized, one has reference to those texts as sources of authority. Whatever the consequence the legitimizing of Confucius would have for China's economic development, it cannot be but good for China's ethical development. The one caveat is that it would be deeply beneficial if the Confucius who is revived bears a close resemblance to the textual Confucius.

The Confucian Revival and the Dialectic

The dialectic, as Hegel taught, has a mind of its own. In the same sense, the *Yijing* has a mind of its own, as well. Regardless of the motives for the Confucian revival in China, the movement of a return to the study of the Chinese Classics is a movement that bears notable promise as a corrective to greed and pursuit of profit making without sufficient regard for humanistic and altruistic values. That a closer examination of the classical writings is required in order to gain a proper understanding of the Confucian heritage goes without saying.

Will such a return to the Confucian canon be a simplistic return to a more authoritarian and patriarchal society? One would hope that a closer examination of the Confucian classics will enable a return to the universalistic, the humanistic Confucius, not the popularized version that tends to emphasize obedience to elders. However, these are questions for later philosophers to contemplate. For the time being, China is in the stage of its development that represents returning and pivoting to the early Mao's egoistic version of Confucianism. It is this contradiction that both currently fuels China's development and represents the enigma for Chinese philosophers to fathom.

Mao would be happy to see that contradiction and disharmony and the current marriage of opposites of Confucianism and egoism characterize present-day China. Mao, as has been clearly demonstrated, was no lover of harmony. In this sense, Mao broke with the Chinese tradition and joined forces with the Hegelian notion of struggle and contradiction as the essence of life and not its resolution in the Great Harmony. Mao represents the beginning of the new world in his effort to combine his exposure to the West, with his early studies of Hegel and his more famous studies of Marx, with his classical beginnings in Chinese thought. Current China mirrors Mao's way. It can never return to the simple and graceful harmony as depicted in Laozi's famous 80th chapter.

Mao's thought resembles that of Zhuangzi more than that of Laozi. Zhuangzi both cries and bangs on his drum when his wife dies. He cries out at the same time that he sings. Disharmony and harmony exist side by side in Zhuangzi.

This is not to say, by any means, that all of Mao's actions are, therefore, justified or that all of his behaviour can be valued. Mao was guilty of enormous excesses. If I read the works of Hitler, it is because I want to understand how his actions evolved from his thinking. I may read Heidegger to see how he seemed to borrow ideas (without accrediting them) from Kierkegaard and to take note of what weaknesses exist in this philosophy that would allow one who embraced it to also embrace Nazism. For example, one can take note of Heidegger's strong endorsement of resoluteness without specifying or qualifying that to which one should be resolute. If his philosophy is liable to such a weakness, it possesses serious flaws, so serious that it may imperil its status as being considered worthy of the label of greatness in the history of philosophy. I may, therefore, not continue to choose to read Heidegger. It is not only because he chose to become a Nazi that I would not read Heidegger, but because his philosophy did not prevent him from embracing Nazism. Its theoretical structure was weak enough to allow its master to embrace the polemics of a racist theory. All of this is alien to the thought of Mao.

In the case of Mao, his thinking is important to understand the course of development of modern China. It is not to eulogize Mao to read his work or to write about his thought. It is not to praise Mao for his brilliance or to expose the definite gaps and flaws in his thinking. That Mao studied philosophy is not all to the good. His reading of Chapter 19 of Laozi may have had some influence on him, whether self-conscious or unconscious, with the initiation of the Cultural Revolution. Not everything that Laozi wrote was good. Not everything that Plato wrote was good. Not everything that Aristotle wrote was good. Even Homer nods.

6

Mao's Marxist Thought and the *Yijing*

Mao's later Marxist works such as 'On Contradiction', reflect a parallel with changes as depicted in the *Yijing* and are not found in Marxist dialectic. Most notably, as we shall see below, passages can be found in 'On Contradiction' in which the continued presence of the opposite exists as opposed to its being transcended. In this sense, 'On Contradiction' possesses more in common with the *Yijing* than with the Marxist dialectic proper. In these passages of 'On Contradiction,' we can see a parallel to the *Yijing* and Mao's denial of Hegel's 'negation of negation', that is the synthesis that is supposed to overcome the opposites. For Hegel, the 'negation of the negation' is a crucial concept. I can vividly recall the great Hegelian scholar and my professor, John Findlay, emphasizing this in a graduate course I took with him in Hegel's *Phenomenology*.[1] Without the concept of the 'negation of the negation' there is no synthesis of opposites. The synthesis is the key element for Hegel. The opposites find their ultimate meaning in the synthesis, the new third element, that they produce. In the *Yijing*, in contrast, the complementary opposites are never totally overcome. The opposition never dissolves. With Mao, the more gradual movement of change in the *Book of Changes* is replaced with more abrupt and more drastic changes. Still, Mao's philosophy is closer to that of the *Yijing* than it is to Hegel. It differs from the *Yijing* since it departs from the value and goal of harmony. In the *Yijing*, seeking a balance or a harmony is a goal, though it is a goal that is never reached. For Mao, balance or harmony is never a goal at all. It is important to realize that while harmony is a goal of the *yi*, that it is never reached. That it is never reached is a significant clue to the nature of change. Harmony is a *motus* to change rather than its ideal realization. Mao eliminates harmony even as a *motus* to change.[2]

Contradiction for Mao should not be construed only as the external collision between two opposites. Contradiction is inherent internally in each thing. This is how change comes about. Each thing is inherently dissatisfied and moves towards dissolution. Consider this statement of Mao's: 'Contradiction is present in the process of development of all things; it permeates the process of development of each thing from beginning to end.'[3] This is why things move and change. They are inherently unstable. The friction of the internal contradictions propels alteration. This is pure Hegel. Did Mao refer to Engels for the concepts that he discusses? No doubt. But, it must be remembered that he had already absorbed those concepts from the imbibing of Hegel's ideas from his youthful reading of Paulsen. In addition, according to his self-report, Mao had read Hegel.[4] There is controversy whether Mao had given up the concept of the 'negation of the negation' in 1964 even though it appears as if he does do so in his 1964 essay, 'On Contradiction'. According to Xu Quanxing, Mao was still making reference to the 'negation of negation' in 1964.[5] Schram, presumably thinking of the essay, 'On Contradiction', claims that Mao abandoned the concept of the 'negation of the negation' in 1964.[6]

Schram writes:

> Then, in the 1960s, Mao went beyond simply renaming and in some degree redefining the negation of the negation to repudiating this basic concept altogether.[7]

Knight argues otherwise. For Knight, Mao continues to use the concept of the negation of the negation under a different name:

By renaming the concept 'affirmation and negation', Mao could leave the substance of the concept unaltered while bringing its title into line with the pervasive idea that the unity of opposite exists in all things and processes.[8]

Here, I am more inclined to agree with Schram rather than Knight. The essential feature of the negation of the negation is the synthesis. This is the element of the negation of the negation that Mao eliminates. It is because Mao does not consider there ever to be resolution that he abandons the concept of the negation of the negation. It is not, therefore, a mere verbal or semantic change. It is a significant, substantive conceptual change.

We may for a moment, reflect on the contrast between the Hegelian unity of opposites and the combination of the yin and the yang of the *Yijing*. The concept of the Hegelian unity of opposites is unrefined when compared to the yin and the yang. The notion of opposites combined into one is a difficult concept to grasp; it is difficult to grasp because it is incoherent. With the *Yijing*, the two opposites retain their distinctness inside the combination. Conceptually speaking, this is perfectly coherent. What is more is that the two opposites in the *Yijing* do not simply oppose each other; they complement and balance each other. They are, in Mao's language, non-antagonistic contradictions. More than likely, this is the source of Mao's concept of non-antagonistic contradictions. In the *Yijing* the opposites also possess a character; they are not simply forces in opposition. The yin character is passive and receptive; the yang character is active and creative. These oppositions are more refined than the Hegelian ones. In addition, the yin and the yang need each other. They are not two opposite forces in battle with each other. They are incomplete complementary forces that seek their totality in a dynamic union.

The Hegelian notion of the unity of opposites is a self-contradictory concept. That is why it is incoherent. From a Marxist point of view, this is its virtue. It is the central idea of Marxist dialectic. The very self-contradictory nature of the concept illustrates and embodies the notion of contradiction that is understood to be at the heart of all reality. The *Yijing* is far subtler. At the heart of reality are two complementary forces. The idea of Hegel and the idea of the *Yijing* are two quite distinct and different ideas. Mao's notion is more akin to that of the *Yijing* than it is to Hegel. Mao diverges from both Hegel and the *Yijing*, because he does not envision either a temporary or a final harmony.

The main point is that Mao was not a mere follower of Hegelian dialectic. It is true that in the original version of 'On Contradiction', Mao repudiates formal logic as incompatible with dialectical logic.[9] In the original text of 'On Contradiction' in referring to the Unity of Opposites, Mao says of the unity of opposites that:

It is opposed to the absolute law of identity of formal logic.[10]

However, this section is not present in the official version. Later, he is to take great pains to distinguish formal logic from Hegelian logic. He employs careful reasoning to demonstrate that the use of formal logic was a necessary condition for the communication of dialectical thinking:

> Formal logic is concerned with the form of thought, and is concerned to ensure that there is no contradiction between separate stages in an argument. It is a specialized science. Any kind of writing must make use of formal logic. ... One cannot acquire much fresh knowledge through formal logic. Naturally one can draw inferences, but the conclusion is still enshrined in the major premise. At present some people confuse formal logic and dialectics. This is incorrect.[11]

Mao's reasoning here is sophisticated. Formal logic is carefully distinguished from dialectics. This is a valuable philosophical contribution.

Famously, Mao takes exception to a major feature of the Hegelian dialectic in his critique of Engels, when Mao proclaims that 'the negation of the negation does not exist at all.'[12] For Žižek, this is precisely Mao's problem. Mao has eliminated the stage of unification, the stage of harmonious resolution. Žižek writes:

His [Mao's] problem was precisely the lack of the 'negation of the negation', the failure of the attempts to transpose revolutionary negativity into a truly new positive Order: all temporary stabilizations of the revolution amounted to so many restorations of the old Order, so that the only way to keep the revolution alive was the 'spurious infinity' of endlessly repeated negation which reached its apex in the Great Cultural Revolution.[13]

Žižek, floating like a butterfly and stinging like a bee, has reference here to Hegel's notion of the 'bad infinity' which goes on endlessly. He does not refer to Hegel's notion of the 'good infinity' which moves in a circle. Žižek's critique is profound and incisive. It pinpoints the key difficulty attending Mao's abandonment of the third phase of the Hegelian dialectic, the synthesis, and the implication for Mao's political actions.

It is a difficult question to discern what Mao meant by the 'negation of negation' whether in affirming or denying it. According to Xu, Engels and Lenin thought that this referred to the spiral nature of development.[14] Xu quotes Mao as saying:

> Practice, knowledge, again practice, again knowledge. This form repeats itself in endless cycles, and with each cycle the content of practice and knowledge rises to a higher level.[15]

This suggests a combination of both the cyclical nature of change characterizing the *Yijing* and the Hegelian spiral moving ever upward.

Holubnychy interprets Mao's view to be more similar to Marx and Engels than the *Yijing* because of the spiral route.[16] What Holubnychy does not note is that Mao's view is a combination of both the Hegelian spiral and the cyclical movement of the *Yijing*. In addition, Mao does not always follow the spiral direction since he does not foresee endless progress.

To make matters murkier, Mao replaces the phrase 'negation of negation' with 'affirmation and negation' a name alteration that comes closer, in my way of thinking, to abandoning the validity of the 'negation of the negation' (if we identify this with a higher synthesis) and thus is more consistent with more of Mao's usages. Xu argues that this innovation of Mao's is an improvement on both Lenin's and Stalin's understanding.[17]

Schram quotes Mao's critique of Stalin's view as it is illustrated in the *Shorter dictionary of philosophy*, fourth edition, compiled in the Soviet Union:

> It is said there: 'There can be no identity between war and peace ... between life and death ... because they are fundamentally opposed to each other and mutually exclusive.' ... This interpretation is utterly wrong. ... In their view, war is war and peace is peace, the two are mutually exclusive and entirely unconnected ... If war is not brewing in peacetime, how can it possibly break out all of a sudden? ... If life and death cannot be transformed into each other, then please tell me where living things come from. Originally there was only non-living matter on earth ... Life and death are engaged in a constant struggle and are being transformed into each other all the time.[18]

Schram strongly notes the similarity of these thoughts to ancient Daoist dialectics of the flow of nature.[19] Does this quotation not also echo the early philosophical musings of the young Mao in the Margins reflected in his reading and commenting upon Paulsen? There is little doubt that there is a continuity in Mao's thinking that extends from his early philosophical thinking to the philosophical thinking of his later years. The middle period of Mao's thinking is dominated by Marxist thinking; the ideas of traditional Western and Chinese philosophy of Mao's youth are never transcended, as in the Hegelian dialectic, but survive in dormant form, to ascend to dominance in his later years. Mao's thinking follows the pattern of the *Yijing*, the *Book of Changes*. The opposites co-exist, for some time one is dominant; at another time, the other takes its place. It is not a smooth and seamless process. It is, like Mao's early commentary on Paulsen, filled with turbulence, explosiveness and contradiction.

Do Mao's ideas of dialectics originate with his Marxism? It can be argued that Mao obtained his key idea, the unity of opposites, from Lenin. Schram writes:

> In 'On Contradiction', Mao Tse-tung had accepted implicitly the 'three basic laws' of Marxist and Hegelian dialectics (the unity and struggle of opposites, the transformation of quantity into quality, and the negation of the negation), but at the same time he had given a hint of a new approach to these problems by characterizing the 'law of the unity of opposites' and the 'fundamental law of thought', thus seemingly placing it in a higher category than the other two. To be sure, Lenin had said, in a passage quoted by Mao in January 1957 'In brief, dialectics can be defined as the unity of opposites.'[20]

Though this may be true, it may also be true that Mao brought with him, to his reading of Lenin, his knowledge of the unity of opposites gleaned from his understanding of the *Yijing*. In other words, in true *Yijing* fashion, both interpretations may be true. Schram, pointing to Mao's 'On Contradiction' takes the position that Mao derives his voluntarism from Lenin.[21] However, Mao's voluntarism, as has been discussed at length above, has been with Mao ever since he studied and commented upon Paulsen's *System of Ethics*. Even Schram emphasizes Mao's stress on the importance of the will as the primary motivator for mankind. In Mao's own words:

> *The will is the antecedent of a man's career.*[22]

If Mao also notices the importance of the will in Lenin, this is clearly a case of both-and thinking (that Mao already placed great emphasis on the will and noticed that Stalin had also emphasized the will), and therefore, another instance of *Yijing* thinking in the mind of Mao.[23]

The importance of the *Yijing* connection is underscored when one considers Mao's critique of Stalin:

> Stalin says that Marxist dialectics has four principle features. As the first feature he talks of the interconnection of things, as if all things happened to be interconnected for no reason at all ... It is the two contradictory aspects of a thing that are interconnected ... As the fourth feature he talks of the internal contradiction in all things, but then he deals only with the struggle of opposites, without mentioning their unity.[24]

In the *Yijing*, the two opposites are internally connected within one. Every one of the sixty-four hexagrams is composed of a combination of yin and yang. This is the standpoint from which Mao is thinking. For Mao, Stalin saw the opposites as only externally connected. This marks a great difference. For Mao, as for Hegel, contradiction is internal to each unity. The difference between Hegel and the *Yijing* is that for Hegel the opposites are antagonistic and need to be reconciled and transcended. In the *Yijing* the opposites exist in a delicate balance, which like a pendulum swings in a back-and-forth complementary movement rather than an upward-moving Hegelian spiral.[25]

One difficulty that lies in the attempt to explicate the Hegelian concept of 'the unity of opposites' stems from the fact that for Hegel, 'the unity of opposites' is achieved through a tripartite process of thesis, antithesis and synthesis. The synthesis is not only a synthesis; it is a movement to a third position that transcends the prior two phases. Mao does not want to incorporate the synthesis that involves the transcendence to a third position. It is in this sense that he denies 'the unity of opposites'. He affirms 'the unity of opposites' in the sense that there is always a unity of opposites, but this unity does not evolve into a new entity. Mao's notion of a 'unity of opposites' is closer to the unity of opposites that characterizes the *Yijing*. Mao's denial of the negation of the negation is in effect the negation of the synthesis that constitutes a new entity. It is not the denial of the unity of opposites. His denial is the denial of the synthesis in the sense of the creation of a stasis without contradiction.

On the other hand, Mao even contradicts his most famous denial of the negation of negation, that is, the existence of the synthesis. For example, in the following passage from 'On the Correct Handling of Contradictions,' Mao writes:

> … in the formula 'unity-criticism-unity' … that means starting from the desire for unity, resolving contradictions through criticism or struggle, and arriving at a new unity on a new basis. In our experience this is the correct method of resolving contradictions among the people.[26]

The above passage is evidence that in some instances Mao makes explicit use of the unity of opposites and even expresses the goal as being that of a new unity. With a contradiction of such a main principle, one cannot account for this simply by appealing to the law of contradiction in general. For this, one needs a subtler and a more particular explanation. In his essay, 'On the Correct Handling of Contradictions Among the People,' Mao provides the answer to this seeming conundrum. Mao points out that there are many contradictions. Like a physician dealing with illnesses, though he does not use this analogy, all contradictions are not the same and each contradiction requires special handling. In Mao's words:

> These contradictions [between proletariat and bourgeoisie, peasantry and urban petty bourgeoisie, etc.] cannot be treated in the same way since each has its own particularity; moreover, the two aspects of each contradiction cannot be treated in the same way since each aspect has its own characteristics.[27]

And again,

> Qualitatively different contradictions can only be resolved by qualitatively different methods.[28]

According to Schram, Mao claims his analyses of antagonistic and non-antagonistic contradictions among the people in 'On the Correct Handling of Contradictions Among the People' are not to be found in Marx, Engels, Lenin or Stalin. Mao claims philosophical originality both for his concept of contradictions among the people and how to handle these contradictions. With regard to Stalin, Mao claims philosophical originality in terms of his [Mao's] proper understanding of antagonistic and non-antagonistic contradictions:

> Contradictions among the people, and how to resolve this problem, is a new problem. Historically, Marx and Engels said very little about this problem, and though Lenin referred to it, he only just referred to it … He said that in a socialist society antagonisms just died away but … there continued to be contradictions among the people. Lenin said there were still contradictions among the people … he didn't have time to analyse this problem systematically. As for antagonism, can contradictions among the people be transformed from non-antagonistic contradictions to antagonistic contradictions? It must be said that they can, but in Lenin's day there was as yet no possibility of investigating this problem in detail. There was so little time allotted to him. Of course, after the October Revolution, during the period when Stalin was in charge, for a long time he mixed up these two kinds of contradictions.[29]

While Mao has in mind contradictions between different social classes, there is no reason why we cannot apply the notion of different methods of resolution to the issue of the unity of opposites. While Mao, to my knowledge, does not apply this reasoning to this issue, it seems a fair adaptation of his approach. While most of the time, there is no unity of opposites, in some special instances, he may have recourse to it when the need for it arises.

Despite these dialectical vagaries, Mao actually considers himself a monist:

> It was said that dialectics had three basic laws and then Stalin said there were four. But I think there is only one basic law – the law of contradiction.[30]

There is one reason, perhaps, that Mao did not appropriate the Hegelian dialectical triad. The notion of a thesis, antithesis and a synthesis is for Mao, a triplicity, not a monism:

> Engels talked about the three categories, but as for me I don't believe in two of those categories. (The unity of opposition is the most basic law, the transformation of quality and quantity into one another is the unity of the opposites, quality and quantity, and the negation of the negation does not exist at all). The juxtaposition, on the same level, of the transformation of quality and quantity into one another, the negation of the negation, and the law of the unity of opposites, is 'triplism' not monism. The most basic thing is the unity of the opposites. The transformation of quality and quantity into one another is the unity of opposites quality and quantity. There is no such thing as the negation of the negation. Affirmation, negation, affirmation, negation … in the development of things, every link in the chain of events is both affirmation and negation.[31]

To take a moment for a philosophical digression, it should be noted that while Hegel introduced the notion of changes of quantity at a critical mass causing changes in quality and offers many examples to illustrate how quantitative changes produce qualitative changes; nevertheless, it is difficult to find examples of qualitative changes producing quantitative changes. Hegel's lack of illustrative examples perhaps illustrates that the alteration is asymmetrical, from quantity to quality, but not vice versa. For example, while water is transformed into ice by lowering the temperature (quantity), its transformation back into water is also effected by quantitative change, that is, raising the temperature. The qualitative change does not by itself effect quantitative changes.

On the conceptual level, Hegel speaks of the mutual transformation of quality and quantity:

> ... we have seen that the alterations of being in general are not only the transition of one magnitude into another, but a transition from quality into quantity and *vice versa*.[32]

In following Hegel, as Mao does, with the phrase, 'the transformation of quality and quantity into one another', Mao implies a mutual transformation which would include the transformation of quality into quantity.

From the empirical examples found in Hegelian dialectics, the transformation, it seems, is always asymmetrical, one way from quantity into quality, not the other way around:

> In the moral sphere, in so far as it is considered under the categories of being, there occurs the same transition from quantity into quality and different qualities appear to be based on a difference of magnitude. It is through a more or less that the measure of frivolity or thoughtlessness is exceeded and something quite different comes about, namely crime, and thus right becomes wrong and virtue vice. Thus states, too, acquire through their quantitative difference, other things being assumed equal, a distinct qualitative character. With the expansion of the state and an increased number of citizens, the laws and the constitution acquire a different significance. The state has its own measure of magnitude and when this is exceeded this mere change in size renders it liable to instability and disruption under that same constitution which was its good fortune and its strength before its expansion.[33]

The alteration from quantity to quality makes sense when one considers these concrete examples. It is difficult, on the other hand, to discover or imagine an example of an alteration in quality producing an alteration in quantity.

The reason behind Mao's proposal of the idea of a mutual transformation may be that his thinking was influenced by the mutual transformation (not necessarily of quantity and quality) that is characterized by the changes of the

Yijing. Mao's dialectic, while self-consciously formulated with Western models in mind, may have been inspired in part or in whole, by the dialectical changes typified in the *Yijing* of ancient Chinese philosophy. Schram even notes that:

> ... it is suggestive that Mao should have stressed, in his philosophical conversations of 1964, that neither Buddhism nor Taoism should be left out of account (in favour of an exclusive concentration on the largely non-dialectical Confucian tradition) in studying the history of Chinese thought. In the same conversations he utterly rejected the principle of the negation of the negation [here, Schram reveals a correct understanding of the equivalence of the concept of the negation of the negation with the concept of synthesis] as an axiom of dialectics, on the grounds of every historical phenomenon was simultaneously or successively affirmation or negation. This remark, too, indicates a certain affinity with the [Chinese] traditional view of history as flux and reflux, rather than purposeful forward movement.[34]

Schram's account would reflect that Mao's dialectic shares more in common with the pendulum movements of the yin and the yang than with the Hegelian clash of opposites. It does not encompass the uniqueness of Mao's account of change in which changes can occur that do not seem to follow either a Hegelian progressive pattern or the pattern of rhythmic, cyclical changes that are embodied in the *Yijing*.

To return to Mao's profession of monism, perhaps, for Mao, triplicity reflected a certain incoherency, a lack of simplicity in explanation. While Mao did not explicitly endorse the concept of simplicity, his critique of triplicity, especially in the works of Engels, puts one in the mind of mathematicians who prefer one theory to another on the grounds of the simplicity of its explanation. Perhaps, this triplicity also represented to Mao a kind of intellectual duplicity, a duplicity that defied the way nature worked, and, hence was artificial and not true to life. To adapt Mao, the triplicity is an intellectual fabrication, a speculative construction. It did not reflect reality. In this respect, Mao is closer to the *Yijing* in which there is always a movement of opposites. Each hexagram is, by its very nature, incomplete and fated, so to speak, to turn into its opposite. Each hexagram is itself a unity of opposites and is unstable. Even the stable hexagrams are instable because stability itself is not a state that can remain the same. Change is paramount. Change is paramount because at the centre of things is opposition and the need to move. Without movement, there is no life. There is no synthesis or settled stage in the *Yijing*. There is no third stage in the *Yijing*. There is no need for a third stage. This is not to say that Mao's thought is the same as the thinking in the *Yijing*. Mao's thought is considerably more turbulent. His concept of change is the thunderstorm, not the morning mist.

Sometimes, Mao's position softens on the issue of whether there is no union of opposites or whether there are temporary reconciliations. In one passage, he writes:

> All processes have a beginning and an end, all processes transform themselves into their opposites. ... we say that the unity of opposite is conditional, temporary and relative, while the mutually exclusive opposite in absolute.[35]

These statements, composed much earlier than his 'Talk on Questions of Philosophy', seem to take a softer stance on the resolution or synthesis than his later thought which denies the existence of the temporary stage altogether.[36] Why not? Mao's thought should not be impervious to the law of change. If it were, the entire concept of continuous change and development would be fraudulent. Here, in his earlier writing, perhaps the thought is more sophisticated. It is not clear that all change is for the better. Mao's thought shows its subtlety when he writes that, 'The constancy of all processes is relative, but the mutability manifested in the transformation of one process into another is absolute.'[37] This distinction seems to suggest that when a process appears to be constant, it can only be temporary while the certainty of its changing is absolute.

In Mao's own words:

> In all things, one divides into two', said Mao in March 1964. I, too, am a case of one divides into two.[38]

Could Mao's position of the one becomes two have been influenced by the 42nd chapter of the Daodejing? The similarity is striking.

> The way begets one;
> One begets two;
> Two begets three;
> Three begets the myriad creatures.[39]

Non-antagonistic and Antagonistic Contradictions

One can, of course, consider the contradictions within Mao's thought examples of non-antagonistic contradictions. Since Mao does not perceive himself as the enemy and is part of the people, in light of his famous distinction between non-antagonistic and antagonistic contradictions, his own self-contradictions would surely be non-antagonistic contradictions:

> The contradictions between ourselves and the enemy are antagonistic contradictions. Within the ranks of the people, the contradictions among the working people are non-antagonistic, while those between the exploited and the exploiting classes have a non-antagonistic as well as an antagonistic aspect.[40]

While Mao may not have been analysing his own self-contradictions in this fashion, it seems that, under his principles, they are susceptible to this analysis.

Mao on Endless Struggle

Mao thought that the Marxist struggle was endless. This notion of the endless struggle of Marxism is a forcible reminder of Mao's early scribbling on the margins in which he proclaimed the endlessness of struggle. In those pre-Marxist days, he did not have Marxism in mind since he was unfamiliar with it. What followed, in his later writings celebrated as Marxist, was Mao's 'negation of a negation', his synthesis of his own early writings and his later immersion in Marxist thought. Perhaps, he himself was not aware of this synthesis. Perhaps, it was altogether unconscious. However, conscious or unconscious, intentional or unintentional, Mao's version of the endless struggle of Marxism is consistent with his pre-Marxist philosophical visions.[41] At the same time, he does not envision a progressive struggle with an inevitable outcome in the manner of either Hegel or Marx. For Schram this is fundamental evidence, in his opinion, that Mao deviates from Marxism:

> By arguing that 'every link in the chain of events is both affirmation and negation', Mao could be held to have seriously undermined the whole Marxist and Hegelian justification, in philosophical terms, for the idea that history moves irreversibly forward. His vision of a random succession of opposites, or in any case the absence in his thought of a continuing progression in a definite direction built into the structure of the dialectical process, may have certain advantages over the original Marxist view of an inexorable trend leading to a communist stage in which the dialectic breaks down or evaporates. ... Mao's ideas on this theme none the less raise serious problems about the conformity of his thinking as a whole to the basic logic of Marxism, and of Leninism.[42]

For Mao, the outcome is indeterminate. All that is clearly determinate is the struggle. The parallel here with his early marginal notes on Paulsen is remarkable. It is a powerful indicator that Mao's early philosophizing, prior to his exposure to Marxism, strongly influences his later interpretation of and deviation from Marxism. Without the pre-Marxist Mao, we would not have Mao's critique of Marxism and his unique formulation of the philosophy of history.

Mao's philosophizing escapes the eventual synthesis, the eventual harmony that characterized the vision of Marx. Though Mao's own method of thinking occasionally incorporates the synthesis (the concept of endless struggle is sublated and retained as a companion to, that is, integrated or harmonized with Marxism), the application of his thinking to the world makes no use of the unity of opposites. In, 'On the Correct Handling of Contradictions among the People', Mao writes:

> The proletariat seeks to transform the world according to its own world outlook, and so does the bourgeoisie. In this respect, the question of which will win out, socialism or capitalism, is still not really settled. Marxists are still a minority among the whole population as well as among intellectuals. Therefore, Marxism must still develop through struggle. Marxism can develop only through struggle, and not only is this true of the past and the present, it is necessarily true of the future as well. What is correct inevitably develops in the struggle with what is wrong.[43]

Mao did not consider that communism would become the final victor. In this regard, he would not have been surprised by the current victory of capitalism, (in his eyes), in the form of SCC over pure communism in his native China. What is surprising, and possibly different from his early philosophizing, is his optimism that right will inevitably triumph over wrong. This, it seems, is at odds with the idea of endless struggle. It also appears to be at odds with his earlier statement that capitalism might triumph. If Mao perceives capitalism as wrong, which he surely does, then, if it triumphs, how can he also maintain that 'what is correct inevitably develops in the struggle with what is wrong.' Perhaps, and this is only a perhaps, Mao is envisioning a far distant future, one in which, even if capitalism had triumphed for many years or centuries, that eventually what is correct will triumph. In any case, Mao was well aware that the triumph of new ideas always required struggle:

> Copernicus' theory of the solar system and Darwin's theory of evolution were once dismissed as erroneous and had to win through bitter opposition.[44]

Mao's early study of Western thought shows itself in this example. Nevertheless, any final victory, capitalism or communism, cannot, in terms of the endless struggle, be final. Perhaps, in this sense, Mao is revealing his realist hand. Struggle will always be necessary. The notion of the ultimate 'winning out' is a provisional notion. The notion of change is what is absolute.

The Principal and the Secondary Aspects of Contradiction

We can make use of Mao's famous discussion of the distinction between the principal and the secondary aspects of the contradiction to address the contradiction between struggle and victory and the contradiction between the abandonment of the unity of opposites and its actual unacknowledged operation in the formulation of Mao's own thinking process. In 'On Contradiction,' Mao writes:

> There are still two points in the problem of the particularity of contradiction which must be singled out for analysis, namely, the principal contradiction and the principal aspect of a contradiction ... of the two contradictory aspects, one must be principal and one secondary ... But this situation is not static; the principal and the non-principal aspects of a contradiction

transform themselves into each other and the nature of the thing changes accordingly. In a given process or at a given stage in the development of a contradiction, A is the principal aspect and B is the non-principal aspect; and another stage or in another process the roles are reversed.[45]

Here, we can take Mao's main view of the principle of contradiction as the principal aspect of contradiction, the absence of the 'negation of negation'. However, in the progression of his own thinking, his development from pre-Marxism to Marxism, Mao has maintained the old within the new; he has synthesized. This is the secondary aspect of the contradiction. No contradiction, as in the *Yijing*, can exist without containing some aspect of the other. In the Hegelian dialectic, in contrast, each negative is negated by the other. This is an essential part of the meaning of Hegel's concept of the negation of the negation (the other part being the production of the synthesis):

> ... this relation in which two specific measures specify themselves in a third something, the exponent, also implies that the one has not passed into the other; that therefore there is not only *one* negation, but that *both* are posited as negative in the relation, and since in this each preserves itself as indifferent towards the other its *negation* is also in turn *negated*.[46]

How very different this is from the combination of opposites within the *Yijing* where each opposite needs the other and is hardly indifferent towards the other. Perhaps, it is this very difference from the *Yijing* that contributes to Mao's abandonment of the idea of the negation of the negation. Just as in the symbol for the yin-yang, inside the yin is a small portion of yang and inside the yang is a small portion of yin. In the formulation of Mao's intellectual development, the secondary reverses roles with the primary.

That Mao's thinking was undoubtedly influenced by the dialectic between the yin and the yang, the cardinal feature of the *Yijing*, is evidenced by this passage from the original text of 'On Contradiction', excised from the official version:

> ... in any contradiction, and at whatever time, the development of the contradictory aspects or profiles ... is uneven (*bu pingheng*). Sometimes they seem to be in equilibrium, which is however only temporary and relative, while unevenness is basic. That is, when they seem to be in equilibrium, there is in fact no absolute equilibrium.[47]

And, in an expurgated passage Mao not only acknowledges the link between ancient Chinese philosophy and his co-temporary Marxism, but also blends the two together in the marvellous phrase, the 'Dao of contradiction,' a phrase which merges ancient thinking with that of Marxist thinking:

> ... what the ancients called 'to be familiar with the Dao (*wen Dao*)', viewed from today's perspective is to be familiar with the Dao of contradiction.[48]

In the dialectic between endless struggle and the question of which will eventually triumph, communism or capitalism, the principal aspect of the contradiction is struggle. Struggle must, however, possess an antagonist. Struggle is always struggle against something for something. The antagonist is the secondary aspect of the contradiction. Whether capitalism or communism wins out is a secondary aspect of the principal contradiction. But, at any one moment in time, in history, the roles of secondary and principal can be reversed.

Mao's discussion of the principal and the secondary aspects of a contradiction show both his early Western philosophical training and the influence of the kind of thinking that is found in the *Yijing* of classical Chinese philosophy. The penetrating quality of the analysis may be traceable to Mao's Western philosophical training. The distinction between two aspects of a contradiction may well be the result of having studied Spinoza. The notion of the principal aspect and the secondary aspect reversing roles is a cardinal feature of the *Yijing*.

At times, Mao's Marxist writings display a striking similarity with the views he first promulgated in the margins to Paulsen's *A System of Ethics* where he showcases his allusions to both Chinese and Western sources. These passages both illustrate that Mao formed his thoughts from his wide reading of the classics of both Chinese and Western literature and that his method of thinking, of analysing the works of the past and the meaning that they possessed for the future, remains embedded in Mao's thought in years far past his pre-Marxist period. In the original text of 'On Contradiction' (expurgated from the official rendition), Mao's writing is sprinkled with allusions to both China and the West:

> Why is it that in his entire life, the greater part of Napoleon's wars were linked to victory, while at the battle of Waterloo, he was roundly defeated, his army beaten and himself taken prisoner? … Don Quixote's mighty battle with the windmill, Su Wukong's somersault of one hundred and eight thousand li [a li is one-third of a mile] over the clouds, Alice's journey through Wonderland, Robinson's wanderings on his lone island, Hegel's Absolute Spirit.[49]

Mao's thinking of his Marxist period even in his comparisons with Chinese and Western literature show the powerful continuing influence of the conceptual framework of the constant presence of the struggle between yin and yang.

Is Mao Influenced by Soviet Sources?

That the transformation of the principal and non-principal aspects of contradiction represents Mao's unique contribution and is not derived from Soviet sources is a view which finds agreement with the analyses of Shi who argues that:

> The Soviet texts ... do not possess reference to notions of the principal and non-principal contradiction, and the transformation of the principal and non-principal aspect of contradiction.[50]

Schram points out that Mao's most notable contribution to dialectics lies in his elaboration of the concepts of 'principal contradiction' and 'principal aspect of the principal contradiction'. Though correct, this does not go far enough in depth or breadth, as discussed above. In my analysis, Mao's contribution in this case, reflects his understanding of the *Yijing*. Schram, on the other hand, attributes Mao's use of the categories of 'principal contradiction' and 'principal aspect of the principal contradiction' to Mao's analysis of economic and political conditions of Chinese society.[51] Schram's analysis is not without merit. There is no doubt that Mao observed and commented upon the changes in social and political conditions in China. However, Mao's discussion of the principal and non-principal aspects of contradiction are so close to the concept of the movement of opposites in the *Yijing* that it is difficult to imagine that these distinctions occurred to him solely by observing changes in social and political conditions. Mao brought with him to his observation the pattern of changes that characterize the *Yijing* and observed them in his China because he already knew the object for which he was searching.

The Superstructure and the Base: Mao's Inversion of Classical Marxism

The most famous instance of the reversal of principal and secondary aspects is Mao's inversion of the economic determinism found in classical Marxism:

> ... in the contradiction between the base and the superstructure, the economic base is the principal aspect ... But it must also be admitted that

in certain conditions, such aspects as the relations of production, theory and superstructure in turn manifest themselves in the principal and decisive role.[52]

In this passage, Mao shows that he understands the importance of theory and thus, philosophy. At times, philosophy is a more important cause of behaviour than economic conditions. This passage is a clear illustration of the influence of Mao's early philosophical development. If Mao had simply started his thinking with later Marxism, it is unlikely that he would have arrived at the conclusion that sometimes idealist causes trump materialist causes.

Did Mao borrow the idea of the inversion of the classical Marxist relationship between the base and the superstructure from Stalin, as Cohen alleges?[53] In answer to this point, Knight comments that:

> Cohen asserted in 1964 that Mao's view on this subject [the relationship between society's base and superstructure] as expressed in the official version of On Contradiction were a thinly disguised copy of Stalin's ideas which had appeared in articles in 1938 and 1950.[54]

However, Knight states that the passage in question is in the original text of 'On Contradiction' so that Mao may actually have anticipated Stalin.[55]

Knight also points out that in the original version of, 'On Practice' (deleted from the official version), Mao comments:

> … each of man's actions (practice) is guided by his thought (*sixiang*) so naturally without thought there can be no action whatsoever.[56]

Karl A. Wittfogel puts forth various arguments to demonstrate that Mao plagiarized some of his ideas, in particular referring to the content of Mao's 'On Dialectical Materialism'.[57] Schram acknowledges this as well.[58] In an earlier work, Schram writes:

> In very large part, they [Mao's lectures on dialectical materialism] amounted (especially in the early sections) to unashamed plagiarism of his Soviet sources and where Mao had expressed himself in his own words, the result was often very crude.[59]

Schram speculates that it was on account of the fact Mao was embarrassed by the amount of plagiarism in which he had engaged with regard to Soviet sources that he famously denied authorship of 'On Dialectical Materialism' in talking with Edgar Snow in 1965.[60]

Knight proposes that the charge of plagiarism by Western scholars is misplaced because copying others' ideas without attribution does not form part of the Chinese tradition.[61] From the viewpoint of the present author, what stands out is that Mao studied the Chinese translations of these Soviet tomes with marked diligence such as: *Dialectical and Historical Materialism* by Mitin, et al., which was 538 pages; *Outline of New Philosophy* by Mitin, et al., which was 454 pages; *A Course on Dialectical Materialism* by Shirokov and Aizenberg which was 582 pages. Knight points out that:

> Mao studied the third edition of this volume [A Course on Dialectical Materialism], covering its margins and any blank spaces with close to 13,000 characters of annotations and commentary [how this reminds us of Mao's Paulsen marginalia of his youthful philosophical studies!] ... he reacted to the text critically, applying its abstract content to the historical situation of the Chinese Revolution.[62]

Schram argues against Cohen that Mao did not derive his ideas from Stalin, but rather from Lenin.[63] (I argue above that Mao derives his ideas from the *Yijing* as well.) Schram points out that the plagiarized sections were summaries of the history of philosophy in Greece and the West by Soviet authors. I draw the conclusion from this that ideas relevant to dialectics are not copied from Stalin. Indeed, if one considers, as pointed out above, both from the evidence that

Mao presents arguments against Stalin's version of dialectics, and the evidence from the original texts of 'On Contradiction' and 'On Practice' that preceded Stalin's writings; then, it becomes less likely that he simply borrowed ideas from Stalin. Lee Feigon takes the view that 'On Contradiction' and 'On Practice' were mainly plagiarized from Stalin.[64] Meisner also states that 'the originality of Mao's writings is questionable', suggesting that they are borrowed from Stalin.[65] However, Meisner supplies neither evidence nor argument to substantiate this claim. Cohen does present evidence and argumentation to support his view that Mao's 'On Practice' first was published in China on 29 December 1950 and 'On Contradiction' was first published in China on 1 April 1952, both dates occurring after Stalin's *Dialectical and Historical Materialism* appeared in Chinese translation in 1939.[66] In contrast, Vsevolod Holubnychy argues along with Knight that Stalin's *Dialectical and Historical Materialism* appeared in Chinese translation in 1939, two years after Mao's writing [as distinct from publishing] 'On Contradiction' and 'On Practice'.[67]

It must be recalled that the early Marx of the 'Paris Manuscripts' was also no simple economic determinist. The early Marx showed a strong predilection towards voluntarism. It was Engels, some have argued, who emphasized economic and material determinism.[68] In terms of my own personal knowledge, when I inquired, the writings of the early Marx were not available at that time in Beijing in 1988.[69] I asked if the library at Peking University held the works of the early Marx such as the 'Paris manuscripts' (the *Economic and Philosophic Manuscripts of 1844*) in 1988. The answer was in the negative. The Marxist corpus was not complete. China was wedded to the Soviet model of Marxism. I was informed that at Peking University, there were no writings of the early, existentialist Marx. If it did possess these works, they were unavailable to the present author. I was also informed by graduate students of economics that they did not know of these works and that they were not part of a special collection of publications (that included *Time Magazine*) that were available in a special library to which graduate students possessed access. If these early writings of Marx were not available to Mao, this would present a plausible explanation of the perception of Mao as inverting the position of classical Marxism as representing the base determining the superstructure.

The entire question of the relationship of superstructure to base is well articulated by Walder in the first of his two articles on Marxism, 'Maoism and Social Change'. For Walder, Marx and Engels did not hold a simplistic position of the base determining the superstructure, but presented a subtle view of the complex interactions between the two. Walder quotes from a letter written by Engels that the simplistic version of the base influencing the superstructure was due to the polemical writing characterizing the *German Ideology*.[70] Walder makes reference to the letter Engels wrote to J. Bloch on 22 September 1890 in which Walder begins in his own words, that, 'human material life was only the "ultimately" determining factor' [followed by this direct (translated) quotation from Engels]:

> More than this neither Marx nor I have ever asserted. If therefore somebody twists this into the statement that the economic element is the *only* determining one, he transforms it into a meaningless, abstract and absurd phrase.

Walder cites many specific illustrations from the writings of Marx, including *Capital*, to support his view that superstructure acts upon the base and vice versa. To be fair, the examples he cites are not pure examples of first-order voluntarism, but fall into the category of second-order voluntarism such as laws (an example of superstructure) created to protect private property which then maintain the existence of private property (base). However, even with this qualification of first- and second-order voluntarism, Walder builds an excellent case of the interaction between superstructure and base already existing in Marxian thought. The problem still remains, however, that in the direct quotation from Engels that Walder cites to support his viewpoint, Engels specifically states that the material conditions are the *ultimate* influences. This is the position that ultimately the base determines the superstructure. Such a position still enables the description of Mao as inverting the classic Marxist position to be a valid description.[71]

In the second of his two articles on Marxism, 'Maoism and Social Change', Walder collapses the distinction between superstructure and base by including nearly all of what is sometimes considered part of the superstructure to be part of the base.[72] While Walder's arguments are not without merit, it remains the case that the superstructure that becomes part of the base at one point in time was separate from the base. It is also the case that much of what Walder discusses as part of the superstructure, e.g. changes in wages, in the beginning were motivated by voluntary motivations, i.e. a desire for a better life. It should also be remembered that even such a base attributed phenomenon as 'relations of production' needed to have first existed as a concept in order to be utilized as a tool to analyse social change. If the changes in relations of production are to be brought about, these changes yet to be made must exist in the first place as ideals to be materialized or realized, that is, as part of the superstructure separate from the base. It could be argued that these relations of production existed in society before they were analysed. However, even pre-existing relations of production had to be first conceived by someone before they were put in place.

Mao saw the value and the priority of philosophy. However, unlike Confucius, he explicitly utilized philosophy as ideology. While this use is not Confucian, it implicitly acknowledges how Mao understood the force of ideas as more important than economic conditions. One has only to remember Mao's little red book to conjure up a vivid illustration of the notion that the pen is mightier than the sword. Liu Kang also considers Mao to place a priority on ideas over material conditions:

Not unlike many Western Marxists, Mao considered the realm of consciousness as the foremost arena for practice. In 'On New Democracy', a programmatic text for alternative modernity, he [Mao] elaborates disproportionally on the role of cultural revolution, leaving little room for economic issues: 'Revolutionary culture is a powerful revolutionary weapon for the broad masses of the people. It prepares the ground ideologically before the revolution comes and is an important, indeed essential fighting front in the general revolutionary front.'[73]

It is interesting and illuminating that Liu compares Mao to a Western Marxist. For Liu, Mao has been influenced by Western ideas. Of course, Marxism is a Western idea and, thus, Liu's statement appears redundant. Nonetheless, it is important to keep in mind the idea that at times Mao emphasized consciousness and thought over material determinations.

What if Other Scholars Wrote the Works Attributed to Mao?

What, however, does one do with the charge that these works of Mao such as his famous 'On Contradiction' were not written by him, but by scholars under his direction? For example, Knight writes:

> Ignatius Ts' ao ... considers Ai's influence on Mao to be such that Ai can be considered (along with Chen Boda) as a co-author of the thought of Mao Zedong.[74]

Would this not detract from the claim that the later Mao continued to be influenced by the early Mao? First of all, this claim has to be substantiated.[75] Secondly, one must consider if Mao commissioned these works that, nevertheless, he might have suggested the development of certain ideas that appear in them. Thirdly, we may also consider Mao's works as texts, not so much as works of Mao, but as reflections of the thought that we may consider to be Maoist thought. We do not know if Shakespeare actually wrote the plays attributed to him. Powerful arguments can be marshalled to show that it is far more likely that they were written by the Earl of Oxford. The authorship is irrelevant to the literary value of the works. In the case of Zhuangzi, there is much dispute as to whether all of the chapters of the *Zhuangzi* were written by one person. Nevertheless, the text of the *Zhuangzi*, especially the inner chapters, can be appreciated as a cherished text of philosophy, quite apart from the question of its authorship.[76]

In any case, we should take into account some of Mao's later writings in order to see the fulfilment of his early philosophical, that is, pre-Marxist educational development. Even if these later works were written by scholars other than Mao, it is nonetheless of great interest to note how the later works owe much to the early writings of Mao, most especially, Mao in the margins. That they do, of course, does tend to support the position that these works, particularly 'On Contradiction' and 'On Practice' are written by Mao.

7

Mao as Metaphysician and *Literatus*

Mao as Metaphysician and Philosopher of Science

Mao is not only a political philosopher. He is also a metaphysical thinker. Consider this statement: 'The myriad things develop continuously and limitlessly, and they are infinite.'[1] This is in accord with the principle of contradiction, but it also goes beyond the principle of contradiction. The principle of contradiction is an attempt to explain the phenomenon of change, but the principle of contradiction does not provide a basis for infinite change. This is a contradiction. If change is infinite, it cannot come to an end. But all things, for Mao, come to an end. In a graphic passage, reminding us of the literary gift Mao displayed in his early marginal notes, he writes in his *Talk on Questions of Philosophy*:

> One thing destroys another, things emerge, develop and are destroyed by others, then they destroy themselves. Why should people die? Does the aristocracy die too? This is a natural law. Forests live longer than human beings, yet even they last only a few thousand years. If there were no such thing as death, that would be unbearable. If we could still see Confucius

alive today, the earth wouldn't be able to hold so many people. I approve of Chuang-Tzu's approach. When his wife died, he banged on a basin and sang. ... Mankind will also finally meet its doom. When the theologians talk about doomsday, they are pessimistic and terrify people. We say the end of mankind is something which will produce something more advanced than mankind. Mankind is still in its infancy.[2]

Anyone reading this passage cannot deny that Mao is a philosopher and is not limited in his thinking to Marxist dogma.[3] In this passage, the concept of the infinite is well contradicted as all things must come to an end. Mao endorses the principle of continuous contradiction, but this continuity is not infinite. He adds a pragmatic note to this metaphysical principle. If there were no death, the earth could not hold so many people. Death has a utilitarian function. His expression of this is literary. He chooses Confucius, the philosophical master of China, to illustrate the reality of death. Such a choice is not necessary; it is a poetic choice. It makes the reality of death more vivid when we consider that even such a master of thought must die. Death trumps philosophy. He then moves on to another philosopher, the one with whom, just as in his early marginal notes, he finds the most in common, Zhuangzi. His reference to Zhuangzi is Zhuangzi's classical action when confronted with his wife's death. Death, while rightly mourned, reflects the nature of things. It must be accepted.

Mao goes even further in his cosmic reflections. He combines his metaphysical vision with political paranoia when he says:

The United States cannot annihilate China with its small stack of atomic bombs. Even if the US atom bombs were so powerful that when dropped on China, they would make a hole right through the earth, or even blow it up, that would hardly mean anything to the universe as a whole, though it might be a major event for the solar system.[4]

Mao's reflections upon death are not limited to metaphysical visions and metaphysical reconciliations. He also contemplates that the state of the human being is not the ultimate evolution. If man has evolved, then what is to stop evolution? Mankind itself is something to be transcended. Such thinking goes far beyond either Marxism or early Chinese philosophy. It extends to the future and augurs the contemporary philosophical discussions of the trans-human.

Mao's concept of evolution is not limited to humans. He points out that animals, too, may evolve. If there is such a phenomenon of evolution, why should it suddenly come to an end? Mao was no simple Marxist. He even repudiates Marx in his discussion of evolution:

> Marx put forward the view that man is a tool-maker, and that man is a social animal. In reality it is only after undergoing a million years [of evolution] that man developed a large brain and a pair of hands. In the future, animals will continue to develop. I don't believe that men alone are capable of having two hands. Can't horses, cows, sheep evolve? Can only monkeys evolve? And can it be, moreover, that of all the monkeys only one species can evolve, and all the others are incapable of evolving? In a million years, ten million years, will horses, cows and sheep still be the same as those today? I think they will continue to change. Horses, cows, sheep and insects will all change.[5]

These thoughts of Mao demonstrate his creative imagination which, at the same time, with the homely Socratic and Zhuangzian illustrations he chooses, show a blend of philosophical speculation with arguments from science. In passing, he denies the ultimate determination of social forces and cedes that to nature.

At times, his metaphysical imagination is capable of entertaining surprising hypothetical situations. In one passage, he imagines a world in space but not in time:

> I can imagine space without time, and feel that I am placed in an infinite, unbounded, broad, and expansive great place that has no present, no past, and no future. In this context, it is possible to maintain the view that both body and spirit are immortal. Is this not an entirely different world?[6]

This is not a commonplace imagination at work. How many philosophers, not to speak of non-philosophers, are capable of such an imagination? Is it possible that it was the possession of such an imagination that enabled Mao to envision the type of transformation of China that he would spearhead?

Mao even speculates on the origin of the concept of time:

> I would say that the discovery of the concept of time comes from a kind of physical mechanical change that exists in the objective world. The earth revolves around the sun and creates day and night. If there were only daylight or only long night, there would be no concept of time, and this proves that there is no such thing as time. The revolution of the earth around the sun is merely motion in space.[7]

Here, Mao comes close to Aristotle's famous definition of time as the number of motion. He comes close to Kant in his conclusion that time does not exist. What more evidence is needed to demonstrate that Mao possessed a philosophical mind?

Sometimes, Mao's philosophical peregrinations exceed rational discourse:

> I say: the concept is reality, the finite is the infinite, the temporal senses are the super-temporal senses, imagination is thought, form is substance, I am the universe, life is death and death is life, the present is the past and the future, the past and the future are the present, small is big, the *yang* is the *yin*, up is down, dirty is clean, male is female, and thick is thin. In essence,

the many are one, and change is permanence. I am the most exalted person, and also the most unworthy person.[8]

It would be philosophical *hubris* to attempt to make sense of this, but the parallels with the topsy-turvy, upside down world of the Cultural Revolution in which tea boys became Chairmen of Philosophy Departments and Chairmen of Philosophy Departments became tea boys could not be clearer.

At the same time, Mao considers that man is part of nature and subject to natural laws:

That human beings are subject to natural law is compatible with my view.[9]

On the other hand, Mao writes:

I would say that the human race has only a spiritual life, and not a bodily life. It is clear that though the spirit has changed frequently, the body has remained unchanged for thousands of years.[10]

And, as if anticipating his own later alteration of the doctrinaire Marxist relationship between the superstructure and the base:

It is concepts that create civilizations. Indeed, indeed.[11]

According to Schram, at an early age Mao thought that changing one's ideas could even change the objective nature of the social class to which one belonged.[12]

The early Mao is no more a stranger to contradiction than the later Mao. Mao seems to go back and forth between the laws of the universe or nature and the power of the mind to conceptualize exactly what *is* the universe. He seems to be attempting to formulate a conception of man and the universe in which the universe is essentially one and our conceptions of the universe are the origins of distinctions. His formulation, in the end, finds resonance with the great philosophy of Spinoza in which distinctions between good and evil are man-made. Consider these philosophical reflections of Mao:

> Reality itself does not make distinctions; the distinctions are only conceptual ... Ethical qualities such as public and personal, great and small, or good or bad, are distinguished according to their usefulness to a person. This is true not just in ethics. All distinctions in the universe are simply those different aspects of it that appear to us when we observe and react to it. In its basic nature it is simply one single form. This is true of such things as the *yin* and the *yang*, of top and bottom, big and small, high and low, this and that, others and self, good and evil, positive and negative, clean and dirty, beautiful and ugly, bright and dark, and victory and defeat. [13]

How does this effect human action? For Mao, one should continue to act virtuously despite this mass of seeming contradictions.

Paulsen writes:

> He who acts virtuously takes only virtue as his goal, and if external happiness eludes him, and his senses suffer hardship, nevertheless his virtuous conduct brings his spiritual happiness. Spinoza said that the reward of virtue is not happiness but virtue.[14]

Mao endorses this view with one word: 'Excellent.' [15]

In his notes, he tends to link his thoughts with the nature of the universe. He does not reflect upon the nature of man in isolation to the universe as a whole. He then also reflects back from the nature of the universe to the nature of society, the state and human life. He then reflects back on the universe again. In these early metaphysical speculations, one is struck by the parallels Mao draws between the fate of the universe and the fate of social and political systems. Consider these philosophical speculations of Mao:

> All phenomena in the world are simply a state of constant change for which there is no birth and death, nor formation and demise. ... The demise of a state is a change in its manifestation. Its land is not destroyed nor are its people. Changes in a state are the germ of its renewal that is necessary for the evolution of society. Today's German Reich is the same as the former German states. ... I used to worry that our China would be destroyed but now I know that this is not so. ... I believe that there must be a complete transformation, like matter that takes form after destruction, or like the infant born out of its mother's womb. The state is like this, and so are nationalities, and so too humanity. In every century, various nationalities have launched various kinds of great revolutions, periodically cleansing the old and infusing it with the new, all of which are great change involving life and death, formation and demise. The demise of the universe is similar. The destruction of the universe is not an ultimate destruction. It is certain that its demise here will necessarily be a formation there. I very much look forward to its destruction, because from the demise of the old universe will come a new universe, and will it not be better than the old universe![16]

One notes Mao's blending of metaphysical observation, metaphysical prediction and Western historical references with the fate of his own China. Is this an adumbration of his own later concept of the need for a transformation of the political face of China? Is it possible to separate Mao's later political ambitions and actions from these early philosophical musings and foundations?

How closely they resemble the philosophical speculations of his old age:

> One thing destroys another, things emerge, develop and are destroyed, everywhere is like this. Why should people die? Does the Aristocracy die too? This is a natural law. Forests live longer than human beings, yet even they last only a few thousand years [here Mao's allusions remind one and even exceed similar thoughts in Zhuangzi]. ... Socialism, too, will be eliminated. ... Then there is the principle, 'From each according to his

abilities, to each according to his needs.' Do you believe they can carry on for a million years with the same economics? ... Mankind will finally meet its doom. ... The myriad things develop continuously and limitlessly, and they are infinite. Time and space are infinite.[17]

In these pronouncements of Mao, his idea of infinity is far from Hegel's notion of the 'good infinite' or the infinite that infinitely proceeds in a circle like a snake whose head can grasp its tail. Mao's infinite is an example of Hegel's bad infinite, the infinite that possesses no end. Regardless of Hegel's honorific or pejorative labels, Mao is very much engrossed with the notion of infinity that is without limits and this idea continues to occupy him in his later period, especially as it pertains to the structure of elementary particles, the infinity of the universe and the origin of life. Such concerns reflect Mao's continuing philosophical ponderings into his late age. Yinghong Chong relates how excited Mao was to converse with the physicists T. D. Lee and my former colleague of many years at The Chinese University of Hong Kong, the Nobel laureate physicist, C. N. Yang:

> He first asked Dr. Yang about the Copenhagen school then asked about Sakata Shoiyouchi. Chairman Mao discussed with Dr. Yang the problem of parity conservation and non-conservation. ... Ten months later on May 30, 1974 Mao met with Dr. T. D. Lee. This time Mao's concern focused on the issue of symmetry, a similar topic he had with Dr. Yang. As Dr. Lee recalled, he received a call at 6:00 am, and was told that Mao would like to see him in one hour. In the meeting, Lee found that he was the only guest, simply accompanied by Zhu Guangya, a Chinese nuclear physicist. This fact may suggest that Mao did not want any other issue to divert the conversation from his real interest, and as a result the meeting proceeded more focused and interactive. ... Mao's curiosity about the fundamental order of the universe seems to be more important than anything in the two meetings.[18]

FIGURE 1 *Mao and C. N. Yang in Mao's study in Zhongnanhai.*

FIGURE 2 *Zhou Enlai, Zhou Peiyuan, Mao and C. N. Yang in Mao's study.*

The first photo of Mao and C. N. Yang and the second photo of Zhou EnLai, Zhou Peiyuan, Mao and C. N. Yang were both taken on 19 July 1973, in Mao's study in Zhongnanhai.[19]

While it may well be argued that Mao's interest in the relevance of the idea of the infinite in science derives from the writings of Engels and Lenin, it remains true that Mao was already thinking in these directions in his pre-Marxist period as evidenced by his marginal notes to Paulsen. His insatiable curiosity about metaphysical knowledge two years before his death is reminiscent of the insatiable curiosity of the young Mao who sequestered himself in 1917–1918 in the Hunan Provincial library for a self-directed, self-study in philosophy for over six months. Perhaps, after a hiatus of a lifetime in practice, Mao's personal philosophical journey is a reflection of his theoretical dialectic of knowledge, practice and again knowledge.

Chinese philosophy figures into Mao's notion of infinity as he quotes from Zhuangzi:

> Take a foot long stick and remove half every day. In ten thousand years, it will not run out.[20]

This, Mao interjects in a conversation that concludes that the universe is infinite macroscopically and microscopically. In the same conversation, he references the findings of Sakata on the divisibility of elementary particles, C. N. Yang and T. D. Lee on the non-conservative nature of parity in the case of weak reactions of elementary particles and raises his own question whether parity is non-conservative in quality conservation and energy conservation. He finishes with a point emblematic of the quintessential Mao:

> There is nothing in the world that is absolutely static. ... Conservation and non-conservation, this is balance and imbalance at once, but there are also some cases that balance are [sic] completely broken.[21]

Here, the syncretic Mao, as usual, mixes the ruminations of ancient Chinese philosophy and the findings of co-temporary physicists with his own metaphysical speculations.

Is Mao a Western or a Chinese Philosopher?

Is Mao a Western philosopher or a Chinese philosopher? Even Stuart Schram is not sure of the answer to this question. At one point, Schram relates that 'it became increasingly hard, especially in his later years, to determine whether the basic structure of "Mao Tse-tung Thought" was Chinese or Western.'[22] The answer is that he is both. The philosophy that he formulates shows profound influences from his early study of both Western and Chinese philosophy.[23] The truth is, he is neither a pure Chinese philosopher nor a pure Western philosopher. His philosophy is built upon two foundations. From the standpoint of Mao's syncretic philosophizing, he stands closer to the Chinese tradition than he does to the Western tradition.[24]

Mao, of course, considers himself to be a Chinese philosopher.[25] His viewpoint sometimes takes on more of the soft view characteristic of the type of change that is described in the *Yijing*. Consider his statement, 'We Chinese often say, "Things that oppose each other also complement each other."'[26] This saying implies that all contradiction need not be antagonistic. One is reminded of the yin and the yang of the *Yijing*. The feminine needs the masculine and the masculine needs the feminine. They oppose each other but at the same time they need each other. They are opposite, but they are complementary. They are opposite to each other, and yet they are necessary to each other in order to complete each other. Raya Dunayevskaya points to this saying of Mao's as an illustration that Mao is not a pure Marxist philosopher.[27] The same could be said of Marx as can be recalled from his quip, *Je ne suis pas Marxiste*.

Mao as *Literatus*

Into his mature years, Mao continued to make active use of his reading of the Chinese literary classics.[28] According to Wang Ruoshui, Mao's frequent reading was of traditional Chinese texts: 'he read *The Mirror of Government* from the Song Dynasty seventeen times, but rarely read any Western books, even a single classic of Marxism.'[29] For Levine, '*The Economic & Philosophic Manuscripts of 1844* and the *Grundrisse der Kritik der Politischen Oekonomie* were not available to Mao.'[30]

Accounts vary. According to Cheek, Mao never learned a foreign language.[31] In contrast,

Tian Chenshan writes that Mao read the English version of the *Communist Manifesto* at the age of sixty-three. According to Tian, Mao also read some texts on logic in English. According to Tian, Mao read *A Critique of the Gotha Program* among other Marxist works … Tian writes further that Mao ordered hundreds of books including *Capital*, *Anti-Dühring*, works by Stalin, Lenin and Western writers including Hegel and Feuerbach. [32]

In 1962, he posed a riddle to the Central Committee, which, according to Terrill, Mao had gleaned from a recent re-reading of the *Journey to the West*:

> 'Why does the monk knock the wooden fish drum when he chants his sutra?" … We must not behave like the black-fish demon.' According to the story, the black-fish demon spat out one word each time it was knocked. The Buddhist legend made Mao's point that Party leaders should not mince words ('spitting out one word at a time').[33]

Mao even improvises his own literary anecdotes to apply to policy making. Short relates the story of the exchange between Liu Shaoqi, Zhou and Mao on the question of how to persuade private businessmen to nationalize. Mao bests Zhou in this exchange that one wag referred to as 'how to make a cat eat pepper approach'.

> Liu begins by saying that 'You get somebody to hold the cat, stuff the pepper into its mouth, and push it down with a chopstick.' Mao was horrified. ... the cat must be persuaded to eat voluntarily ... Premier Zhou enters in with, 'I would starve the cat. Then, I would wrap the pepper with a slice of meat. If the cat is sufficiently hungry, it will swallow it whole.' Again, Mao shook his head. 'One must not use deceit. Never fool the people.' His own answer, he explained, was very simple. 'You rub the pepper into the cat's backside. When it starts to burn, the cat will lick it off – and be happy to be permitted to do so.'[34]

Mao was an avid reader of Chinese literary masterpieces. According to Terrill, by 1964, he had just finished his fifth reading of the *Dream of the Red Chamber*.[35] According to Richard Kraus, one of Mao's favourite quotations from the *Dream of the Red Chamber* was 'He who is not afraid of death by a thousand cuts dares to unhorse the emperor'.[36]

In the end, Mao's philosophy comes full circle. He returns to the Chinese philosophy and literature of his youth. According to Frederick Wakeman, who, in turn, derives his information from Mao's autobiographical account to be found in Edgar Snow's classic, *Red Star Over China*, among Mao's favourites by the age of eight were the fourteenth century novel, *The Romance of the Three Kingdoms*, and the eighteenth-century novel, *Dream of the Red Chamber*. Mao reported: 'I believe that perhaps I was much influenced by such books read at an impressionable age.'[37] Lam makes much of the inclusion of *The Romance of the Three Kingdoms* (*Three Kingdoms*). In particular, Lam points to the oft repeated line:

> The world phenomena under the heavens is that long united, it must divide; and vice-versa[38]

For Lam, Mao's later political policy of the global order of the tripolar powers (Russia, China and the United States) was based on this early model that he read in the *Three Kingdoms*. Lam writes:

At the beginning of the 1970s, inspired by the theme of the historical novel, Mao was convinced that both the United States and China 'long divided, must unite'.³⁹

Lam relates in Orwellian fashion how Mao switches between primary and secondary enemies exchanging Russia with the United States depending upon the political situation. Mao deviates even from the *Three Kingdoms*' Zhuge's 'rigid' international order of tripolarity:

> Thus, considering the novel's theme as 'dialectic', Mao corrected what he viewed as its fundamental principle's limitation through making the positions of the primary and the secondary enemy in a tripolar situation flexibly interchangeable for the contemporary world.⁴⁰

On the other hand, speaking of the *Dream of the Red Chamber*, Mao himself states, 'I have read the *Dream of the Red Chamber* five times and have not been influenced by it.'⁴¹ Nevertheless, Wakeman points out that the post-Marxist saying of Mao's, 'Either the east wind prevails over the west wind or the west wind prevails over the east wind' was drawn directly from the pages of the *Dream of the Red Chamber*.⁴² However Mao twisted or turned Chinese philosophy to serve his purposes, until the end of his life, Mao remained attached to the Chinese Classics despite his claims to the contrary. According to the biographer, Philip Short, 'His speeches in later life were packed with allusions to Confucius, to the Daoist thinker, Zhuangzi, to the Mohists and other early philosophical schools, far outnumbering those references to Lenin and Marx. Theirs were the ideas with which he grew up, and which he knew better than any other. The Confucian legacy would prove at least as important to him as Marxism, and in his last years of his life it became once more ascendant.'⁴³

Short continues in this vein:

> Later in life Mao developed a genuine delight in philosophical speculation, and his conversation, whether in private or political discussion, became so studded with arcane analogy and enigmatic references to abstruse debating points that even his Politburo colleagues often scrambled to keep up with him.[44]

Does this mean that in later life we tend to return to the concerns that occupied our youthful selves? If so, then this illustrates Mao's love for and interest in philosophy both began his intellectual development and formed its culmination.

In no less measure did Mao ever diverge from his devotion to classical Chinese literature. One must not forget that Mao himself both practiced calligraphy and built a reputation for being a good poet. Mao chose to write his poetry in one of the more sophisticated and difficult meters of the classical style. According to the Rausner Library Site at Dartmouth College, Mao used brush and ink to draft the majority of his letters, party documents and his poetry. In the opinion of Professor Chen Chuangxi, Chairprofessor at Renmin University and a well-known art critic and art historian, Mao was the greatest cursive style calligrapher of the past three hundred years.[45] Mao's aesthetic theory was not in line with Walter Pater or Oscar Wilde's 'art for art's sake'. In a recent article, Johannes Kaminsky quotes from Mao's writings to sum up Mao's attitudes regarding Chinese literature:

> We should take over the rich legacy and the good traditions in literature and art that have been handed down from past ages in China ... but the aim must still be to serve the masses of the people. Nor do we refuse to utilize the literary and artistic forms of the past, but in our hands these old forms, remoulded and infused with new content, also become something revolutionary in the service of the people.[46]

Mao is famous for his denunciations and disavowals of Confucianism. Nevertheless, Mao's thought, over time, retained an interest in Confucian philosophy. The Rauner Library site at Dartmouth University reported on 7 November 2014 that it had purchased a rare edition of the *Twenty-Four Histories* with Mao's extensive annotations in his calligraphy in the margins, demonstrating that Mao read the *Histories* over the last twenty years of his life.[47] Mao's scholarly habit of writing in the margins, inculcated with his marginal notes to Paulsen's *A System of Ethics* in his early years, did not desert him later in life.

What of early Western influences on Mao? Mao's early reading of the Great Man from Western books, his studies of such world historical figures as George Washington and Napoleon, the embodiment of this concept in the writings of Paulsen and his interpolation of this concept from Mencius together with his own personal integration of this concept was to sustain and stay with him for the course of his life.

That Mao's life mirrors his philosophy is evident even in the latter days of Mao's life. Meisner relates the story that Kissinger tells about meeting Mao on the historic Nixon visit of 1972:

> Kissinger, a student of power, and much enamoured of his subject, stood in awe of the elemental political power that the aged Chairman embodied. When Kissinger saw Mao's study in 1972, ... it was cluttered with books and manuscripts, covering the walls, the table, and even the floor. Kissinger noted, 'It looked more like the retreat of a scholar than the audience room of the all-powerful leader of the most populous nation on earth ... There was no ceremony. Mao just stood there ... I have met no one, with the possible exception of Charles de Gaulle, who so distilled raw concentrated will power ... He dominated the room – not by the pomp that in most states confer a degree of majesty on the leaders, but by exuding in almost tangible form the overwhelming drive to prevail.'[48]

This description is a testimony to Mao's dedication to and embodiment of the idea of the primacy of the will.

In Kissinger's own words:

> Mao's residence appeared no different, though it stood slightly apart from the others. There were no visible guards or other appurtenances of power. A small anteroom was almost completely dominated by a Ping-Pong table. … Mao's study, a room of modest size with bookshelves lining three walls filled with manuscripts in a state of considerable disarray. Books covered the tables and were piled up on the floor. A simple wooden bed stood in the corner. The all-powerful ruler of the world's most populous nation wished to be perceived as a philosopher-king who had no need to buttress his authority with traditional symbols of majesty.[49]

FIGURE 3 *Mao and Kissinger in Mao's Study.*

One may interpolate from the following poem that Mao composed to commemorate Nixon's historic visit to China that he presented to the US President in honour of his visit that Mao saw Nixon as a world historical figure:

The old man sits on a stool.

Chang-o ascends to the moon.

Flowers are viewed from a galloping horse.

According to Terrill's interpretation:

'The old man on the stool was imperialism. Chang-o (a mythological character of the third millennium B.C.E. who flew to the moon to escape her nasty husband) was a charming image for a satellite. Nixon himself, in briefly visiting China, [for eight days] was the one viewing flowers from horseback.'[50]

8

Mao's Contributions to Philosophy

Mao's Philosophical Contributions to Marxism

What of the philosophical contributions of Mao to Marxism? His contributions to Marxism proper are debated. For example, Cohen states:

> … nowhere in *On Practice* does Mao introduce a genuinely novel idea or make a constructive contribution to dialectical materialist doctrine on practice.[1]

Cohen goes on to say:

> To sum up, the claims for Mao as a contributor to the theory of dialectical materialism are largely spurious.[2]

On the other hand, Holubnychy claims that Mao's insight that the law of the universality of contradiction was the only law of dialectics and the one from which all others can be derived is an insight unique to Mao.[3] Holubnychy states that:

In the form presented in *On Contradiction* this law has no precedent in Marxist-Leninist literature. ... Prior to Mao such a law was discussed in details only by Hegel. But Mao has probably not read Hegel.[4]

Knight seems to concur with Mao's originality regarding the law of contradiction citing Shi's arguments:

In *On Contradiction*, Mao provided an elaboration of the abstract category of contradiction which went beyond that to be found in the Soviet sources ... Shi goes on to assert that the Soviet texts on philosophy did not contain mention of the concepts of the relationship of the principal and non-principal aspects of a contradiction.[5]

Cohen himself acknowledges the originality of the distinction between the principal and non-principal aspects of contradiction to belong to Mao, but denigrates the distinction:

Mao does indeed seem to have come up with one novel formulation, namely the contention that any contradiction has a 'principal aspect' which is the determinant of qualitative change; but this rather suspect idea is the extent of his originality as a dialectical materialist and Marxist philosopher.[6]

The reason that Cohen discounts the value of the idea of the distinction between the principal and non-principal aspects of contradiction is that this distinction does not form part of traditional, Russian intellectual culture. This distinction is highlighted by Mao, because the distinction between the principal and non-principal aspects of contradiction constitute an integral part of traditional, Chinese intellectual culture.

Shi Zhongquan also points out that the Soviet texts do not possess reference to notions of the principal and non-principal contradiction, and the transformation of the two.[7]

The reason that Soviet texts did not mention the relationship between the principal and non-principal aspects of contradiction is because the Soviet writers were not nourished from their early youth with the ancient Chinese ideas of the exchange of dominance between yin and yang that permeates the structure of the *Yijing*. The uniqueness of Mao's contribution to dialectics is due to his understanding of yin and yang that he brings to his study of Marxism.

Schwartz discounts Mao's originality, but does consider that Mao was innovative in his thinking that a communist party can exist without an actual proletariat and that China can pass from New Democracy to socialism without a dictatorship of a proletariat.[8] Meisner argues that Mao rejects the central Marxist position that socialism presupposes capitalism.[9] Are these deviations from Marxism, contributions to Marxism or developments of Marxism?

Mao's Reduction of All Laws of Dialectics to One

Mao's reduction of all laws of dialectics to one possesses the merit of theoretical elegance and, following Ockham's razor, of simplicity. On the other hand, one may wonder if such a reduction suffers from making the plausibility of the law of dialectical change less apparent. To offer a brief example of such a reduction, consider my imaginative 'reconstruction'. The example is originally Hegel's, expounded by Engels, and it serves to illustrate Mao's reduction. Hegel's law of quantity turning into quality is illustrated by water that changes into steam when the temperature reaches 212 degrees Fahrenheit and to ice when the temperature reaches 32 degrees Fahrenheit. The quantitative alteration in temperature produces a qualitative change of state.[10] If one analyses this in terms of the law of contradiction, one can argue that water possesses an inherently self-contradictory or oppositional nature. Under the presence of certain circumstances such a nature cannot but change into its opposite, from solid to liquid, from liquid to vapour. While it may well be argued that these changes of state are not logical opposites in term of formal logic, this is the kind of dialectical oppositions to which Hegel is referring.[11] The question is: Does this reduction of the law of quantity changing into quality to the basic law of contradiction serve to clarify dialectics or does this reduction remove some of the clarity and explanatory power of dialectical explanation? I think that the point remains moot. On the one hand, I think that the demonstration that the law of quantity changing into quality derives from the essential nature of contradiction possesses the merit of philosophical soundness. On the other hand, it possesses the danger of making the law of contradiction the sole law of dialectics too cryptic and, thus, less explicative. Engels's further examples from chemistry illustrating how quantity alters quality are excellent examples of Hegel's law of quantity altering quality, but do not support Mao's contention that the law of quantitative change resulting in qualitative change can be reduced to the law of contradiction. Engels's examples from chemical changes are much more specific than those chosen by Hegel. For example, Engels points out that by increasing oxygen by five times, the chemical compound nitrogen monoxide, a gas, becomes nitrogen pentoxide, a solid crystalline substance at ordinary temperatures.[12] This example and others would be less easily reducible to the law of contradiction itself and support the contention that the law of quantity altering quality cannot be reduced to the law of contradiction.

Mao provides an example of quantity affecting quality when he points out that communism itself will change after millions of years:

> I don't believe that it [communism] can remain qualitatively the same, unchanging for millions of years.[13]

Mao's example is not as persuasive as Engels's examples from chemistry because the putative change in communism which did take place, but did not require the millions of years that Mao estimated, was not due to the passage of years, that is, the quantity of years, but was due to qualitative changes that occurred within those years. The quantity of years did provide the occasion for qualitative changes to take place, but the quantity of years, unlike the quantitative alterations that produce chemical changes, did not on its own cause the qualitative changes.

There are numerous philosophical contributions that can be attributed to Mao, but whether these are contributions should be classified as contributions to Marxism proper or deviations from Marxism depends upon what one defines as Marxism. If Marxism is defined as Marxist-Leninism, then Mao's innovations are deviations. If Marxism is defined as a continuing tradition, then Mao's innovations can be defined as developments to or within Marxist thought. For Shi, Mao's formulations of the relationship between the principal and non-principal aspects of a contradiction and their transformation into each other can be regarded as a development of Marxist dialectics.[14]

Schram adopts the point of view that Mao's innovations are deviations and, hence, Mao is neither Marxist nor Hegelian. In particular, Schram points to Mao's deviation from the inevitability of progress that sharply demarcates his thinking from that of either Hegel or Marx.[15] John E. Rue writes that Mao's application of Marxist theory to Chinese society is mistaken:

> From the Marxist point of view, Mao's analysis of classes was full of errors. He divided Chinese society into upper, middle and lower strata primarily on the basis of wealth and property. Thus he identified the big landlords (which Marxists identify as a feudal class) with the big urban bourgeoisie (which Marxists identify as a capitalist class). He thereby confused two distinct stages in the Marxist theory of historical development. Mao had yet to master the distinction between feudalism and capitalism. He saw the bourgeoisie simply as owners of property and the proletariat as the propertyless. Therefore, he put landlords in the same class with capitalists, and landless peasants in the same class with modern industrial workers. The only characteristic distinguishing soldiers, bandits, robbers, beggars, and prostitutes from all other persons who owned no property was that

members of these groups, usually through no fault of their own, had lost access to respectable ways of earning a living.[16]

Rue's criticism of Mao relates to Mao's alleged confusions between the distinctions between feudalism and capitalism and between different stages of historical development. These putative confusions in any case do not seem to represent Mao's intentional deviations from Marxism. In any case, this analysis is unfair because China did not have a large industrial proletariat with which to begin. Mao had to work with the large class of peasants, because that is what he had at the start. One might say that this was Mao's creative interpretation of Marxism or Mao's adaptation of Marxist analysis to the particular conditions of his country. According to an article in *China Now*:

> ... there's no doubt that [Mao's] insistence that the revolution could rely on the peasant farmers and not simply on an industrial proletariat, was something which was quite unorthodox from the prevalent Marxist point of view. China didn't have a vast industrial proletariat.[17]

The historian Maurice Meisner makes the additional comment that 'It would be difficult to imagine a more fundamental revision of Marxist theory than [Mao's] proposition " ... the more backward the economy, the easier ... the transition to socialism."'[18]

The question of Mao's relationship to Marxism is complex. According to Meisner:

> The means which Maoists have employed to achieve what they perceive to be ultimate ends are unprecedented in the history of Marxist-Leninism ... there is nothing Leninist, much less Stalinist, in the Maoist willingness to sacrifice economic development ... and even to abandon the Party itself as the indispensable means to Marxist ends .... Maoism is primarily

concerned with the relationship between intellectuals and peasants ... rather than with the traditional Marxist focus on the proletariat and the bourgeoisie, relatively weak classes in modern Chinese society and only marginally involved in the communist revolution.[19]

John M. Koller points to a number of comparisons and contrasts of Mao with Marxism. As I have also maintained throughout this volume, Koller emphasizes that Mao stresses the priority of thought over economic determinism. Koller mentions the Maoist emphasis on struggle within classes and within individuals themselves as opposed to struggle between classes; and, he mentions, as I have also emphasized, that Maoist thought takes opposites to be complementary rather than, as Marxist thought held, to be exclusive. Koller points out that in Marxist thought, the contradiction between classes requires the destruction of one of the classes, the bourgeoisie. Marx posited the end-goal to be a classless, peaceful society; Mao, on the other hand, considered that there would be a continuous struggle, a permanent revolution.[20] Koller comments that Mao's two most famous creative developments of, or deviations from, Marxism are the Maoist ideological definition of class and the concept of permanent revolution based on intra-personal class struggle.[21] For Koller, Mao does not assume that changes in the mode of production will automatically bring about necessary changes in society. For Schram, 'Mao continued [after the death of Stalin] to speak in bolder terms than they [the Soviet ideologists] of the contradictions under socialism. In particular, it was he [Mao] who put forward the revolutionary idea that there might be contradictions not only among the "people" but between the government and the people.'[22] Schram continues, 'In his [Mao's] view, man and society will be re-shaped in a never-ending process of struggle which will continue even after full communism has been established.'[23] According to both Mao and traditional Confucianism, it is within the cultivation of self-conscious awareness that practice and theory come together to form a unity.[24]

It is difficult to separate completely Mao's contributions to Marxism from his contributions to philosophy proper. Hence, some discussions below of Mao's relationship to Marxism will continue in the discussion of Mao's philosophical contributions to philosophy proper.

Mao's Philosophical Contributions to Philosophy Proper

I think we can single out three main philosophical contributions of Mao to philosophy proper. Whether they are contributions to or deviations from Marxism is a moot point. These contributions are: The primacy of the will, the continuous struggle without resolution, the use of complementary rather than contradictory opposites.

The Primacy of the Will

This emphasis, nurtured by the young Mao's reading of Paulsen, influences both Mao's theoretical thinking and his belief in his own decision-making, and by extension, the will of the masses, as historical determinants. For Timothy Cheek, the emphasis on will, both individual and collective, differentiates Mao from both Stalin and Lenin.[25] I would add to this Hegel as well. However, Hegel's thought, particularly the Hegel of *The Phenomenology of Mind*, is more aligned to Mao's thought in this respect than the thought of Lenin and Stalin. That Mao's thought is so differentiated from that of Lenin and Stalin adds fuel to the argument that Mao did possess a unique contribution to Marxism. That this aspect of Mao's thinking is derived from his reading of Paulsen is striking and demonstrates the influence of Mao's early training in philosophy on his later thinking.

Mao's belief in the primacy of the will is inextricably linked both with his idea of freedom and his idea that history is made by men. This belief of Mao's separates Mao from doctrinaire Marxism in which a particular pattern of historical change is inevitable. In 1964 Mao attacks the determinism of Engels:

> Engels spoke of moving from this realm of necessity to the realm of freedom, and said that freedom is the understanding of necessity. This sentence is not complete.[26]

This sentence of Engels is completed by Mao by the actions of men. These free actions of men comprise at least one-half of why the perceived determinism of Engels is not followed by Mao. The other half of why the perceived determinism of Engels is not followed by Mao is that Mao believed that there is no inevitability to the course of events. The inevitability of a definite direction of a progression of change is replaced by Mao by the random succession of opposites. These two innovations, of the primacy of the will and the rule of chance, move Mao far away from Marxism.[27]

For Meisner, Mao diverges from Marxist-Leninism politically because of Mao's trust in the masses, and his populism, as opposed to the priority Marxist-Leninism reserved for the Party.[28] Schwartz points to Mao's 1927 Hunan Report to stress that while the critique of the independent revolutionary role of the peasantry is common to all Marxist-Leninist literature, such a critique is lacking in Mao's analysis.[29]

Most dramatically, Meisner writes in 1971 that 'In the Maoist view, China, two decades after the victory of the revolution, can as easily revert to capitalism as proceed to communism; it depends entirely on the consciousness, the will, and the activities of man.'[30]

Andrew Walder, as we have pointed out above, argues that Mao has misinterpreted Engels and, therefore, Mao's thought does not represent an innovation to Marxism. Walder's arguments are copious, but in the mind of the present author, not decisive. In any case, if one considers, rightly or wrongly, that Engels's thought is deterministic, from that standpoint, Mao's thinking deviates from Engels's. However one decides this issue, the point made here is that there is a strong voluntaristic element in Mao's thinking and that it can be traced to his early study of Paulsen.[31]

On the other hand, Mao's elevation of the will also merges the will and conscience. In his marginal notes, Mao takes great exception to the notion that conscience should be separate from the ego. As argued above, this view of Mao's derives from his interpretation of both Confucius and Mencius. For Confucius, the self one strives to express is the moral self, the rectified self, not the raw self that has undergone no moral reflection. For Confucius, the true self is always guided by what is right, not by what one desires. The self or the ego and conscience are sharply differentiated in Confucius. In Mencius, the Great Man is the man who follows a moral direction, not the man who follows his egoistic desires. Mao wants to integrate ego with morality and argues against the separation of altruism from egoism. His argument against the separation of egoism from altruism derives from his critical reaction to Western philosophers such as Schopenhauer and Kant, especially Kant. Mao integrates his understanding of Confucius and Mencius with his opposition to the moral philosophy of Kant to forge a philosophy which perilously submerges conscience under will. The problem with this merger is that there is no separate conscience to limit the actions of the will. It is this philosophical weakness that may well account for the excesses of Mao's Cultural Revolution. When one submerges conscience under will, one may well think one's actions moral. This would explain Chen Yung-fa's revealing comment. 'The danger in Mao's personal ethics lies not in the lack of morality but in its excessive morality.'[32]

There are two philosophical mistakes: there is an identification of will with the unreflected self; two, there is no separate conscience to check the will. With conscience engulfed by the will, there is no checkpoint on excesses. Perhaps, Mao needed to retain more of the dialectic here, more of the *Yijing*. Instead of two, he has succumbed to the mistake of dividing two into one.

Mao's Deviation from Confucius

There is another way in which Mao deviates from Confucius, although the deviation in this case may turn out to be in Mao's favour. This deviation of Mao's from Confucius, therefore, cannot be termed, strictly speaking, a mistake. This deviation of Mao's is his notion that the masses can be made to understand the policies that are to be carried out. In terms of rulership, according to Confucius, the masses can be led, but they cannot be made to understand why they are being led:

> The people may be made to follow a path of action, but they may not be made to understand it.[33]

Mao wanted to go farther than this. He wanted the masses to make ideas their own and not simply blindly follow them. Schram writes:

> … it must be recognized that Mao's view according to which ordinary people may be a source of ideas from which correct policies are elaborated, and that they in turn understand these policies, rather than blindly applying them, marked a very great rupture with one of the central themes of traditional Chinese thought.[34]

This may be interpreted as Mao's extension of voluntarism to the collective. In this, Mao departs from Orwell's approach in *1984* in which blind obedience and loyalty were what were required of the masses, and not understanding. In this respect, Confucius, who thought the masses could not understand, would seem to stand closer to Orwell's *1984*. This is not the case, since, for Confucius, he thought that the masses were incapable of understanding, not that they should be manipulated so that they would not understand.

On the other hand, if the ideas in question are simply propaganda, the extension of voluntarism is or becomes a euphemism. In this case, if the masses' incorporation of ideas is simply an uncritical acceptance, then we cannot consider this a substantive improvement on Confucius. Such a mass self-incorporation of unexamined ideas would remind us more of a *1984* than of an improvement upon the values of Confucius. More than anything, this reminds us of Oscar Wilde's memorable line spoken by the character Algernon Moncrieff in Wilde's play, *The Importance of Being Earnest*, that the truth is never pure and rarely simple.

Cohen even argues that the idea of the mental transformation of the masses is another one of Mao's original ideas, though, in Cohen's description, it does not have a favourable connotation:

> It remained for Mao, however, to formulate the idea that the capitalists, as a class, would be transformed mentally into workers in a socialist society. This was a novel concept indeed, and its implementation was aided by the development of the equally new Marxist technique of mass 'thought remolding' or 'brainwashing'.[35]

Mao's Notion of Continuous Struggle without Resolution

The second of Mao's main philosophical contributions is the notion of continuous struggle. This theme, strongly emphasized as a young man in his marginal notes to Paulsen, remains with him his entire life and informs his mature idea of contradiction. With this mature idea, contradiction is permanent and desirable. This idea diverges strongly from Hegel whose dialectic always resolved itself into syntheses or resolutions. In addition, for Hegel, since the dialectic is the unfolding of the development of the Absolute Spirit, the dialectic is hardly directionless. For Mao, in terms of a good part of his writing, contradiction is king. The dialectic can move forward, backward and sidewise. There is no necessity of an upward direction. There are clear statements by Mao in which he sometimes does argue that the dialectic moves ever upward in what commentators refer to as a spiral. On the other hand, it does not seem that this is a *necessary* direction. That upward change is not necessary, as it is in Hegel, appears to give the nod to contradiction as the essential drive to alteration, not improvement. Indeed, since Mao often illustrates his version of dialectics with cyclical change, despite his occasional denials that it is cyclical, Mao's dialectics, from this point of view shares more in common with the *Yijing* than it does with Hegel. For Hegel, changes are not cyclical. On the other hand, in terms of Mao's inversion of the classical Marxist formula regarding the order of primacy between superstructure and base, Mao (perhaps, not self-consciously) looks backwards through Marx to Hegel. Hegel is the *locus classicus* for the notion that the origin of changes is located in conceptual development that is prior to material determinations. Marx, in his own words, did not turn Hegel upside down. He found Hegel standing on his head and turned him right side up again. Mao seems to have turned Marx upside down, and then right side up in a permanent series of somersaults. The notion of the permanent somersault, Mao's unique contribution, may be likened to the permanent turning of the earth. For some scholars, this is seen as parallel to the Jewish, Marxist theoretician and revolutionary Trotsky's notion of the permanent revolution.[36] Mao himself strongly differentiates his idea of a permanent revolution from that of Trotsky mostly on the grounds that it is important to go through stages including a democratic stage before arriving at socialism. However, he did utilize the use of this term 'permanent revolution' as he thought it would serve to maintain the revolutionary enthusiasm of the people.[37]

If one interprets Hegel's ultimate as the dialectic itself, then it could be argued that Mao's never-ending contradiction is a second cousin to Hegel's dialectic. Mao's dialectic has no syntheses. This lack of syntheses is unlike Hegel. Like Hegel and unlike Marx, for Mao there is no final end. For Mao, the process is one of endless change. The tonality of the endless change is for Mao characterized more by struggle and for Hegel more by inevitability. This is the factor of voluntarism which looms larger in Mao than it does in Hegel. In this respect, Mao is closer to Marx, particularly the young Marx, than he is to Hegel. Hegel has his world-historical men who move history. However, the voluntarism of their actions is reduced when one considers that they are but tools of the Absolute Spirit, or what Hegel sometimes calls *Die List der Vernuft* ('the Cunning of Reason'). For Mao, there is no supervening force that drives men forward. For Mao, it is their indomitable will driven by their vision and fuelled by their self-image.

Theory and Practice

By the same token, like Hegel, for Mao, it could be argued that the primal factor of the determination is the conceptual vision. Unlike Hegel, the material conditions do play a significant role for Mao. However, if we also examine Mao's statement regarding theory and practice, if we look closely, we notice that it also "ends" in theory, not practice. For Mao, practice always generates theory because we reflect upon practice. Then, post reflection, we apply theory again to practice. It is, in a way, despite Mao's own occasional protestations to the contrary, a never-ending cycle. However, it is a cycle in which theory or ideas end each cycle and then begin each cycle anew. Knowledge and practice are partners and Mao seems to be inconsistent in his multiple explications of the intricate relationship between the two. In the very last paragraph of 'On Practice', he seems first to invert his famed inversion between superstructure and base back into the Marxist-Leninist model, but then contradicts himself and tips his hand to the primacy of theory and knowledge over practice. While the two are inextricably connected, it is interesting to take note of the primacy Mao seems to accord theory in terms of how the cycle ends and what causes the cycle to recommence:

Discover the truth through practice, and again through practice verify and develop the truth. Start from perceptual knowledge and actively develop it into rational knowledge; then start from rational knowledge and actively guide revolutionary practice to change both the subjective and the objective world. Practice, knowledge, again practice, *again knowledge. This form repeats itself* in endless cycles, and with each cycle the content of practice and knowledge raises itself to a higher level. Such is the whole of the dialectical-materialist theory of knowledge, and such is the dialectical-materialist theory of the unity of knowing and doing.[38]

On the other hand, Mao makes it clear that the priority should be given to practice, not theory:

The truth of any knowledge or theory is determined not by subjective feelings, but by objective results in social practice. Only social practice can be the criterion of truth. The standpoint of practice is the primary and basic standpoint in the dialectical-materialist theory of knowledge.[39]

This would seem to contradict the end paragraph of 'On Practice' quoted above. However, it is wise to examine closely the reasoning behind the primacy accorded practice:

The dialectical-materialist theory of knowledge places practice in the primary position, holding that human knowledge can in no way be separated from practice and repudiating all the erroneous theories which deny the importance of practice or separate knowledge from practice. Thus, Lenin said '*Practice is higher than (theoretical) knowledge*, for it has not only the dignity of universality but also of immediate actuality'.[40]

For Lenin, in addition to the greater dignity and immediate actuality of practice, the main reasoning for according primacy to practice is to avoid the error of the denial of the importance of practice and separating knowledge from practice. The two must always be considered together.

Is this once more an illustration of Mao's contradictory pronouncements? It reflects this and it reflects perhaps more the complementary nature of oppositions that characterize Mao's thinking. What is complementary includes the relative position of the primary and the secondary nature of the contradiction and the contradiction of theory and practice does not escape this continuous changing of place between primary and secondary. That primary and secondary continuously change places does not demonstrate that there is not a distinction between what is primary and what is secondary. In fact, if there were no hierarchy of determination, there would be insufficient impetus to change. It is the complementary and contradictory relationship between the primary and the secondary that creates the dynamic of change. However, the existence of this dynamic does not negate the fact of the temporary ascendance of one side of the contradiction over the other; it illustrates it. Tian presents correlativity as the Chinese opposite to Western dualistic and deterministic, hierarchical thinking. In my view, correlativity, a brilliant Chinese conceptual contribution to philosophy, requires disequilibrium as a partner to provide impetus to change. That correlativity requires disequilibrium does not negate the internality of contradiction; it supplements it.[41]

It is important to remember that in any case when superstructure determines base or vice versa, the determination is not a *final* determination. Strictly speaking, in my view, the nature of the determination is also different. In the case of base determining superstructure, the base does not *cause* the superstructure. Without the base there would be no need for the superstructure to arise. Without the existence of unfair working conditions, there would be no need for a change in laws regulating working hours. Thus, the base is a necessary, but not a sufficient condition for the superstructure. In the case of the superstructure determining the base, the superstructure is a sufficient condition for the base as in the case of lowering working hours creating better working conditions. In this case, the lowering of working hours is the cause of the better working conditions.

Mao and Heraclitus

We could say that Mao is close to Heraclitus in the Heracleitian emphasis on the primacy of flux. In Heracleitus's famous phrase, 'One can never step twice into the same river'. However, Mao's antipathy to harmony makes his approach even more radical than Heracleitus. Heracleitus speaks of harmony as underlying strife, but for Mao there is no underlying harmony. Mao is the opposite to Heracleitus. It is disharmony which underlies harmony, not the reverse:

> The cycle, which is endless, evolves from disequilibrium to equilibrium and then to disequilibrium again. Each cycle, however, brings us to a higher level of development. Disequilibrium is normal and absolute whereas equilibrium is temporary and relative.[42]

Here, Mao refers to an endless cycle which is reminiscent of the *Yijing*. (Despite his sometime disclaimers of the existence of a cycle.) The notion of a continuing upward spiral is reminiscent of the Hegelian dialectic, not of the *Yijing*. We see both Eastern and the Western philosophical influences. However, the key phrase here is the first clause of the last sentence in the passage quoted above. Disequilibrium is given primacy. This is not Heracleitus, Hegel or the *Yijing*. This is Mao. While Mao's thinking in the end is closer to the *Yijing* than to any other framework of understanding opposition and change, it contains the element of underlying disharmony that diverges from all previous frameworks.

Mao's Use of Complementary rather than Contradictory Opposites

This brings us to what stands out as the third of Mao's philosophical contributions, namely, Mao's use of complementary rather than contradictory opposites. This is very much in line with the treatment of opposites in the *Yijing*, in which opposites are not antagonistic to each other, but are necessary to the existence of each other. They are not simply non-antagonistic; complementary opposites complete each other. One significant aspect of the notion of opposition as complementary is that it brings opposite views together rather than keeping them apart in adversarial positions. If a position that opposes one's own is not antagonistic, there is a greater chance that the relationship between the opposing positions will not be conflictual. Given the ideological strife and physical violence that threaten the possibility of peaceful life on earth, it behooves us to consider the value of adopting a view of difference that is complementary rather than oppositional. The Western 'either-or' approach to belief systems can gain much from a Chinese perspective of 'both-and'.

One may wonder why it was that Mao's thought, directed as it was by the notion of complementary opposition, spawned a period of history marked by violent change. It is difficult, naturally, to attribute all the violence sparked by the Cultural Revolution to Mao's philosophical concepts. When portions of a population have been repressed for many generations, it is not surprising that they would erupt with violence when accorded more freedom. This cannot be attributed to Mao's philosophy. A revolution, as Mao famously said, is not a dinner party.[43]

Mao, perhaps influenced by his early exposure to Western thought, especially by his early exposure to the stories of George Washington, the American Revolution and the idea of the Great Man, saw himself as the means of liberating those belonging to the lower socio-economic class from their position of economic inequality. The problem of economic inequality was already there and the unhappiness that came with it was already present. Mao took it upon himself to be the primal agent of change. He accelerated the change that in terms of the *yi* was already incipient. If it were not already there, he could not have awakened it, harnessed it and brought it into fruition. The need for the change was already there. In a sense, the people were too passive, too yin. Mao was the yang force that aroused and channeled the movement to change from passivity to activity. This is not to say that everything Mao did was good, or bad. His actions produced both consequences that were in some instances beneficial and in other, instances, extremely harmful. What can be said is that without Mao, China would not have gone through the remarkable transitions that it has seen in the twentieth and now into the twenty-first century.

Mao's ideas of the origin of political rights should also not be overlooked. His development of the idea of rights is vintage Mao. On the one hand, he deviates from the conventional version of the Chinese tradition that does not base itself on the idea of rights. (This conventional version does not take into account Mencius's famous right of rebellion.) On the other hand, he critiques the idea of natural rights that arises in the West and he replaces it with the idea that man creates and bestows the idea of rights. The idea of rights does not arise from nature. In Mao's words:

> The natural rights of man represents, of course, an erroneous line of thought. Is there such a thing as rights bestowed by nature? Our rights were bestowed by the common people, and primarily by the working class and the poor and lower-middle peasants.[44]

This represents an interesting blend of a demythologizing the idea of right as stemming from nature and existentialism, emphasizing that rights belong to man to assert with the Marxian emphasis on the working class. Mao, as always, combines the expression of will with his devotion to Marxian concerns. Such a stance on human rights belongs to the philosophy of Mao; whether or not it found its way into policy is an entirely different matter. The philosophy itself is not free from flaws; it privileges a certain class, the working class, whereas the concept that rights are bestowed by nature is more universal.

For future inspiration, one should look to the writings of Mao that encourage complementary opposites, his encouraging, for example of democratic rather than violent processes to forward political aims. All of his thinking was not exclusively focused on revolution. Even if one finds his endorsement of democratic means disingenuous, the point is that it is found in his writing and possesses the permanent influence of the pen rather than of the sword. Mao saw no antagonistic contradiction between promoting the use of democratic means of persuasion such as discussion to forward his economic agenda. Mao saw through the false dichotomy of either-or oppositional thinking and it is this philosophical development that holds the most promise for the resolution of present and future conflict.

The story of China provisionally ends here, back at the very beginning of Mao's study of the classics of Chinese philosophy. Though Mao may not have predicted the changes that were to overtake China, it must be said that his thought played a key role in the history of China in the twentieth century.[45] It starts in 1917–1918 with his forging of the beginning of his own philosophical development from both the Chinese and the Western classical tradition. It ends at the latter part of the century when Mao has brought China itself to a *point d'appui* from which it reaches a *rapprochement* with the very Western world that formed part of Mao's early intellectual heritage.

Mao's thought, from its beginning to its end, can be seen as a bridge which connects China both back to its original Confucian heritage, through the struggle to shake off that heritage, to finally, in its post-Mao era, to regain that heritage that Mao both held onto and transmogrified in the period that constituted one of the greatest periods of social upheaval in the twentieth century. While the Confucian heritage to which China is returning is not a return *simpliciter* to the values of Confucius that one finds in the texts of Confucius, such a return does afford scholars the opportunity to find the real teachings of Confucius in the texts of Confucius.[46]

NOTES

Winter Clouds

1 Jerome Ch' en, *Mao and the Chinese Revolution*, Thirty-seven Poems by Mao Tse-tung, trans. Michael Bullock and Jerome Ch' en, London, Oxford, New York: Oxford University Press, Part Two, Thirty-Seven Poems by Mao Tse-Tung, 1965, 358. Reproduced with permission of the Licensor through PLSclear.

Preface

2 *Cf.*, Herrlee G. Creel, *Chinese Thought from Confucius to Mao Tse Tung*, Chicago: The University of Chicago Press, 1953.

3 Frederick Wakeman, Jr., *History and Will, Philosophical Perspectives of Mao Tse-tung's Thought*, Center of Chinese Studies, Berkeley: University of California Press, 1973.

4 Wing-tsit Chan, 'Chinese Philosophy in Communist China', *Philosophy East & West*, Vol. 11, No. 3, October 1961, 115. Mao's philosophical writings are included in *The Sources of the Chinese Tradition*, edited by Wm. Theodore de Bary, New York: Columbia University Press, 2001, and his philosophy is referenced in the *Encyclopedia of Chinese Philosophy*, edited by Antonio S. Cua, London and New York: Routledge, 2003. Father O. J. Briere includes Mao in his *Fifty Years of Chinese Philosophy from 1898–1948*, New York and London: Routledge, 1965.

5 This Confucianism is not to be identified with Confucianism viewed as a defence of feudal ethics and male chauvinism.

Chapter 1

1 *Cf.*, Andrew G. Walder takes a critical view of Mao. *Cf.*, *China Under Mao, A Revolution Derailed*, Cambridge and London: Harvard University Press, 2015. A more qualified view of Mao appears in the essays collected in Gregor Benton and Lin Chun, (eds.), *Was Mao Really a Monster? The Academic Response to Chang and*

Halliday's Mao: The Unknown Story, London and New York: Routledge, 2010. (In the Chinese version, the subtitle is altered to 'The Little-Known Story'.)

2   Nick Knight, 'Introduction: The Study of Mao Zedong's Philosophical Thought in Contemporary China,' *Chinese Studies in Philosophy*, Vol. 23, No. 3-4, 1992, p. 7.

3   *Cf.*, Arthur Waldron, 'Mao Lives', Gregor Benton and Lin Chun, (eds.), *Was Mao Really a Monster? The Academic Response to Chang and Halliday's Mao: The Unknown Story*, London and New York: Routledge, 2010, p. 167.

4   *Cf.*, Frank Dikötter, *Mao's Great Famine, The History of China's Most Devastating Catastrophe*, London: Bloomsbury, 2012; Frank Dikötter, *The Tragedy of Liberation, A History of the Chinese Revolution, 1945-57*, London, New Delhi, New York, Sydney: Bloomsbury, 2013; Zhou Xun, *Forgotten Voices of Mao's Famine, 1959-1962*, New Haven and London: Yale University Press, 2013; Ralph Thaxton, Jr., *Catastrophe and Contention in Rural China*, Cambridge: Cambridge University Press, 2008.

5   *Cf.*, Gregor Benton and Lin Chun, *Was Mao Really a Monster? The Academic Response to Chang and Halliday's Mao: The Unknown Story*, London and New York: Routledge, 2010, p. 8.

6   Lee Feigon, *Mao, A Reinterpretation*, Chicago: University of Chicago Press, 2002, p. 179. *Cf.*, Andrew G. Walder, *China Under Mao, A Revolution Derailed*, Cambridge and London: Harvard University Press, 2015, pp. 320-321.

7   Lee Feigon, p. 183.

8   *Cf.*, Andrew G. Walder, *China Under Mao, A Revolution Derailed*, Cambridge and London: Harvard University Press, 2015, pp. 320-321.

9   John Bryan Starr, '"Good Mao", "Bad Mao": Mao Studies and the Re-Evaluation of Mao's Political Thought,' *The Australian Journal of Chinese Affairs*, No. 16, July 1986, p. 4.

10 *Cf.*, Andrew G. Walder, *China Under Mao, A Revolution Derailed*, Cambridge and London: Harvard University Press, 2015, pp. 335-341.

11 Stuart Schram, *The Thought of Mao Tse-Tung*, Cambridge: Cambridge University Press, 1989, p. 195. *Cf.*, Francis Y. K. Soo, *Mao Tse-Tung's Theory of Dialectic*, Vol. 44, Dordrecht, Boston, London: D. Reidel Publishing Company, 1981, p. 25. Ignatius Ts' ao adds the interesting point that 'Even when schools and universities were closed for years, their staff still received their salaries.' *Cf.*, Ignatius J. H., Ts' ao, 'Mao Tse-Tung and China's Fate,' *Asian Thought & Society*, Vol. 2, No. 1, 1977, p. 142.

12 Edward Friedman, 'Einstein and Mao: Metaphors of Revolution,' *The China Quarterly*, No. 93, March, 1983, p. 58. Mao proposed the new policy known as the 'Great Leap Forward' in the Autumn of 1957.

13 Lee Feigon, *Mao, A Reinterpretation*, Chicago: University of Chicago Press, 2002, p. 182. One must always consider the question of distinguishing between personal sexual habits and the merits of leadership for the country. There are numerous examples of the need to make such a distinction in the United States of America. One needs only to think of Kennedy and Clinton in recent years.

14 Frank Dikötter, *The Cultural Revolution, A People's History, 1962–1976*, New York: Bloomsbury Press, 2016, p. xi. Dikötter does not reference any source to corroborate this assertion.

15 Stuart Schram, *The Thought of Mao Tse-Tung*, Cambridge: Cambridge University Press, 1989, p. 202.

16 *Cf.*, Bill Wilmott, 'From Wild Swans to Mao: The Unknown Story,' Gregor Benton and Lin Chun, (eds.), *Was Mao Really a Monster? The Academic Response to Chang and Halliday's Mao: The Unknown Story*, London and New York: Routledge, 2010, p. 185.

17 Stuart Schram, *The Thought of Mao Tse-Tung*, Cambridge: Cambridge University Press, 1989, p. 206.

18 Stuart R. Schram, 'The Formative Years: A Preliminary Reassessment,' 1917–1937, *Mao Zedong, A Preliminary Assessment*, Hong Kong: The Chinese University Press, 1983, p. 77. Deng Xiaoping, victimized by Mao, made the following comment: 'Meiyou Mao zhuxi jiu meiyou xin Zhongguo (Without Chairman Mao, there would be no new China).' *Cf.*, Bill Willmott, 'From Wild Swans to Mao: The Unknown Story,' Gregor Benton and Lin Chun, (eds.), *Was Mao Really a Monster? The Academic Response to Chang and Halliday's Mao: The Unknown Story*, London and New York: Routledge, 2010, p. 185.

19 Henry Kissinger, *On China*, New York: Penguin Books, 2012, p. 92.

20 *Cf., Christian Science Monitor*, 4 June 1986. https://m.csmonitor.com/1986/0604/opoem.html

21 C. P. Fitzgerald, 'Mao and the Chinese Cultural Tradition,' *Il Politico*, Vol. 42, No. 3, September, 1977, p. 487.

22 As Francis Soo notes, 'Since most of his [Mao's] writings are essentially political, they tend to be polemical. For this reason, it is hard to distill what is philosophical from his political writings.' *Cf.*, Francis Y. K. Soo, *Mao Tse-Tung's Theory of Dialectic*, Vol. 44, Dordrecht, Boston, London: D. Reidel Publishing Company, 1981, p. 5. The purpose of this present volume is primarily to elucidate the individual philosophical thinking of Mao and secondarily how it may have influenced his political philosophy. There is no intention of justifying Mao's political philosophy or his political policies.

23 Stuart Schram, *The Thought of Mao Tse-Tung*, Cambridge: Cambridge University Press, 1989, pp. 65–66.

24 Hereafter, whenever there is reference to 'Mao's thought', the intention is to refer to Mao's philosophical thought. This appellation is an attempt to distinguish Mao's individual philosophical thinking from the use of the phrases 'Mao Zedong Thought' or 'Mao Zedong Philosophical Thought' as phrases utilized to refer to the official ideological version of Mao as configured by the CCP.

25 Stuart Schram, *The Thought of Mao Tse-Tung*, Cambridge: Cambridge University Press, 1989, p. 10.

26 Timothy Cheek, 'Mao, Revolution, and Memory', *A Critical Introduction to Mao*, Cambridge: Cambridge University Press, 2010, p. 13.

27 Liu Rong, 'Mao Zedong Philosophical Thought Is the Application and Development of Marxist Philosophy in China,' *Chinese Studies in Philosophy*, Vol. 23, Nos. 3–4, Spring–Summer, 1992, p. 78.

28 Edgar Snow, *Red Star Over China*, New York: Grove Press, 1968, p. 155.

29 *Cf.*, Alexander V. Pantsov and Steven L. Levine, *Mao: The Real Story*, New York and London: Simon & Schuster, 2012, p. 64.

30 Stuart R. Schram, (ed.), *Mao's Road to Power, Revolutionary Writings*, 1912–1949, Vol. I, The Pre-Marxist Period, 1912–1920, Armonk, New York, London: M. E. Sharpe, 1992, pp. 378–379.

31 Stuart R. Schram, 'The Formative Years: A Preliminary Reassessment,' 1917–1937, Mao Zedong, *A Preliminary Assessment*, Hong Kong: The Chinese University Press, 1983, p. 6.

32 Stuart Schram, *The Thought of Mao Tse-Tung*, Cambridge: Cambridge University Press, 1989, p. 8. The investigation of things is a part of traditional Chinese philosophy, and it dates back at least as far as the *Great Learning*. *Cf.*, also, my late colleague, Shu-hsien Liu's discussion of Wang Yangming in his *Understanding Confucian Philosophy: Classical and Sung-Ming*, Westport, CT: Praeger Publishers, 1998, pp. 238–239.

33 Ibid., p. 9.

34 Ibid., p. 185.

35 Schram arrives at a similar set of distinctions by first singling out Mao's own thinking and then dividing the stages of official thinking differently, dividing a stage of orthodox Maoist writing from the rectified corpus which explicitly excludes Mao's later writings 'that reflect the errors from his later years'. *Cf.*, Ibid., pp. 185–186. The implications of these divisions remain substantially the same as those of Knight.

36 Nick Knight, 'Introduction: The Study of Mao Zedong's Philosophical Thought in Contemporary China,' *Chinese Studies in Philosophy*, Vol. 23, Nos. 3–4, 1992, p. 21.

37 Ibid., p. 21.

38 Ibid., p. 22.

39 Ibid., p. 22.

40 Zhang Wenru, 'Mao Zedong's Critical Continuation of China's Fine Philosophical Inheritance,' *Chinese Studies in Philosophy*, Vol. 23, Nos. 3–4, Spring–Summer 1992, p. 117.

41 Ibid., 120. *Cf.*, *Selected Works of Mao Tse-Tung*, Foreign Languages Press, Vol. II, p. 209.

42 Nick Knight, (1992), 'Introduction: The Study of Mao Zedong's Philosophical Thought in Contemporary China', *Chinese Studies in Philosophy*, Vol. 23, No. 3–4, pp. 23–24.

43 *Cf.*, *Analects*, IV, 16; XIV, 12; XVI, 10; XIX, 1.

44 Maurice Meisner, *Mao Zedong, A Political and Intellectual Portrait* (hereafter, referenced as *Mao Zedong*) Cambridge: Polity Press, 2007, p. 15.

45 While it is more accurate, in terms of conforming to contemporary usage of terminology, to use descriptions such as 'socialism with Chinese characteristics' or 'market socialism' to refer to China's economic system, it is sometimes necessary to use the term 'capitalism' to provide philosophical coherency in terms of relating Mao's views on capitalism to current conditions in China, in order to maintain the continuity of the Marxist discourse of the relation of communism to capitalism, to relate changes to the rubric of the *Yijing*, and to accommodate the usage of the term 'capitalism' by other writers. For brevity's sake, I have mainly used the acronym SCC (socialism with Chinese characteristics) as well as the phrase, 'market socialism'. According to the *China Daily* in 2010, more than 70 per cent of Chinese workers were employed in the private sector.

Chapter 2

1 Maurice Meisner, *Mao Zedong*, Cambridge: Polity Press, 2007, p. 3. Mao defied his father to attend this school. Mao's account is quoted virtually verbatim from Mao's autobiography as he recounts it to Edgar Snow in Snow's *Red Star Over China*. *Cf.*, *Red Star Over China*, New York: Grove Press, 1968, p. 137. Meisner recounts how Mao read books about the 1898 Reform movement of Kang Youwei. *Cf.*, p. 3.

2 Snow, *Red Star Over China*, 254.

3 Rebecca E. Karl, *Mao Zedong and China in the Twentieth Century World, A Concise History*, Durham, NC: Duke University Press, 2010, p. 6. The source of this information is Mao's own account of his childhood given in interviews with Edgar Snow and later recorded in Edgar Snow, *Red Star Over China*, New York: Grove Press, 1968, p. 132.

4 Mao Tse-Tung, Chairman Mao's Conversation with Comrades Ch' en Pota and K' ang Shen, quoted in Frederic Wakeman, Jr., *History and Will, Philosophical Perspectives of Mao Tse-Tung's Thought*, Center of Chinese Studies, Berkeley: University of California Press, 1973, p. 182. For Mao's direct quotations from the *Yijing*, *cf.*, Stuart R. Schram, (ed.), *Mao's Road to Power, Revolutionary Writings, 1912-1949, The Pre-Marxist Period, 1912-1920*, Vol. I, Armonk, New York, London: M. E. Sharpe, 1992, pp. 27, 46, 83, 446. *Cf.*, 'Talk on Questions of Philosophy', Stuart Schram, (ed.), trans. John and Tieyun Chinnery, *Mao Tse-tung Unrehearsed, Talks and Lectures, 1956-1971*, Harmondsworth: Penguin Books, 1975, p. 213.

5 Ross Terrill, *Mao*, New York: Harper & Row, 1980, pp. 40-41. The source of this information is most likely Mao's own account recounted in Edgar Snow, *Red Star Over China*, New York: Grove Press, 1968, p. 153.

6 *Cf.*, Jerome Ch' en, *Mao and the Chinese Revolution*, trans. Michael Bullock and Jerome Ch' en, London, Oxford, New York: Oxford University Press, 1965, p. 20.

7 *Cf.*, Ibid., p. 356.

8   Stuart R. Schram, (ed.), *Mao's Road to Power, Revolutionary Writings, 1912–1949, The Pre-Marxist Period, 1912–1920*, Vol. I, Armonk, New York, London: M. E. Sharpe, 1992, Introduction, p. xx.

9   *Cf.*, Jerome Ch' en, *Mao and the Chinese Revolution*, trans. Michael Bullock and Jerome Ch' en, London, Oxford, New York: Oxford University Press, 1965, p. 50.

10 *Cf.*, Edgar Snow, *Red Star Over China*, New York: Grove Press, 1968, p. 146.

11 She was to be arrested, tortured and executed by the Kuomingtang in 1930 after refusing to reveal Mao's whereabouts. She was twenty-nine years old. She is still heralded as a local heroine in Hunan.

12 *Cf.*, Howard L. Boorman, 'Mao Tse-Tung as Historian', *The China Quarterly*, Cambridge: Cambridge University Press, No. 28, October–December 1966, p. 85.

13 Jerome Ch' en, *Mao and the Chinese Revolution*, trans. Michael Bullock and Jerome Ch' en, London, Oxford, New York: Oxford University Press, 1965, p. 48.

14 For much of this information on Mao's educational background, I am indebted to Ross Terrill's *Mao*, the biography of Mao of which no less of an authority than John Fairbank of Harvard considered 'the most illuminating synthesis on Mao since Snow's *Red Star Over China* of 1938'. *Cf.*, Ross Terrill, *Mao*, New York: Harper & Row, 1980, pp. 37–38.

15 Frederick Wakeman, *History & Will: Philosophical Perspectives of Mao Tse Tung's Thought*, Berkeley, Los Angeles, London: University of California Press, 1973, p. 165.

16 Maurice Meisner, *Mao's China and After, A History of the People's Republic*, Third Edition, New York: The Free Press 1999, pp. 14–15. (emphasis added) According to Meisner, Chen Duxiu, the founder of *New Youth*, was influential for Mao's conversion to Marxism. *Cf.*, Meisner, *Mao Zedong*, 7, 28–29, p. 179.

17 Ibid., p. 16.

18 This table is adapted from Frederic Wakeman, Jr., *History and Will, Philosophical Perspectives of Mao Tse-Tung's Thought*, Center of Chinese Studies, Berkeley: University of California Press, 1973, pp. 164–165.

19 Edgar Snow, *Red Star Over China*, New York: Grove Press, 1968, p. 151.

20 Sir Joseph Needham, obituary for Mao Zedong, http://www.sacu.org/maoobituary.html, p. 4. Sir Joseph was to personally invite me to come as a Fellow to his Institute, the Needham Research Institute at his College, Robinson College at the University of Cambridge, to work on his multi-volumed *Science and Civilization in China*. It turned out that later I did work on the section on Logic that was to become part of Volume VII.

21 *Cf.*, Tian Chenshan, *Chinese Dialectics from Yijng to Marxism*, Lanham: Lexington Books, 2005, p. 146.

22 *Cf.*, Stuart R. Schram, *Mao's Road to Power, Revolutionary Writings*, 1912–1949, Vol. I, The Pre-Marxist Period, 1912–1920, Armonk, New York, London: M. E. Sharpe, 1992, Introduction, p. xxx; Howard Boorman, 'Mao Tse-Tung: The Lacquered Image', *The China Quarterly*, No. 16, October–December 1963, p. 5, and Li Jiu, *The Early Revolutionary Activities of Comrade Mao Tse-Tung*, White Plains, New York: M. E.

Sharpe, 1977, pp. 8, 16, 19; Jerome Ch' en, *Mao and the Chinese Revolution*, trans. Michael Bullock and Jerome Ch' en, London, Oxford, New York: Oxford University Press, 1965, p. 48.

Rebecca Karl writes that Mao's reading of Herbert Spencer was of Spencer's *Principles of Sociology*. *Cf.*, *Mao Zedong and China in the Twentieth Century World, A Concise History*, Durham, NC: Duke University Press, 2010, p. 10. For Meisner, Mao was much influenced by Spencer's social Darwinism, '... with its enormous emphasis on the inevitability of struggle.' *Cf., Mao Zedong*, p. 4.

23   Li Jiu, *The Early Revolutionary Activities of Comrade Mao Tse-Tung*, White Plains, New York: M. E.Sharpe, 1977, p. 8.

24   *Cf.*, Jerome Ch' en, *Mao and the Chinese Revolution*, trans. Michael Bullock and Jerome Ch' en, London, Oxford, New York: Oxford University Press, 1965, p. 32.

25   Li Jiu, *The Early Revolutionary Activities of Comrade Mao Tse-Tung*, White Plains, New York: M. E.Sharpe, 1977, pp. 8, 277–278. Wakeman imaginatively reconstructs Mao's lessons from his reading of Yang's philosophy book, *Hsi-yang lun-li chu-I shu-p'ing*, [*A Critique of Western Ethical Theories*], Shanghai: Commercial Press, 1923.

26   Edgar Snow, *Red Star Over China*, New York: Grove Press, 1968, pp. 94–95. Jerome Ch' en adds Greek mythology, world history and geography to the list. *Cf.*, Jerome Ch' en, *Mao and the Chinese Revolution*, trans. Michael Bullock and Jerome Ch' en, London, Oxford, New York: Oxford University Press, 1965, p. 32.

27   Much of this information is to be found in Edgar Snow, *Red Star Over China*, New York: Grove Press, 1968, p. 138.

28   Ross Terrill, *Mao*, New York: Harper & Row, 1980, pp. 20–21.

29   *Cf.*, Chapter Seven below for varying accounts of Mao's command of English.

30   *Cf.*, Howard Boorman, 'Mao Tse-Tung: The Lacquered Image, *The China Quarterly*, No. 16, October–December 1963, p. 4 and Philip Short, *Mao, A Life*, New York: Henry Holt and Co., 1999, p. 55.

31   Marginal Notes, p. 194.

32   *Cf., The Portable Nietzsche*, trans. Walter Kaufmann, Harmondsworth, Middlesex: Penguin, Books, 1959, p. 507.

33   Stuart R. Schram, (ed.), *Mao's Road to Power, Revolutionary Writings*, 1912–1949, Vol. I, The Pre-Marxist Period, 1912–1920, Armonk, New York, London: M. E. Sharpe, 1992, pp. 128–129 (hereafter to be referred to as Schram).

Chapter 3

1   There are many influences on Mao's thought and this present work focuses only on selected major influences. Jerome Ch' en mentions other influences as well.

Ch' en mentions classical works such as the *Complete Works of Han Yü*, the *Tzu-chih T'ung-chien* and the *Tu-shih Fang-yü Chi-yao*. *Cf.*, Jerome Ch' en, *Mao and the Chinese Revolution*, trans. Michael Bullock and Jerome Ch' en, London, Oxford, New York: Oxford University Press, 1965, p. 45.

2. Stuart R. Schram, (ed.), *Mao's Road to Power, Revolutionary Writings*, 1912–1949, Vol. I, The Pre-Marxist Period, 1912–1920, Armonk, New York, London: M. E. Sharpe, 1992, Introduction, p. xxix. (emphasis added).

3. Ibid.

4. For example, Wakeman did not have access to Mao's marginal notes to Paulsen at the time of the writing of his *History and Will, Philosophical Perspectives on Mao's Thought*.

5. Li Jiu, *The Early Revolutionary Activities of Comrade Mao Tse-Tung*, White Plains, New York: M. E. Sharpe, 1977, p. 36.

6. Ibid., p. 37.

7. There are a number of studies of Mao's Marxist philosophical perigrinations. Two examples are Chapter IV, 'The Philosophical Basis of Mao Tse-Tung's Thought', and 'The Thought of Mao-Tse Tung in Relation to Traditional Philosophy' found in S. K. Chin, *The Thought of Mao Tse-tung, Form and Content*, trans. Alfred H. Y. Lin, Centre of Asian Studies, Hong Kong: University of Hong Kong, 1979.

8. Marginal Notes to Friedrich Paulsen, *A System of Ethics* (1917–1918), pp. 175, 177 (hereafter referred to as Marginal Notes).

9. In his introduction to Li Jui's work, Stuart Schram writes that 'Both the emphasis on the importance of subjective forces, and the eclecticism in the choice of his authorities, persist in Mao's later writings.' *Cf.*, Li Jiu, *The Early Revolutionary Activities of Comrade Mao Tse-Tung*, White Plains, New York: M. E. Sharpe, 1977, p. xxv.

10. Marginal Notes, p. 179.

11. Ibid., p. 189.

12. Ibid., p. 189.

13. Ibid., p. 200.

14. For simplicity, instead of qualifying 'Mao' with 'the early Mao' in every usage, it is understood that whenever Mao is referenced in this chapter (except in obvious cases when the context will signify otherwise), it is the early Mao that is intended.

15. Marginal Notes, p. 205.

16. Ibid., p. 236.

17. Ibid., p. 257.

18. Ibid., p. 261.

19. Ibid., p. 207.

20. *Cf.*, Christos Lynteris, *The Spirit of Selflessness in Maoist China, Socialist Medicine and the New Man*, London: Palgrave Macmillan, 2013.

21 *Cf.*, http//www.marxists.org/reference/archive/mao/selected_works/volume-2/mwv2_25.htm
22 K. T. Fann, 'Mao and the Chinese Revolution in Philosophy', *Studies in Soviet Thought*, Vol. 12, 1972, pp. 11–123.
23 Marginal Notes, pp. 251–252.
24 Ibid., p. 208.
25 *Cf.*, the early writings of Marx such as the Paris Manuscripts (the *Economic and Philosophical Manuscripts of 1844*). When I was Visiting Professor to Peking University in 1988, the library's collection of Marx did not include the Paris manuscripts (in German or Chinese) and when I interviewed graduate students in economics, they did not know of these works. Existentialist themes were not politically correct at that time. Despite this or perhaps because of it, when I was invited to give lectures on existentialism to the graduate students in philosophy at Peking University, they were so eager to learn about existentialism that the room became so full of students that the doorway itself was blocked with the bodies of students crammed side by side attempting to hear the lectures.
26 Marginal Notes, p. 285.
27 Stuart R. Schram, (ed.), *Mao's Road to Power, Revolutionary Writings*, 1912–1949, Vol. I, The Pre-Marxist Period, 1912–1920, Armonk, New York and London: M. E. Sharpe, 1992, Introduction, p. xxiv. I cannot but agree with this assessment.
28 Marginal Notes, p. 177.
29 Ibid., p. 273.
30 Ibid., p. 303.
31 Ibid., p. 260.
32 Ibid., p. 260.
33 Ibid., p. 260.
34 Ibid., p. 260.
35 Ibid., pp. 261–262.
36 Ibid., p. 262.
37 Ibid., p. 262.
38 Ibid., p. 261.
39 Ibid., p. 268.
40 Ibid., p., 268.
41 In another context Mao cites examples from American, Chinese and European history in the same sentence. 'For example, a great new continent to the West confronted Columbus, Yu was faced with a great flood, and a host of European nations rose up to surround Paris and defeat Napoleon.' Marginal Notes, p. 235.
42 Marginal Notes, p. 268.
43 Ibid., pp. 261–262.

44 Ibid., p. 262.
45 Ibid., p. 262.
46 Ibid., pp. 200–201.
47 Ibid., p. 201. Mao even refers to noble Egoism, or the Egoism of the spirit.
48 Ibid., p. 202.
49 Ibid., p. 278.
50 Ibid., p. 279.
51 Ibid., p. 200.
52 Ibid., p. 200.
53 Ibid., p. 201.
54 Ibid., p. 203.
55 Ibid., p. 203.
56 Ibid., p. 205.
57 Ibid., p. 280.
58 Ibid., p. 280.
59 Ibid., p. 239.
60 Ibid., p. 241.
61 Ibid., p. 243.

Chapter 4

1 *Cf.*, Robert Elliott Allinson, "'Aristotle and Economics,'" and "'Confucianism and Taoism'", Luk Bouckaert and László Zsolnai, (eds.), *The Palgrave Handbook of Spirituality and Business*, New York: Palgrave Macmillan, 2011, pp. 69–79, 95–102, for an extended analysis of the comparison between Aristotle and Confucius.
2 'In order to be good, one must do [ethical acts] … for the sake of the acts themselves.' *Cf., Nicomachean Ethics* 1144a 14–20.
3 *Nicomachean Ethics*, 1105a 16–17.
4 Ibid., 1098a 16.
5 Ibid., 1099a 17–18.
6 *Cf. Mencius*, translated with an Introduction by D. C. Lau, London: Penguin Books, 1970, Introduction, p. 27.
7 *Cf., Classroom Notes*, October–December 1913, *Self-Cultivation*, 13 November, ibid., pp. 9, 21. *Mencius*, VI, 1, XIV, 1 *et passim*.
8 Ibid., p. 79.

9   *Cf., Great Learning*, 4–5. (The passage continues to add that a study of external things was necessary to become sincere in one's thoughts, but the goal was sincerity and this is a key difference between Mao and Confucius.)

10 Marginal Notes, p. 202. This is in reference to the *Great Learning*, 4–5.

11 In later Chinese Marxism, Liu Shaoqi adapted Confucian self-cultivation to Marxist purposes. *Cf.*, 'How to Be a Good Communist', July 1939. *Cf.*, https://www.marxists.org/reference/archive/liu-shaoqi/1939/how-to-be/ch02.htm

12 *Cf.*, Schram's argument both in his Introduction to Li Jui's, *The Early Revolutionary Activities of Comrade Mao Tse-tung*, White Plains, New York: M. E. Sharpe, 1977, p. xxv and in Stuart Schram, *The Political Thought of Mao Tse-tung*, New York: Praeger, 1969, p. 159 in reference to *Analects*, XV, 21.

13 *Cf., Analects*, XII, 1.

14 *Mencius*, VII, A, 45. (D. C. Lau translation). *Cf.*, also, III, A, 5.

15 *Analects*, I, 6. (This is D. C. Lau's translation.) Legge renders it as 'He should overflow in love to all…'.

16 *Analects*, XII, 2; XV, 23; V, ll.

17 *Cf., Analects*, XVII, 2.

18 *Analects*, 12, 5.

19 *Analects*, XIII, 18.

20 *Analects*, XV, 23. For a thoroughgoing analysis of the relationship between the single thread and the single saying, *cf.*, Robert E. Allinson, 'The Ethics of Confucianism and Christianity: The Delicate Balance', *Ching Feng, Quarterly Notes on Christianity and Chinese Religion and Culture*, Vol. XXXIII, No. 3, Hong Kong, September 1990, pp. 158–175.

21 *Cf.*, Robert Elliott Allinson, 'Six Arguments for the Primacy of the Proscriptive Formulation of the Golden Rule in the Jewish and Chinese Confucian Ethical Traditions', Peter Kupfer, (ed.), *Youtai- Presence of Jews and Judaism in China*, Frankfurt am Main, Berlin, Bruxelles, New York, Oxford, Vienna: Peter Lang, 2008, pp. 289–308.

22 *Cf., Analects*, IV, 15; XV, 3.

23 *Cf., Analects*, II, 5–8; *Cf.*, also, I, 11; XVII, 21. The notion of filial piety and fraternal submission (in Legge's rendition) being at the root of morality is Yu Tzu's saying, not Confucius', *Analects*, I, 2. This point is overlooked by many scholars. In any case, filial piety is the place where one first learns love which is then extended to all persons. It does not mean that it disappears when it is so extended. It is only that, if we credit Yu Tzu's saying as representing the view of Confucius, that the family is the first venue for learning love. That the family is the first venue for learning love, would be, in any case, an empirical fact based on the cultural existence of the nuclear family unit.

24 *Mencius*, IV, A, 27. Even in this passage, when one considers the textual context, it may well be that Mencius is specifying how one relates to one's parents morally (by

serving them), and how one relates to one's elder brothers (by obeying them) and not limiting morality to these applications. In VII, A, 15, similarly, he may be citing filial and fraternal behavior as moral examples.

25 While Mencius considers morality to be natural to human beings, one could argue that the roots of what is explicit in Mencius are implicit in Confucius. Consider, for example, *Analects*, VII, 30. 'No sooner do I desire it [benevolence] than it is here.' There is no mention of learned behavior here. All one has to do is to aspire to morality and it is immediately available. For Mao's incorporation of morality into human nature, please see Chapter 3, above.

26 Ross Terrill, *Mao*, New York: Harper & Row, 1980, p. 36. (This could also reflect Buddhist sentiments in equal measure.)

27 *Analects*, II, 4. While on the one hand, this passage could be criticized as reflecting an uncommon instance of self-praise in Confucius, such self-congratulation could be diminished by the argument that one has set the bar too low by achieving a harmony between nature and morality only at the age of seventy.

28 *Analects*, IV, 16; XIV, 12; XVI, 10; XIX, 1.

29 *Analects*, XV, 24.

30 *Mencius*, II A: 6.

31 Marginal Notes, p. 271.

32 Ibid., p. 271.

33 Ibid., pp. 263–264.

34 *Mencius*, translated with an Introduction by D. C. Lau, London: Penguin Books, 1970, Introduction, p. 25.

35 *Mencius*, II, Pt. 1, Ch. 11, 16. (emphasis in Legge, p. 190).

36 *Mencius*, III, Pt. 2, Ch. 11, 3. (emphasis in Legge, p. 265.)

37 Marginal Notes, pp. 263–264.

38 Marginal Notes, p. 207.

39 Ibid., pp. 306–307.

40 Ibid., p. 308.

41 Ibid., pp. 286–287.

42 This question is not unique to Mao as it also pertains to Lenin whose philosophical tracts, it may be argued, are more technical than Mao's. However one decides this issue, the fact remains that Mao was both schooled in philosophy and actively constructed his philosophy.

43 Ibid., pp. 246–247.

44 Schram asserts that '… Mao is not original, nor even competent; and yet, he has a profoundly philosophical turn of mind.' *Cf.*, Stuart Schram, 'Mao Tse-tung and the Theory of the Permanent Revolution, 1958–1969', *The China Quarterly*, No. 46, April–June 1971, p. 223. I am not sure that I agree with Schram's assessment of Mao's lack of originality.

45 Marginal Notes, p. 292.
46 Ibid., p. 294.
47 Friedrich Nietzsche, *Beyond Good & Evil, Prelude to a Philosophy of the Future*, translated with Commentary by Walter Kaufmann, New York: Random House, 1989, p. 90.
48 *The Portable Nietzsche*, p. 493. (emphasis in the original)
49 Friedrich Nietzsche, *Thus Spoke Zarathustra*, trans. Walter Kaufman, New York: Random House, 1995, p. 27.
50 Ibid.
51 *Cf*., Robert E. Allinson, 'Having Your Cake and Eating It, Too: Evaluation and Transvaluation in Chuang Tzu and Nietzsche', *Journal of Chinese Philosophy*, Vol. 13, No. 4, December 1986, pp. 419–443 for a more detailed exposition of Nietzsche.
52 Walter Kaufmann, *Nietzsche*, 4th Edition, Princeton: Princeton University Press, 1974, p. 309.
53 *Cf*., Ross Terrill, *Mao*, New York: Harper and Row, 1980, p. 9.
54 Edgar Snow, *Red Star Over China*, New York: Grove Press, 1968, p. 132. The interpolations I am drawing regarding Mao's description of his father and his later aversion to capitalism are of my own devising.
55 Ibid., p. 135.
56 Burton Watson, *The Complete Works of Chuang Tzu*, New York: Columbia University Press, 1968, p. 200. Watson's translation carries more of the point of the story than the translation of Angus Graham. While I had the privilge of knowing both of these great translators, in the main, I have always preferred the translations of my humble, learned and charming former colleague, the late Burton Watson, a sincere and authentic *literatus*.

Chapter 5

1 According to Xiao Yanzhong, Mao Zedong Thought is no longer part of SCC. In this present volume, this is not relevant because the phrase 'Mao Zedong Thought' is used to refer to Mao's official philosophy and does not form a part of our study which is focused on Mao's individual philosophy. *Cf*., Xiao Yanzhong, 'Recent Mao Zedong Scholarship in China', Timothy Cheek, (ed.), *A Critical Introduction to Mao*, Cambridge: Cambridge University Press, 2010, p. 274, 5 *et passim*.

2 The cyclical movement of the *yi* is epitomized by the fact that there is no hexagram for completion. The cycle of changes is never complete. There is Hexagram 63 which is before completion followed by Hexagram 64 which is after completion. One nearly reaches completion and then completion is over. There is never actually any completion. In Hexagram 63, water is over fire; in Hexagram 64, the final hexagram, fire is over water. This is a change of opposites and reminds us of the change that takes

place from the first to the second hexagram. There is a continuous movement from yang or the predominance of yang to yin and yin or the predominance of yin back to yang. This is the cyclical nature of the *yi*. There is much more detail in terms of the movement of the lines, but such considerations take us beyond the scope of this work.

3   The philosophy of the *Yijing* is characterized by the theory of yin-yang complementarity and cyclical change in order to achieve a balance when either the yin or the yang becomes too strong. For a study of how the philosophy of yin-yang influenced Niels Bohr's influential concept of complementarity in Western physics, *cf.*, Robert Elliott Allinson, 'Complementarity as a Model for East-West Integrative Philosophy', *Journal of Chinese Philosophy*, Vol. 25 No. 4, 1998, pp. 505–517. The present author was amazed to discover from a personal interview with Bohr's grandson, Christian, that Bohr was familiar with the *Daodejing* and a copy of it in Danish translation was in their home. The discovery of a letter written by Bohr to a Danish school teacher also revealed Bohr's acquaintance with the *Daodejing*. In the article cited above, evidence is drawn from Bohr's life and education to illustrate the influence of yin-yang philosophy on Bohr's thinking.

4   The principal and secondary aspects of the contradiction will be discussed in the sequel.

5   Stuart Schram, *The Thought of Mao Tse-Tung*, Cambridge: Cambridge University Press, 1989, p. 237.

6   Ibid., pp. 237–238. Mao does refer to the end goal of reaching Great Harmony in his 'On the People's Democratic Dictatorship,' on 30 June, 1949 in *Selected Works of Mao Tse-tung*, https://www.marxists.org/reference/archive/mao/selected-works/volume-4/mswv4_65.htm, accessed 31 March 2019.

7   Mao Zedong, 'Spring Festival Day on Education', Jerome Ch' en, (ed.), *Mao Papers, Anthology and Bibliography*, London: Oxford University Press, 1970, p. 95.

8   On the other hand, there is a difference in that while Laozi possessed the intention of a return to the Dao, Mao had no such intention. I am grateful to the celebrated historian of China, Irene Eber, for pointing this out to me.

9   The aftermath of Mao's Cultural Revolution had many ironic twists. When I was offering a seminar to the Department of Philosophy on 'What is Living and Dead in Marxism' at Nanjing University in 1984, one only saw the Chinese people outfitted in the ubiquitous blue cotton jackets, sometimes complemented by black trousers. By 1988, when I was Visiting Professor at Fudan University in Shanghai, all of this was to change. The students were all regaled in more fashionable, colourful Western style clothing.

10 Mao introduced the People's Commune system in the summer of 1958. *Cf.*, Francis Y. K. Soo, *Mao Tse-Tung's Theory of Dialectic*, Vol. 44, Dordrecht, Boston, London: D. Reidel Publishing Company, 1981, p. 25.

11 The dialectic, while the invention of Fichte and not Hegel, is commonly attributed to Hegel, as Hegel's philosophy was to give it historical prominence.

12 Stuart Schram, *The Thought of Mao Tse-Tung*, Cambridge: Cambridge University Press, 1989, p. 63.

13 Ibid., p. 137.
14 Ibid., p. 139. (emphasis in original)
15 *Selected Works of Mao Tse-Tung*, 'On Contradiction', Vol. I, Peking: Foreign Languages Press, 1967, p. 321.
16 Stuart Schram, *The Thought of Mao Tse-Tung*, Cambridge: Cambridge University Press, 1989, p. 137.
17 Stuart Schram, *The Thought of Mao Tse-Tung*, Cambridge: Cambridge University Press, 1989, p. 141. *Cf*., 'Oppose Book Worship', *Selected Readings*, 34. (*Analects*, VII, 2); Legge, *The Chinese Classics*, Taipei: SMC Publishing Inc., 1998, I, p. 195; Mao, *Selected Works*, Peking: Foreign Languages Press, 1968, pp. 4, 378; (*Analects*, V, 14); Legge, 1, 178.
18 The late philosopher Charles Fu depicted 'Mao's Thought as a dialectical synthesis of Marxism-Leninism and Confucian ethical humanism.' *Cf*., Charles W. H. Fu, 'Confucianism, Marxist-Leninism and Mao: A Critical Study', *Journal of Chinese Philosophy*, Vol. 1, 1973–1974, p. 340.
19 Slavoj Žižek, 'Three Notes on China: Past and Present', *Positions*, Vol. 3, No. 19, Winter 2011, p. 718.
20 Robert Elliott Allinson, 'Circles Within a Circle: The Condition for the Possibility of an Ethical Business Enterprise Within a Market System', *Journal of Business Ethics*, 54, 2004, pp. 261–277.

Chapter 6

1 Findlay had planned to offer a graduate seminar in Hegel's *Logic*. Since I had already studied Hegel's *Logic* in a graduate seminar with the great Hegelian, Errol E. Harris, I wrote a letter to Findlay who was at the University of London and asked him if he would offer a course in Hegel's *Phenomenology* instead. To my great surprise and delight, he graciously agreed.
2 For this reason, it is difficult to follow Tian's argument that Mao's vision of the dialectic is guided by the notion of continuity. *Cf*., Tian Chenshan, 'Mao Zedong: The Mature Formulation of Dialectical Materialism', *Chinese Dialectics from Yijng to Marxism*, Lanham: Lexington Books, 2005, pp. 143–172.
3 'On Contradiction', August 1957, Mao Tse-Tung, *Four Essays on Philosophy*, Peking: Foreign Languages Press, 1968, p. 35.
4 He related this in an answer to Edgar Snow's question as to whether he had read Hegel. *Cf*., Edgar Snow's Interview with Chairman Mao Tse-Tung, http://www.marxistsfr.org/reference/archive/mao/selected-works/volume-9/appendix.htm The interview was held on 9 January 1965.

5   Xu Quanxing, 'From the "Negation of the Negation" to "Affirmation and Negation" in Mao Zedong's Thought,' *Chinese Studies in Philosophy*, Vol. 23, Nos. 3–4, Spring–Summer 1992, p. 221.

6   Stuart Schram, *The Thought of Mao Tse-Tung*, Cambridge: Cambridge University Press, 1989, p. 65.

7   Ibid., 140.

8   Nick Knight, (ed.), *Mao Zedong on Dialectical Materialism, Writings on Philosophy, 1937*, Armonk, New York: M. E. Sharpe, Inc., 1990, p. 23.

9   Stuart Schram, *The Thought of Mao Tse-Tung*, Cambridge: Cambridge University Press, 1989, p. 64, n. 112.

10 Nick Knight, 'On Contradiction and on Practice: Pre-Liberation Texts,' *China Quarterly*, No. 84 December 1980, p. 648.

11 Mao Zedong, 'Speech at Hangchow', 21 December 1965, Stuart Schram, (ed.), trans. John Chinnery and Tieyun Chinnery, *Mao Tse-tung Unrehearsed, Talks and Lectures, 1956–1971*, Harmondsworth: Penguin Books, 1975, pp. 240–241. This is substantially the same point I argued (without knowing Mao's argument) in my 'Self-Contradictory Propositions in Logic', presented for The National Meeting of the Society for the Philosophical Study of Marxism, Miami University, Oxford, Ohio, 18 April 1975.

12 'Talk on Questions of Philosophy' 18 August 1964, Slavoj Žižek, *On Practice and Contradiction, Mao tse-Tung*, London and New York: Verso, 2007, p. 181.

13 Ibid., p. 21.

14 *Cf.*, n. 12, p. 225.

15 Ibid., p. 226. *Cf.*, Mao Tse-Tung, *Selected Works of Mao Tse-tung*, Vol. I, Peking: Foreign Languages Press, p. 273.

16 Vsevolod Holubnychy, 'Mao Tse-tung's Materialistic Dialectics', *The China Quarterly*, No. 19, July–September 1964, p. 31.

17 Xu Quanxing, 'From the "Negation of the Negation" to "Affirmation and Negation" in Mao Zedong's Thought,' *Chinese Studies in Philosophy*, Vol. 23, Nos. 3–4, Spring–Summer 1992, p. 229.

18 Stuart Schram, *The Thought of Mao Tse-Tung*, Cambridge: Cambridge University Press, 1989, p. 137. Arthur Cohen considers that these philosophical ruminations of Mao are superficial, but they do not strike me this way. *Cf.*, Arthur Cohen, *The Communism of Mao Tse-tung*, Chicago: University of Chicago Press, 1964, p. 22.

19 Ibid., p. 137. *Cf.*, Schram's observation that 'his [Mao's] understanding of dialectics was strongly marked by Taoism and other currents in traditional Chinese thought.' Ibid., p. 63.

20 Ibid., p. 136.

21 Ibid., p. 67. The concept of the will is hardly absent even in Hegel. One only needs to have recourse to Hegel's discussion of world historical men such as Napoleon in his

Philosophy of History to realize how much Hegel attributed the movement of history to the wilful and willed action of such men as Napoleon. One recalls Hegel's famous saying, 'Nothing great in the world has ever been accomplished without passion.'

22 Ibid., p. 17. (emphasis in original) It is difficult, when one reads passages such as this, not to consider the primary place of voluntarism in the development of Mao's individual philosophy. Tian seems to argue that the elevation of voluntarism in the voluntarism-determinism debate arises because of a lack of understanding of Marxism on the part of Mao's commentators, particularly Schram. However, it is clear from Mao's own pre-Marxist writing that voluntarism is for Mao a key determinant of human behaviour. *Cf.*,Tian Chenshan, *Chinese Dialectics from Yijng to Marxism*, Lanham: Lexington Books, 2005, pp. 1–19, *et passim*.

23 The unlikelihood that Mao derived his voluntarism from Lenin is heightened when one takes note of the fact that the official version of Mao Zedong thought criticizes Mao's philosophy for placing too much emphasis on the role of subjective will and effort. *Cf.*, Su Shaozhi, 'The Study of Mao Zedong Thought in Contemporary China,' *The Philosophical Thought of Mao Zedong, Studies from China*, 1981–1989, p. 60.

24 *Cf.* n. 22., p. 136.

25 For comparisons between the dialectic of the *Yijing* and Hegel, *cf.*, Robert E. Allinson, 'Complementarity as a Model for East-West Integrative Philosophy', *Journal of Chinese Philosophy*, Vol. 25, No. 4, December 1998, pp. 505–517.

26 Mao Tse-Tung, *Four Essays on Philosophy*, Peking: Foreign Languages Press, 1968, p. 87.

27 'On the Correct Handling of Contradictions Among the People,' Mao Tse-Tung, *Four Essays on Philosophy*, Peking: Foreign Languages Press, 1968, 79. According to Soo, Mao gave his celebrated speech, 'On the Correct Handling of Contradictions among the People' in February of 1957. *Cf.*, Francis Y. K. Soo, *Mao Tse-Tung's Theory of Dialectic*, Vol. 44, Dordrecht, Boston, London: D. Reidel Publishing Company, 1981, p. 25.

28 Ibid., p. 78.

29 Stuart Schram, *The Thought of Mao Tse-Tung*, Cambridge: Cambridge University Press, 1989, p. 152. Schram notes that in the official version of the 27 February 1957 speech, Mao's judgment of Lenin is turned into its opposite: Lenin, it reads, 'gave a very clear exposition of this law'. Ibid., p. 152, n. 166.

30 Mao Zedong, 'Speech at Hangchow' 21 December 1965,' Stuart Schram, (ed.), trans. John and Tieyun Chinnery, *Mao Tse-tung Unrehearsed, Talks and Lectures*, 1956–1971, Harmondsworth: Penguin Books, 1975, p. 240.

31 Mao Zedong, 'Talk on Questions of Philosophy,' Stuart Schram, (ed.), trans. John and Tieyun Chinnery, *Mao Tse-tung Unrehearsed, Talks and Lectures*, 1956–1971, Harmondsworth: Penguin Books, 1975, p. 226.

32 *Hegel's Science of Logic*, trans. A. V. Miller, Foreword by my beloved late professor, J. N. Findlay, Amherst, New York: Humanity Books, 1969, p. 370. (emphasis in original)

33 Ibid., pp. 370–371.

34 Stuart Schram, (ed.), trans. John Chinnery and Tieyun Chinnery, *Mao Tse-tung Unrehearsed, Talks and Lectures*, 1956–1971, Harmondsworth: Penguin Books, 1975, p. 26.

35 Mao Tse-Tung, *Four Essays on Philosophy*, Peking: Foreign Languages Press, 1968, pp. 66–67.

36 In the interview with Edgar Snow, he revealed that he had written both 'On Contradiction' and 'On Practice' in the summer of 1937 and had stayed up to write them both during the course of the night. In the famous interview with Edgar Snow, Snow relates that 'I myself [Snow] seem to recall having seen unpublished longhand translations of those essays ['On Contradiction' and 'On Practice'] in the summer of 1938. Would you give me your own opinion about when you composed these two essays? He [Mao] replied that he had indeed written them in the summer of 1937 ... Mao said he wrote most of the night and slept during the day. What he had written over a period of weeks he delivered in lecture form in a matter of two hours' *Cf.*, Francis Soo, *Mao Tse-Tung's Theory of Dialectic*, Dordrecht, Boston, London: D. Reidel Publishing Company, Vol. 44, 1981, p. 162. Soo quotes from Snow's, *The Long Revolution*, New York: Random House, 1972, pp. 205–207. What is striking to the present author is that Mao wrote these seminal essays in a matter of a few weeks.

37 Mao Tse-Tung, *Four Essays on Philosophy*, Peking: Foreign Languages Press, 1968, p. 66.

38 Stuart Schram, *The Thought of Mao Tse-Tung*, Cambridge: Cambridge University Press, 1989, p 187. *Cf.*, *Selected Works of Mao Tse-tung*, Vol. II, pp. 765–786. For a detailed history of The One Divides into Two Controversy, *Cf.*, marxistphilosophy.org/ChinTrans1221html

39 D. C. Lau translation.

40 'On the Correct Handling of Contradictions Among the People,' *Four Essays on Philosophy*, Peking: Foreign Languages Press, 1968, p. 81.

41 Wakeman points out that in 1920 Mao was acquainted with Kirkup's, *History of Socialism* which describes socialism as undergoing continuous transformation. *Cf.*, Frederick Wakeman, *History & Will: Philosophical Perspectives of Mao Tse Tung's Thought*, Berkeley, Los Angeles, London: University of California Press, 1973, p. 216.

42 Stuart Schram, 'The Marxist,' Dick Wilson, (ed.), *Mao Tse-Tung in the Scales of History, A Preliminary Assessment Organized by the China Quarterly*, Cambridge: Cambridge University Press, 1978, pp. 63–64.

43 Mao Tse-Tung, *Four Essays on Philosophy*, Peking: Foreign Languages Press, 1968.

44 Ibid., p. 114.

45 Ibid., p. 51, 54. *Cf.*, On Contradiction, *Selected Works of Mao Tse-Tung*, Vol. I, Peking: Foreign Languages Press, 1968, p. 333.

46 *Hegel's Science of Logic*, trans. A. V. Miller, Foreword by Professor J. N. Findlay, Amherst, New York: Humanity Books, 1969, p. 354. (emphasis in original)

47 Nick Knight, 'Mao Zedong's on Contradiction and on Practice: Pre-Liberation Texts,' *China Quarterly*, No. 84, December 1980, p. 648.

48 Ibid., p. 655.

49 Ibid., pp. 654–655.

50 Shi Zhongquan, 'A New Document for the Study of Mao Zedong's Philosophical Thought: Introducing *The Philosophical Annotations of Mao Zedong*', *Chinese Studies in Philosophy*, Vol. 23, Nos. 3–4, 1992, p. 138.

51 Stuart Schram, *The Thought of Mao Tse-Tung*, Cambridge: Cambridge University Press, 1989, p. 66.

52 *Cf.*, n. 50, p. 58.

53 Arthur Cohen, *The Communism of Mao-tse tung*, Chicago: University of Chicago Press, 1964, p. 23.

54 Nick Knight, 'Mao Zedong's on Contradiction and on Practice: Pre-Liberation Texts,' *China Quarterly*, No. 84, December 1980, p. 650. *Cf.*, Cohen, *The Communist Thought of Mao Tse-Tung*, p. 23.

55 Ibid., p. 651.

56 Ibid., p. 653.

57 Karl A. Wittfogel, 'Some Remarks on Mao's Handling of Concepts and Problems of Dialectics', *Studies in Soviet Thought*, Vol. III, No. 4, December 1963, pp. 251–269. Mao denies authorship of *Dialectical Materialism*. *Cf.*, Stuart Schram, *The Thought of Mao Tse-Tung*, Cambridge: Cambridge University Press, 1989, p. 62.

58 Ibid., p. 62.

59 Stuart Schram, 'The Formative Years: A Preliminary Reassessment,' 1917–1937, Mao Zedong, (ed.), *A Preliminary Assessment*, Hong Kong: The Chinese University Press, 1983, p. 20.

60 Stuart Schram, review article, 'Mao Tse-tung as a Marxist Dialectician,' review of Arthur A. Cohen, 'The Communism of Mao Tse-tung', *The China Quarterly*, No. 29, January–March 1967, p. 158.

61 Nick Knight, (ed.), *Mao Zedong on Dialectical Materialism, Writings on Philosophy, 1937*, Armonk, New York: M. E. Sharpe, Inc., 1990, p. 37.

62 Ibid., pp. 33–34.

63 Stuart Schram, *The Thought of Mao Tse-Tung*, Cambridge: Cambridge University Press, 1989, pp. 66–67.

64 Lee Feigon, Mao, *A Reinterpretation*, Chicago: University of Chicago Press, 2002, p. 72.

65 Maurice Meisner, *Mao Zedong*, Cambridge: Polity Press, 2007, p. 94.

66 Arthur A. Cohen, 'How Original Is "Maoism"?' *Problems of Communism*, Vol. X, No. 6, 1961, p. 35. *Cf.*, John E. Rue, 'Is Mao Tse-tung's "Dialectical Materialism" A Forgery?' *The Journal of Asian Studies*, Vol. 26, No. 3, May, 1967, pp. 464–468.

67 Vsevolod Holubnychy 'Mao Tse-tung's Materialistic Dialectics', *The China Quarterly*, No. 19, July–September 1964, p. 12.

68 *Cf.*, Adam Schaff, *Marxism and the Human Individual*, New York: McGraw-Hill Book Company, 1970. For a comparison between the two, *cf.*, Normal Levine, *The Tragic Deception: Marx Contra Engels*, Oxford: Clio Books, 1975.

69 According to Vsevolod Holubnychy, Marx's, *Economic and Philosophical Manuscripts of 1844* were not available in Chinese in China in 1964. 'Mao Tse-tung's Materialistic Dialectics', *The China Quarterly*, No. 19, July–September 1964, p. 11.

70 Andrew G. Walder, 'Marxism, Maoism and Social Change', *Modern China*, Vol. 3, No. 1–2, January 1977, p. 110. Schram refers to Marx's comment that he was happy to consign the *German Ideology* to the 'gnawing criticism of the mice'. *Cf.*, Stuart Schram, 'Some Reflections on the Pfeffer-Walder "Revolution: In China Studies"', *Modern China*, Vol. 3, No. 2, April 1977, p. 171.

71 Andrew G. Walder, 'Marxism, Maoism and Social Change', *Modern China*, Vol. 3, No. 1–2, January 1977, pp. 111–112 (the word 'only' is emphasized in original).

72 Andrew G. Walder, 'Marxism, Maoism and Social Change: A Reexamination of the "Voluntarism" in Mao's Strategy and Thought', *Modern China*, Vol. 3, No. 2, April 1977, pp. 125–160. For Schram, the inner connections between superstructure and base are already part of Marx's thinking. *Cf.*, Stuart Schram, 'Some Reflections on the Pfeffer-Walder "Revolution"', in China Studies, *Modern China*, April 1977, Vol. 3, No. 2. Schram also presents the view that for Marx, historical causality was more deterministic in the feudal and capitalist stages than after the socialist revolution. Ibid., pp. 179–180.

73 Liu Kang, 'Poeticizing Revolution: Žižek's Misreading of Mao and China,' *Positions*, Vol. 19, No. 2, 2011, p. 635. The original source for this quotation is, Mao Tse-Tung, 'On New Democracy,' *Selected Works of Mao Tse-tung*, Vol. I, Peking: Foreign Languages Press, p. 382.

74 Nick Knight, *Mao Zedong on Dialectical Materialism, Writings on Philosophy, 1937*, Armonk, New York: M. E. Sharpe, Inc., 1990, pp. 60–61.

75 Knight thinks that the essays *On Contradiction* and *On Practice* were apparently written by Mao himself. *Cf.*, Nick Knight, *Mao Zedong on Dialectical Materialism, Writings on Philosophy, 1937*, Armonk, New York: M. E. Sharpe, Inc., 1990, p. 31.

76 Robert E. Allinson, *Chuang-Tzu For Spiritual Transformation: An Analysis of the Inner Chapters*, Albany: State University of New York Press at Albany, 1989, 2006.

Chapter 7

1 Slavoj Žižek, *On Practice and Contradiction, Mao tse-Tung*, London and New York: Verso, 2007, p. 184.

2 Ibid., p. 182. Mao has omitted the fact that Zhuangzi first cries when his wife dies before he bangs on a basin and sings.

3   Friedman writes that, 'Philosophy of science was of continuing interest to Mao from his youth onwards. He wanted to be sure he understood the nature of biology, microphysics, epistemology, of life, of matter, knowledge and the universe. ... Mao ... had concluded that his Marxism, his revolutionary theory, was true because it was Einsteinian [here, Mao was mistaken in his attribution of the new physics to Einstein]. As Mao saw it, knowledge and revolution both advanced in waves of new practice followed by waves of newer practice ... He seemed knowledgeable about the arcane as well as the prosaic, the theoretical as well as the concrete. It was difficult to contend that Mao did not understand the dynamics of the universe.' *Cf.*, Edward Friedman, 'Einstein and Mao: Metaphors of Revolution,' *The China Quarterly*, No. 93, March 1983, pp. 51–57.

4   *Cf.*, n. 1, pp. 106–107.

5   Ibid., p. 176. Even Marxism, according to Mao, would have its birth, development and death. *Cf.*, Friedman Edward, 'Einstein and Mao: Metaphors of Revolution', *The China Quarterly*, No. 93, March 1983, p. 62. According to the historian Maurice Meisner, Mao suggests to Snow in their 1965 interview the possible future bourgeois corruption of his own revolution. *Cf.*, Maurice Meisner, 'Leninism and Maoism: Some Populist Perspectives on Marxist-Leninism in China,' *The China Quarterly*, No. 45, January–March 1971, p. 25. It is difficult to reconcile these writings of Mao with Tian's interpretation of Mao's thought as emphasizing continuity. *Cf.*, Tian Chenshan, *Chinese Dialectics from Yijng to Marxism*, Lanham: Lexington Books, 2005, pp. 143–172, *et passim*.

6   Marginal Notes, p. 303.

7   Ibid., p. 304.

8   Ibid., p. 306.

9   Ibid., p. 307.

10 Ibid., p. 322.

11 Ibid., p. 322.

12 Stuart R. Schram, 'The Formative Years: A Preliminary Assessment,' 1917–1937, *Mao Zedong, A Preliminary Assessment*, Hong Kong: The Chinese University Press, 1983, p. 15.

13 Marginal Notes, p. 284.

14 Ibid., p. 294.

15 Ibid., p. 294.

16 Ibid., p. 250.

17 Mao Zedong, 'Talks on Questions of Philosophy,' Stuart Schram, (ed.), trans. John and Tieyun Chinnery, *Mao Tse-tung Unrehearsed, Talks and Lectures*, 1956–1971, Harmondsworth: Penguin Books, 1975, pp. 227–229.

18 Cheng Yinghong, 'Maoist Discussion on Physics and the Cultural Revolution,' Nancy Chunjuan Wei and Darryl E. Brock, (eds.), *Mr. Science and Chairman Mao's*

Cultural Revolution, Science and Technology in Modern China, New York: Lexington Books, 2014, pp. 210–211. *Cf.*, Edward Friedman, 'Einstein and Mao: Metaphors of Revolution,' *The China Quarterly*, No. 93, March 1983, pp. 51–75. I remember a lecture given by C. N. Yang at The Chinese University of Hong Kong in which he related that the idea for which he was awarded the Nobel prize came to him while he was brushing his teeth.

19   These photographs have come to me via the courtesy of Professor Zuoyue Wang, Professor of History at California State Polytechnic University at Pomona. First photograph: Mao Zedong and C. N. Yang, 19 July 1973, from C. N. Yang, *Dushu jiaoxue sishinian (Learning and teaching for four decades)*, Hong Kong: Hong Kong Branch of Sanlian Press, 1985, p. 148. Second photograph: Zhou Enlai, Zhou Peiyuan, Mao Zedong and C. N. Yang, 19 July 1973, from Liu Huaizu, *Beijing zhengfu dianzi duizhuangji (Beijing electron positron collider)*, Beijing: Science Press, 1994, p. 12. 杨振宁,《读书教学四十年》(香港:三联书店香港分店, 1985), 148. 柳怀祖(主编),《北京正负电子对撞机》(北京:科学出版社, 1994), p. 12.

20   *Cf.*, n. 18, p. 202. Western readers are familiar with this paradox as it is formulated by Zeno.

21   Ibid., p. 202.

22   Stuart Schram, *The Thought of Mao Tse-Tung*, Cambridge: Cambridge University Press, 1989, p. 96. *Cf.*, also, Robert Elliott Allinson, 'An Overview of the Chinese Mind,' *Understanding the Chinese Mind: The Philosophical Roots*, Oxford and New York: Oxford University Press, 1989, 2000 (tenth impression), pp. 1–25.

23   According to Friedman, Mao would lecture those around him on Kant. *Cf.*, Edward Friedman, 'Einstein and Mao: Metaphors of Revolution,' *The China Quarterly*, No. 93, March 1983, p. 54.

24   I am indebted to the renowned historian of China, Irene Eber, for this insight. The opposite view is held by Arndt who thinks that in the synthesis of Chinese and Marxist philosophy that Marxism plays the dominant role. *Cf.*, Andrea Arndt's review of Francis Soo's, 'The Synthesis of Chinese and Western Philosophy in Mao Tse-Tung's Theory of Dialectics', *Studies in Soviet Thought*, Vol. 22, No. 3, August 1981, p. 203. There is the view that Mao's philosophical grounding in science had priority over his Marxist ideas. *Cf.*, Edward Friedman, 'Einstein and Mao: Metaphors of Revolution,' *The China Quarterly*, No. 93, March 1983, p. 68.

25   This is in accord with the view of Francis Soo, who, reflecting on the tradition of Chinese philosophy, concludes that by the standards of Chinese philosophy, Mao should rightly be considered as a philosopher *per se*. *Cf.*, Francis Y. K. Soo, *Mao Tse-Tung's Theory of Dialectic*, Vol. 44, Dordrecht, Boston, London: D. Reidel Publishing Company, 1981, p. 136. Soo concludes that Mao differs from the Chinese philosophical tradition post Confucius, Laozi, etc. that tends always to comment on the Classics, because Mao does not comment on the Classics. On the other hand, since Mao's writings are unsystematic, humanistic, and emphasize the unity of theory and action, they fit closely within the Chinese philosophical tradition. In this regard, I would add, since Mao's writings are original and not commentaries, Mao

most closely resembles the Masters of the classical period. Further, Mao's writings do include systematic essays.

26 *Cf.*, n. 24, p. 68. This might be an example of what the French call la *sagesse chinoise*.

27 Raya Dunayevskaya, *Philosophy and Revolution, from Hegel to Sartre, and from Marx to Mao*, New York: Delacorte Press, 1973, p. 164.

28 Mao was familiar with Chinese history as well. Joseph Liu quotes from Mao's accounts of peasant rebellions in China from the Third century BCE through the Seventeenth century CE. To choose only one example of Mao's historical reflections: 'Li Tzu-cheng, also called King Chuang (the Dare-All King), native of Michih, northern Shensi, was the leader of a peasant revolt which led to the overthrow of the Ming Dynasty. The revolt first started in northern Shensi in 1628. Li joined the forces led by Kao Ying-hsiang and campaigned through Honan and Anhwei and back to Shensi. After Kao's death in 1636, Li succeeded him, becoming King Chuang, and campaigned in and out of the provinces of Shensi, Szechuan, Honan and Hupeh. Finally, he captured the imperial capital of Peking in 1644, whereupon the last Ming emperor committed suicide. The chief slogan he spread among the masses was "Support King Chuang, and pay no grain taxes." Another slogan of his to enforce discipline among his men ran: "Any murder means the killing of my father, any rape means the violation of my mother." Thus he won the support of the masses and his movement became the main current of the peasant revolts raging all over the country. As he, too, roamed about without ever establishing relatively consolidated base areas, he was eventually defeated by Wu San-kuei, a Ming general, who colluded with the Ching troops in a joint attack on Li.' *Cf.*, Joseph Liu, 'Mao's On Contradiction,' *Studies in Soviet Thought*, Vol. 11, 1971, p. 87. Liu's source for Mao's historical accounts is Mao Tse-Tung, *Selected Works of Mao Tse-tung*, Vols. II and III, Foreign Language Press, 1967.

29 *Cf.*, Wang Ruoshui, *Xin faxian de Mao Zedong: Puren yanzhong de weiren* (*A Newly Discovered Mao Zedong: The Great Man in the Eyes of His Servant*), Hong Kong: Mingbao chubanshe, 2002, pp. 2–3. *Cf.*, Xiao Yanzhong, 'Recent Mao Zedong Scholarship in China,' Timothy Cheek, (ed.), *A Critical Introduction to Mao*, Cambridge: Cambridge University Press, 2010, p. 278.

30 Norman Levine, 'Non-Marxist Elements in the Communism of Mao,' *Asian Thought & Society*, Vol. 1, No. 3, 1976, p. 209.

31 *Cf.*, Timothy Cheek, 'Mao, Revolution and Memory,' Timothy Cheek, (ed.), *A Critical Introduction to Mao*, Cambridge: Cambridge University Press, 2010, p. 7.

32 *Cf.*,Tian Chenshan, *Chinese Dialectics from Yijng to Marxism*, Lanham: Lexington Books, 2005, pp. 144–145. *Cf.*, Lin Ke, 'Memoirs of Mao Studying English,' Gong Yuzhi, et al., (eds.), *Mao Zedong's Reading Life*, Sanlian shudian, 1987, pp. 249–251.

33 Ross Terrill, *Mao*, New York: Harper and Row, 1980, p. 294. *Cf.*, Mao Zedong, 'Speech at the Tenth Plenum,' Stuart Schram, (ed.), trans. John and Tieyun Chinnery, *Mao Tse-tung Unrehearsed, Talks and Lectures*, 1956–1971, Harmondsworth: Penguin Books, 1975, p. 193.

34 Philip Short, *Mao, A Life*, New York: Henry Holt and Company, 1999, p. 448.

35 *Cf.*, n. 33, 1980, p. 295.

36 Richard Kraus, *The Cultural Revolution*, New York: Oxford University Press, 2012, p. 35.

37 Frederick Wakeman, *History & Will: Philosophical Perspectives of Mao Tse Tung's Thought*, Berkeley, Los Angeles, London: University of California Press, 1973, p. 98. Edgar Snow, *Red Star Over China*, New York: Grove Press, 1969, p. 133. *The Dream of the Red Chamber* is not included in the original list of books Mao recites to Snow of the books that influenced him but *The Romance of the Three Kingdoms* (*San Kuo*) is included. According to Francis Y. K. Soo, Mao frequently quoted 'from the writings of Confucius, Mencius, Lao-Tzu, Hsün-tze, Ssu-ma Chien, Chu Hsi and others … and made reference to 'the Book of Odes, the Tso-chuan, … The Heroes of the Marshes, and The Pilgrimage of the West.' *Cf.*, Francis Y. K. Soo, *Mao Tse-Tung's Theory of Dialectic*, Vol. 44, Dordrecht, Boston, London: D. Reidel Publishing Company, 1981, p. 36.

38 Lam, Lai Sing, *Conservatism and the Kissinger-Mao Axis, Development of the Twin Global Orders*, Lanham: Lexington Books, 2015, p. xiii.

39 Ibid., p. xiv.

40 Ibid., p. 33.

41 Mao-tse Tung, 'Talk on Questions of Philosophy,' Stuart Schram (ed.), trans. John and Tieyun Chinnery, *Mao Tse-tung Unrehearsed, Talks and Lectures*, 1956–1971, Harmondsworth: Penguin Books, 1975, p. 223.

42 *Cf.*, n. 37, p. 98.

43 Philip Short, *Mao, A Life*, New York: Henry Holt and Company, 1999, p. 27. (The author's last name and the modest title of his monograph are belied by the scope and detail of his comprehensive 782 page biography.)

44 Ibid., p. 359.

45 https://sites.dartmouth.edu/library/2014/11/07/mao-zedongs-calligraphic-art-2/

46 Johannes Kaminsky, 'Toward a Maoist Dream of the Red Chamber: Or, How Baoyu and Daiyu Became Rebels Against Feudalism,' *Journal of Chinese Humanities*, Vol. 3, 2017, p. 190. I am indebted to Irene Eber for the source of this quotation.

47 https://sites.dartmouth.edu/library/2014/11/07/mao-zedongs-calligraphic-art-2/; According to Tu Weiming, '… Mao time and time again acknowledged that six years of Confucian education in his youth had a profound influence in shaping his world view. He was familiar with the Four Books and the Five Classics. … he could recite long passages from *The Book of Poetry*. … On the Chinese New Year of 1964 … Mao made references to the Confucian "six arts" (ceremonies, music, archery, carriage-driving, writing, and mathematics). He expressed regret that the "main stream" (*chu-liu*) of Confucianism had been lost and urged his followers not to throw away the Confucian heritage. *Cf.*, Tu Wei-Ming, *Humanity and Self-Cultivation, Essays in Confucian Thought*, Boston: Cheng & Tsui Company, pp. 275–6. Tu draws much of his material from what he refers to as *Mao's Unpublished Statements*, Hoover Institute Version, 1968, pp. 550, 627, 461, 463. *Cf.*, Ibid., p. 293–4. In addition, Tu points out that 'Mao noted that his knowledge about warfare did not come from the *Sun Tzu*,

as many suspected, but from books much closer to the Confucian tradition, such as *Tso-chuan* (The Tso Commentary to the Spring and Autumn Annals), *Tzu-chih t'ung-chien* (General Mirror for the Aid of Government), and *San-kuo yen-i* (Romance of the Three Kingdoms). In a footnote, Tu adds that Mao claimed that these books did not help him in his military campaign. For that, he relied upon his direct involvement. Ibid., p. 294. Tu also asserts that there is no evidence of Mao making any systematic effort at eradicating the Confucian influence in his thought. As evidence of a seemingly open-minded attitude toward the Confucian tradition, Tu cites an article written in a journal published in 1972 by a close, personal friend of Mao's for decades, Kuo mo-jo, the president of the Academy of Science, that is written '… on a handwritten scroll of the Confucian Analects, dated 710 with poems and miscellaneous notes added toward the end.' Ibid., pp. 275–6.'

48 *Cf.*, Meisner, *Mao Tse Tung*, p. 189.

49 Henry Kissinger, *On China*, New York, Penguin Books, pp. 256–257. I am indebted to the Society for Anglo-Chinese Understanding for their kind authorization of the use of the photo of Mao and Kissinger.

50 Philip Short, *Mao, A Life*, New York: Henry Holt and Company, 1999, p. 365. Mao's classical education was not lost on him nor had he lost his literary talent.

Chapter 8

1 *Cf.*, Arthur Cohen, *The Communism of Mao-tse tung*, Chicago: University of Chicago Press, 1964, p. 13.

2 Ibid., p. 27.

3 Vsevolod Holubnychy, 'Mao Tse-tung's Materialistic Dialectics', *The China Quarterly*, No. 19, July–September 1964, p. 29.

4 Ibid., p. 29. Holubnychy's claim that Mao had not read Hegel is disputed by the account Mao gives to Edgar Snow as noted above.

5 Nick Knight, (ed.), *Mao Zedong on Dialectical Materialism, Writings on Philosophy, 1937*, Armonk, New York: M. E. Sharpe, Inc., 1990, p. 45. *Cf.*, Shi, 'A New Document for the Study of Mao Zedong's Philosophical Thought: Introducing *The Philosophical Annotations of Mao Zedong*,' *Chinese Studies in Philosophy*, Vol. 23, No. 3–4, 1992. *Cf., Hongqi* (Red Flag), No. 17, trans. Nick Knight, 1987, 138. Shi Zhongquan, 'A New Document for the Study of Mao Zedong's Philosophical Thought: Introducing *The Philosophical Annotations of Mao Zedong*', *Hongqi (Red Flag)*, trans. Nick Knight, No. 17, 1987, p. 138.

6 Arthur A. Cohen, 'How Original is 'Maoism'? *Problems of Communism*, Vol. X, Issue 6, 1961, p. 35. *Cf.*, Benjamin Schwartz, 'On the "originality" of Mao Tse-Tung', *Foreign Affairs*, Vol. 34, October 1955, p. 74.

7   Cf., Shi Zhongquan, 'A New Document for the Study of Mao Zedong's Philosophical Thought: Introducing *The Philosophical Annotations of Mao Zedong*,' *Hongqi (Red Flag)*, trans. Nick Knight, No. 17, 1987, p. 138.

8   Cf., Benjamin Schwartz, 'On the 'originality' of Mao Tse-Tung', *Foreign Affairs*, Vol. 34, October 1955, p. 74. Some scholars have argued that the Cultural Revolution represented a dictatorship of the proletariat. In this case peasant farmers are the stand-in for an industrial proletariat.

9   Maurice Meisner, 'The Advantage and Burden of Backwardness on Maoism and Marxism at the Close of the Maoist Era', *Asian Thought & Society*, Vol. 2, No. 1, 1977, p. 40. Meisner emphasizes Mao's departures from Marxism and comments that, 'His [Mao's] intellectual and theoretical contributions to Marxism were meagre, at best.' Cf., Meisner, *Mao Zedong*, p. vii. I cannot agree with this assessment.

10 *Hegel's Science of Logic*, trans. A. V. Miller, Foreword by my professor J. N. Findlay, Amherst, New York: Humanity Books, 1969, p. 369.

11 Cf., https://www.marxists.org/archive/marx/works/1883/don/ch02.htm

12 https://www.marxists.org/archive/marx/works/1883/don/ch02.htm

13 Stuart Schram, (ed.), trans. John and Tieyun Chinnery, *Mao Tse-tung Unrehearsed, Talks and Lectures, 1956–1971*, Harmondsworth: Penguin Books, 1975, p. 227.

14 Nick Knight, (ed.), *Mao Zedong on Dialectical Materialism, Writings on Philosophy, 1937*, Armonk, New York: M. E. Sharpe, Inc., 1990, pp. 45–46.

15 Stuart Schram, 'The Marxist,' Dick Wilson, (ed.), *Mao Tse-Tung in the Scales of History, A Preliminary Assessment Organized by the China Quarterly*, Cambridge: Cambridge University Press, 1978, pp. 63–64.

16 John E. Rue, *Mao Tse-tung in Opposition 1927–1935*, Stanford: Stanford University Press, 1966, p. 49.

17 *China Now*, 65, October 1976, p. 2.

18 Cf., Maurice Meisner, 'Mao and Marx in the Scholastic Tradition', *Modern China*, Vol. 3, No. 4, October 1977, p. 402.

19 Cf., Maurice Meisner, 'Communism and Maoism: Some Populist Perspectives on Marxist-Leninism in China', *The China Quarterly*, January–March, 1971, pp. 30, 33.

20 Levine points to certain statements of Mao that suggest Mao valued the achievement of the Great Harmony, but this point of view does not cohere with the majority of Mao's writing. Cf., Norman Levine, 'Non-Marxist Elements in the Communism of Mao,' *Asian Thought & Society*, Vol. 1, No. 3, 1976, p. 315.

21 The late philosopher Charles Fu presented an intriguing interpretation of Mao's permanent revolution as.... 'permanent revolution in the **superstructure,** [which] should be looked upon as exposing the *ultimate* meaning of Marxism-Leninism as fundamentally a moralistic working ideology of revolutionary praxis, based on the Marxian moral judgment about what man and society ought to be.' Cf., Charles Wei-Hsun Fu, 'Rejoinder to Professor Parson's Critical Remarks', *Journal of Chinese Philosophy*, Vol. 2, 1975, p. 447. (both emphases in the original)

22 Stuart Schram, 'Mao Tse-tung as Marxist Dialectician', A Review Article, Arthur Cohen, 'The Communism of Mao Tse-tung', *The China Quarterly*, No. 29 (January–March 1967) pp. 62–63. Whether the contradictions that continue to exist are antagonistic or non-antagonistic is a subject of interest.

23 Stuart Schram, 'Mao Tse-tung as Marxist Dialectician,' A Review Article, Arthur Cohen, *The Communism of Mao Tse-tung, The China Quarterly*, No. 29 (January–March 1967), p. 164.

24 *Cf.*, John M. Koller, 'Philosophical Aspects of Maoist Thought', *Studies in Soviet Thought*, Vol. 14, No. 1/2, March–June 1974, pp. 47, 56, 58. For Levine, Mao utilized Marxism as a means to achieve '…. the old Confucian ideal' *Cf.*, Norman Levine, 'Non-Marxist Elements in the Communism of Mao,' *Asian Thought & Society*, Vol. 1, No. 3, 1976, p. 319.

25 Timothy Cheek, 'Mao, Revolution and Memory,' Timothy Cheek, (ed.), *A Critical Introduction to Mao*, Cambridge: Cambridge University Press, 2010, p. 13.

26 Mao Tse-Tung, 'Talk on Questions of Philosophy,' ed. Stuart Schram, trans. John and Tieyun Chinnery, *Mao Tse-tung Unrehearsed, Talks and Lectures*, 1956–1971, Harmondsworth: Penguin Books, 1975, p. 225.

27 *Cf.*, Stuart Schram, 'The Marxist,' Dick Wilson, (ed.), *Mao Tse-Tung in the Scales of History, A Preliminary Assessment Organized by the China Quarterly*, Cambridge: Cambridge University Press, 1978, pp. 62–64. *Cf.*, Andrew G. Walder, 'Marxism, Maoism and Social Change', *Modern China*, Vol. 3, No. 1–2, January 1977; Andrew G. Walder, 'Marxism, Maoism and Social Change: A Reexamination of the "Voluntarism" in Mao's Strategy and Thought', *Modern China*, Vol. 3, No. 2, April 1977.

28 *Cf.*, Maurice Meisner, 'Communism and Maoism: Some Populist Perspectives on Marxist-Leninism in China', *The China Quarterly*, January–March, 1971, p. 18. Meisner's discussion of Mao's endorsement of capitalism for a limited period along the lines of Sun Yat-sen's notions and at the same time wishing to maintain his Nineteenth century Russia type Populist convictions is revelatory of this dilemma. *Cf.*, Meisner, *Mao Zedong*, p. 90.

29 *Cf.*, Benjamin Schwartz, *Chinese Communism and the Rise of Mao*, Cambridge: Harvard University Press, 1952, p. 76.

30 *Cf.*, Maurice Meisner, 'Communism and Maoism: Some Populist Perspectives on Marxist-Leninism in China', *The China Quarterly*, January–March, 1971, p. 31. Meisner interestingly writes that, 'The capitalist revolution that has transformed China over the past quarter-century would have been impossible without the achievements of the Mao period, especially national unification and land reform.' *Cf.*, Meisner, *Mao Zedong*, p. 196.

31 *Cf.*, Andrew G. Walder, 'Marxism, Maoism and Social Change', *Modern China*, Vol. 3, No. 1–2, January 1977; Andrew G. Walder, 'Marxism, Maoism and Social Change: A Reexamination of the "Voluntarism" in Mao's Strategy and Thought', *Modern China*, Vol. 3, No. 2, April 1977.

32 *Cf.*, 'Jung Chang and Jon Halliday, *Mao: The Unknown Story, A Review*', trans. Bi Wenjuan with Christopher A. Reed, Gregor Benton and Lin Chun, *Was Mao Really a*

Monster? The Academic Response to Chang and Halliday's Mao: The Unknown Story, London and New York: Routledge, 2010, p. 116.

33   Confucius, *Analects*, VIII, 9.

34   Stuart R. Schram, 'The Formative Years: A Preliminary Reassessment', 1917–1937, *Mao Zedong, A Preliminary Assessment*, Hong Kong: The Chinese University Press, 1983, p. 39.

35   Arthur A. Cohen, 'How Original is 'Maoism'? *Problems of Communism*, Vol. X, No. 6, 1961, p. 41. Cohen makes no mention of Orwell's masterpiece, *1984*, published in 1949.

36   Lynch makes this connection to Trotsky's notion of permanent revolution. *Cf.*, Michael Lynch, *Mao*, London: Routledge, 2004, p. 233. Trotsky was born Lev Davidovich Bronstein.

37   *Cf.*, Stuart Schram, 'Mao Tse-tung and the Theory of the Permanent Revolution, 1958–1969,' *The China Quarterly*, No. 46, April–June, 1971, pp. 221–244.

38   'On Practice,' *Selected Works of Mao Tse-tung*, Vol. I, Peking: Foreign Languages Press, 1967, p. 308 (emphasis added).

39   Ibid., p. 297. One must be careful, in my view, not to equate the dialectical relationship between theory or knowledge and practice with the dialectical relationship between superstructure and base. In the former, practice includes voluntary action; in the latter, the base may only refer to existing structural conditions such as the institution of private property.

40   Ibid., p. 297 (emphasis in original).

41   For Tian's discussions, *cf.*, Tian Chenshan, *Chinese Dialectics from Yijng to Marxism*, Lanham: Lexington Books, 2005, pp. 10, 159, 166–167.

42   Jerome Ch' en, *Mao Papers, Anthology and Bibliography*, London: Oxford University Press, 1970, p. 66.

43   In Snow's account of Mao's observation to him of the nature of revolution, his translation of this much-repeated phrase, 'dinner party' is rendered as 'tea party'. The meaning is much the same. *Cf.*, Edgar Snow, *Red Star Over China*, New York: Grove Press, 1968, p. 186.

44   Mao Zedong, 'Speech at Hangchow,' 21 December 1965, Stuart Schram (ed.), trans., John and Tieyun Chinnery, *Mao Tse-tung Unrehearsed, Talks and Lectures*, 1956–1971, Harmondsworth: Penguin Books, 1975.

45   This is not to say that Mao's thought was singularly influential in causing China's future. It is only to bring out the parallels between his thinking and what was to happen in his China. It is intended to demonstrate how Mao's philosophical overview can serve to assist to comprehend the myriad of changes that characterize China's growth now and into the future.

46   The propagation of Confucius Institutes throughout the world is a good example of this (though external propagation would not appear to be in line with traditional Chinese custom). Some have viewed the founding of these institutes as possible,

potential instruments of propaganda. Recent examples such as the University of Chicago terminating its Confucius Institute program may be perceived as illustrations of this viewpoint. Some have viewed these institutes as opportunities to share Chinese culture similar to the Goethe Institutes sharing German culture or the Alliance Française sharing French culture. They can also be viewed as opportunities for the scholarly study of the textual Confucius and Chinese culture in general. When I was personally invited to speak at the inaugural conference for Confucianism in Qufu, Shandong, in the early 1980s, I faced this issue along with my late Chair, colleague, co-editor and friend, Liu Shuxian. Since then, I have been willing to accept invitations to speak at Confucius Institutes.

SELECTED LIST OF REFERENCES

Allinson, R. (1991), 'A Cross-Cultural Understanding of Chinese Thought' (in Chinese translation), *Times and Trends of Thought, Dialectics of Cultural Traditions*, Shanghai: Communication & Research Center on Chinese-Western Philosophy and Culture, Shanghai, 71–80.

Allinson, R. (2011), 'Aristotle and Economics,' L. Bouckaert and L. Zsolnai (eds.), *The Palgrave Handbook of Spirituality and Business*, New York: Palgrave Macmillan.

Allinson, R. (1989), *Chuang-Tzu for Spiritual Transformation: An Analysis of the Inner Chapters*, 2006, Albany: State University of New York Press.

Allinson, R. (2004), 'Circles within a Circle: The Condition for the Possibility of an Ethical Business Enterprise Within a Market System', *Journal of Business Ethics*, 54: 261–277.

Allinson, R. (1998), 'Complementarity as a Model for East-West Integrative Philosophy,' *Journal of Chinese Philosophy*, 25 (4): 505–517.

Allinson, R. (1988), 'Confucius' Golden Rule' (Chinese translation), *History and Theory*, No. 3: 92–97, Bejing: Chinese Academy of Social Sciences, The Institute of World History.

Allinson, R. (1991), 'Contemporary Viewpoints on Compassion in the Case of the Small Child About to Fall in the Well in Mencius' (Chinese translation), *Journal of Fudan University*, Special Issue on 'Confucianism for the Future', 1st Edition, 107–117, Shanghai: Fudan University.

Allinson, R. and Liu, Shu-hsien, eds. (1988), *Harmony and Strife: Contemporary Viewpoints, East and West*, Hong Kong: Chinese University Press.

Allinson, R. (1986), 'Having Your Cake And Eating It, Too: Evaluation and Trans-Evaluation in Chuang Tzu and Nietzsche,' *Journal of Chinese Philosophy*, 13: 429–443.

Allinson, R. (2003), 'Hegelian, *Yi-Jing* and Buddhist Transformational Models for Comparative Philosophy', Mou, B. (ed.), *Comparative Approaches to Chinese Philosophy*, 60–85, Aldershot (UK), Burlington (USA), Sydney, Singapore: Ashgate Publishers.

Allinson, R. (2002) (Encyclopaedia Entry) 'Intercultural Hermeneutics, Chinese and Western Philosophy', A. S. Cua (ed.), *Encyclopaedia of Chinese Philosophy*, 315–320, London and New York: Routledge.

Allinson, R. (1996), 'Moral Values and the Chinese Sage in the *Tao de Ching*' (concluding chapter) B. Carr (ed.), *Morals and Society in Asian Philosophy*, Curzon Studies in Asian Philosophy, 156–168, London: Curzon Press.

Allinson, R. (1989, 2000), 'An Overview of the Chinese Mind' (opening chapter), R. E. Allinson (ed.), *Understanding the Chinese Mind: The Philosophical Roots*, 1–25, Oxford and New York: Oxford University Press.

Allinson, R. (1975), 'Self-Contradictory Propositions in Logic', The National Meeting of the Society for the Philosophical Study of Marxism, Oxford, Ohio: Miami University.

Allinson, R. (2008), 'Six Arguments for the Primacy of the Proscriptive Formulation of the Golden Rule in the Jewish and Chinese Confucian Ethical Traditions', P. Kupfer (ed.), *Youtai-Presence of Jews and Judaism in China*, 289–308, Frankfurt am Main, Berlin, Bruxelles, New York, Oxford, Vienna: Peter Lang.

Allinson, R. (1989), 'The Debate Between Mencius and Hsün-Tzu: Contemporary Applications', *Journal of Chinese Philosophy*, 25 (1): 31–50.

Allinson, R. (1990), 'The Ethics of Confucianism and Christianity: The Delicate Balance,' *Ching Feng, Quarterly Notes on Christianity and Chinese Religion and Culture*, Hong Kong, XXXIII (3): 158–175.

Arndt, A. (1981), Review of Francis Soo's, 'The Synthesis of Chinese and Western Philosophy in Mao Tse-Tung's Theory of Dialectics', *Studies in Soviet Thought*, 22 (3): 203.

Benton, G. and Lin, Chun (2010), *Was Mao Really a Monster? The Academic Response to Chang and Halliday's Mao: The Unknown Story*, London and New York: Routledge.

Billioud, S. and Thoraval, J. (2008), 'The Contemporary Revival of Confucianism, *Anshen Liming* or the Religious Dimension of Confucianism', trans. Christopher Storey, *Chinese Perspectives*, 3: 88–106.

Billioud, S. and Thoraval, J. (2014), *The Sage and the People, The Confucian Revival in China*, Honolulu: University of Hawaii Press.

Boorman, H. L. (1966), 'Mao Tse-Tung as Historian', *The China Quarterly*, Cambridge: Cambridge University Press, No. 28: 85.

Boorman, H. L. (1963), 'Mao Tse-Tung: The Lacquered Image' Vol. 16, *The China Quarterly*, Cambridge: Cambridge University Press.

Bowe, A. (1977), *Mao Tse-Tung, A Guide to His Thought*, New York: St. Martin's Press.

Briere, O. J. (1965), *Fifty Years of Chinese Philosophy from 1898–1948*, New York and London: Routledge.

Chan, W. T. (1961), 'Chinese Philosophy in Communist China,' *Philosophy East & West*, 11 (3): 115.

Cheek, T., ed. (2010), *A Critical Introduction to Mao*, Cambridge: Cambridge University Press.

Ch'en, J. (1965), *Mao and the Chinese Revolution*, trans. Michael Bullock and Jerome Ch'en, London, Oxford, New York: Oxford University Press.

Ch'en, J., ed. (1970), *Mao Papers, Anthology and Bibliography*, London: Oxford University Press.

Cheng, A. (1997), *Histoire de La Pensée Chinoise*, Paris: Éditions du Seuil.

Chin, S. S. K. (1979), *The Thought of Mao Tse-Tung, Form and Content*, trans. A. H. Y. Lin, Hong Kong: Centre of Asian Studies, University of Hong Kong.

China Now, 65, no. 2, October 1976: 2.

Chisholm, H., ed. (1911), 'Friedrich Paulsen', *Encyclopaedia Britannica*, 11th Edition, Cambridge: Cambridge University Press.

Christian Science Monitor, 4 June 1986. Available online: https://m.csmonitor.com/1986/0604/opoem.html

Chunjuan, N. W. and Brock, D. E. (2014), *Mr. Science and Chairman Mao's Cultural Revolution, Science and Technology in Modern China*, New York: Lexington Books.
Cohen, A. A. (1961), 'How Original Is "Maoism"?' *Problems of Communism*, X (6): 41.
Cohen, A. A. (1964), *The Communism of Mao Tse-Tung*, Chicago: The University of Chicago Press.
Confucius (2002), *The Analects*, trans. D. C. Lau, Hong Kong: The Chinese University Press.
Creel, H. G. (1953), *Chinese Thought from Confucius to Mao Tse Tung*, Chicago: University of Chicago Press.
Cua, A. S. ed. (2003), *Encyclopedia of Chinese Philosophy*, New York and London: Routledge.
Davin, D. (2013), *Mao, A Very Short Introduction*, Oxford: Oxford University Press.
De Bary, W. T., ed. (2001), *The Sources of the Chinese Tradition*, New York: Columbia University Press.
Dikötter, F. (2012), *Mao's Great Famine, The History of China's Most Devastating Catastrophe*, London: Bloomsbury.
Dikötter, F. (2016), *The Cultural Revolution, A People's History, 1962–1976*, New York: Bloomsbury Press.
Dikötter, F. (2013), *The Tragedy of Liberation, A History of the Chinese Revolution, 1945–57*, London, New Delhi, New York, Sydney: Bloomsbury.
Dirlik, A., P. Healy and Knight, Nick (1997), *Critical Perspectives on Mao Zedong's Thought*, Atlantic Highlands, NJ: Humanities Press.
Dunayevskaya, R. (1973), *Philosophy and Revolution, From Hegel to Sartre, and from Marx to Mao*, New York: Delacorte Press.
Engels, F. (1940), *Dialectics of Nature*, trans. and edited by C. Dutt, London: Lawrence and Wishart.
Fann, K. T. (1972), 'Mao and the Chinese Revolution in Philosophy,' *Studies in Soviet Thought*, 12: 111–123.
Friedman, E. (1983), 'Einstein and Mao: Metaphors of Revolution,' *The China Quarterly*, 93: 58.
Fitzgerald, C. P. (1977), 'Mao and the Chinese Cultural Tradition,' *Il Politico*, 42 (3): 483–493.
Fu, C. W. H. (1973-74), 'Confucianism, Marxist-Leninism and Mao: A Critical Study,' *Journal of Chinese Philosophy*, 1: 339–371.
Fu, C. W. H. (1975), 'Rejoinder to Professor Parson's Critical Remarks,' *Journal of Chinese Philosophy*, 2: 447.
Fu, Z. (1993), *The Autocratic Tradition in Chinese Politics*, Cambridge: Cambridge University Press.
Griffin, N. (2014), *Ping-Pong Diplomacy, The Secret History Behind the Game That Changed the World*, New York: Scribner.
Hegel, G. (1969), *Hegel's Science of Logic*, trans. A. V. Miller, Foreword by Professor J. N. Findlay, Amherst, NY: Humanity Books.
Heilmann, S. and Perry, E. J., eds. (2011), *Mao's Invisible Hand, The Political Foundations of Adaptive Governance in China*, Cambridge, MA: Harvard University Press.

Holubnychy, V. (1964), 'Mao Tse-tung's Materialistic Dialectics', *The China Quarterly*, 19 (July–September): 3–37.
Ji, X, et. al. (2016), *The Cowshed Memories of the Chinese Cultural Revolution*, New York: New York Review of Books.
Kaminsky, J. (2017), 'Toward a Maoist Dream of the Red Chamber: Or, How Baoyu and Daiyu Became Rebels Against Feudalism,' *Journal of Chinese Humanities*, 3: 190.
Karl, R. E. (2010), *Mao Zedong and China in the Twentieth Century World, A Concise History*, Durham: Duke University Press.
Kaufmann, W. (1974), *Nietzsche*, 4th Edition, Princeton: Princeton University Press.
Kaufmann, W. (1959), *The Portable Nietzsche*, edited and trans. W. Kaufmann, Harmondsworth, Middlesex: Penguin Books.
Kennedy, E. M. (2009), *The Compass, A Memoir*, New York: Hachette Book Group.
Kissinger, H. (2012), *On China*, New York: Penguin Books.
Kissinger, H. (2014), *World Order*, New York: Penguin Books.
Knight, N. (1992), Introduction: The Study of Mao Zedong's Philosophical Thought in Contemporary China,' *Chinese Studies in Philosophy*, 23 (3–4): 7.
Knight, Nick, ed. (1990), *Mao Zedong on Dialectical Materialism, Writings on Philosophy, 1937*, Armonk, NY: M. E. Sharpe, Inc.
Knight, N. (1980), 'On Contradiction and on Practice: Pre-Liberation Texts,' *China Quarterly*, 84 (December): 641–68.
Knight, N. (2007), *Rethinking Mao*, Lanham, MD: Lexington Books.
Koller, J. M. (1974), 'Philosophical Aspects of Maoist Thought,' *Studies in Soviet Thought*, 14 (1/2): 47, 56, 58.
Kraus, R. (2012), *The Cultural Revolution*, New York: Oxford University Press.
Kung, Y. C. (1983), '"Shih-chien" lun san t'i,' (Three points regarding 'On Practice), *Lun Mao Tse-tung che-hsüeh ssu-hsiang* (On Mao Tse-Tung's philosophical thought), 66–86, Peking: Jen-min ch'u-pan-she.
Lam, L. S. (2015), *Conservatism and the Kissinger-Mao Axis, Development of the Twin Global Orders*, Lanham: Lexington Books.
Lao Tzu, (1963), *Tao Te Ching*, trans. D. C. Lau, Harmondsworth, Middlesex: Penguin Books.
Lee, F. (2002), *Mao, A Reinterpretation*, Chicago: University of Chicago Press.
Legge, J. (1998), *The Chinese Classics in Five Volumes*, Taipei: SMC Publishing Inc.
Levine, N. (1976), 'Non-Marxist Elements in the Communism of Mao,' *Asian Thought & Society*, 1 (3): 307–332.
Levine, N. (1975), *The Tragic Deception: Marx Contra Engels*, Oxford: Clio Books.
Li, J. (1977), *The Early Revolutionary Activities of Comrade Mao Tse-tung*, J. C. Hsiung (ed.), trans. Antony W. Sariti, Introduction by Stuart R. Schram, White Plains, NY: M. E. Sharpe, Inc.
Lin, ke (1987), 'Memoirs of Mao Studying English', Yuzhi Gong, et al., (eds.), *Mao Zedong's Reading Life*, Beijing, China: Sanlian shudian.
Liu, H. (1994), *Beijing zhengfu dianzi duizhuangji* (*Beijing electron positron collider*), Beijing: Science Press.
Liu, J. (1971), 'Mao's On Contradiction,' *Studies in Soviet Thought*, 11: 71–89.

Liu, K. (2011), 'Poeticizing Revolution: Žižek's Misreading of Mao and China,' *Positions*, 19 (2): 627–651.

Liu, S. H. (1998), *Understanding Confucian Philosophy: Classical and Sung-Ming*, Westport, CT: Praeger Publishers.

Loewe, M. (2005), *Everyday Life in Early Imperial China*, Cambridge, MA: Hackett Publishing Company.

Lynch, M. (2004), *Mao*, London: Routledge.

Lynteris, C. (2013), *The Spirit of Selflessness in Maoist China, Socialist Medicine and the New Man*, London: Palgrave Macmillan.

MacFarquhar, R. and Schoenhals, Michael (2008), *Mao's Last Revolution*, Cambridge: Harvard University Press.

MacFarquhar, R. (1997), *The Origins of The Cultural Revolution*, Oxford and New York: Oxford University Press and Columbia University Press.

MacFarquhar, R. (1994, 1997, 2011), *The Politics of China, Sixty Years of the People's Republic of China*, Cambridge: Cambridge University Press.

Mao Tse-Tung (1988), *che-hsüeh p'i-chu-chi* (Mao Tse-tung's collected annotations on philosophy), Peking: Chung-yang wen-hsien yen-chiu-shih.

Mao Tse-Tung (1986), *chu-tso hsuan-tu* (selected readings from Mao-tse tung's writings), 2 vols. Peking: Jen-min ch'u-pan-she.

Mao Tse-Tung (1968), *Four Essays on Philosophy*, Peking: Foreign Languages Press.

Mao Tse-Tung (1981), *Mao Zedong's On Contradiction, An Annotated Translation of the Pre-liberation Text*, Nick Knight, Griffith Asian Papers, No. 3, Queensland: National Library of Australia, Griffith University.

Mao Tse-Tung (1967), *Selected Works of Mao Tse-Tung*, Vol. 1, Peking: Foreign Languages Press.

Mao Tse-Tung (1967), *Selected Works of Mao Tse-Tung*, Vol. 2, Peking: Foreign Languages Press.

Mao Tse-Tung (1967), *Selected Works of Mao Tse-Tung*, Vol. 3, Peking: Foreign Languages Press.

Mao, Tse-Tung (2004), http://www.marxistsfr.org/reference/archive/mao/selected-works/volume/9.

Marx, K. (1967), *Capital*, 3 vols. edited by F. Engels, trans. Samuel Moore and Edward Aveling, New York: International Publishers.

Marx, K. (1972), *A Contribution to the Critique of Political Economy*, New York: International Publishers.

Marx, K. (1973), *Grundrisse*, trans. Martin Nicolauss, New York: Random House.

Meisner, M. (1971), 'Communism and Maoism: Some Populist Perspectives on Marxist-Leninism in China,' *The China Quarterly*, 45: 30, 33.

Meisner, M. (1999), *Mao's China and After, A History of the People's Republic*, 3rd Edition, New York: The Free Press.

Meisner, M. (2007), *Mao Zedong, A Political and Intellectual Portrait*, Cambridge: Polity Press.

Meisner, M. (1970-71), 'Maoist Utopianism and the Future of Chinese Society,' *International Journal*, 26: 535–55.

Meisner, M. (1977), 'The Advantage and Burden of Backwardness on Maoism and Marxism at the Close of the Maoist Era', *Asian Thought & Society*, 2 (1): 40.
Meisner, M. (1999), 'The Significance of the Chinese Revolution in World History', *LSE Asia Research Centre Working Papers*, 1: 1 and 12.
Melby, J. F. (1872), 'Maoism as a World Force,' *The Annals*, 402: 26–39.
Munroe, D. J. (1971), 'The Malleability of Man in Chinese Marxism,' *China Quarterly*, 48: 609–640.
Nietzsche, F. (1989), *Beyond Good & Evil, Prelude to a Philosophy of the Future*, Translated with Commentary by Walter Kaufmann, New York: Random House.
Nietzsche, F. (1995), *Thus Spoke Zarathustra*, translated with a Preface by Walter Kaufmann, New York: Random House.
Nixon, R. (2012), Presidential Library and Museum Pantsov, Alexander V. and Levine, Steven L., *Mao: The Real Story*, New York & London: Simon & Schuster.
Paulsen, F. (1894), *System der Ethik*, Berlin: Verlag von Wilhelm Hertz.
Puett, M. and Gross-Loh, C. (2017), *The Path, What Chinese Philosophers Can Teach Us*, New York: Simon & Schuster.
Rudolph, J. and Szonyi, M., eds. (2018), *The China Questions, Critical Insights into a Rising Power*, Fairbank Center for Chinese Studies, Cambridge, MA: Harvard University Press.
Rue, J. E. (1967), 'Is Mao Tse-tung's "Dialectical Materialism" A Forgery?' *The Journal of Asian Studies*, 26 (3): 464–68.
Rue, J. E. (1966), *Mao Tse-tung in Opposition 1927–1935*, Stanford: Stanford University Press.
Sandel, M. J. and D' Ambrosio, P. J., eds. (2018), *Encountering China: Michael Sandel and Chinese Philosophy*, Cambridge: Harvard University Press.
Schaff, A. (1975), *Marxism and the Human Individual*, New York: McGraw-Hill Book Company.
Schram, S. (1971), 'Mao Tse-tung and the Theory of the Permanent Revolution, 1958–1969,' *The China Quarterly*, 46: 221–44.
Schram, S. (1967), 'Mao Tse-tung as a Marxist Dialectician,' review of Arthur A. Cohen, *The Communism of Mao Tse-tung*, *The China Quarterly*, 29 (January–March): 155–65.
Schram, S., ed. (1975), trans. John and Tieyun Chinnery, *Mao Tse-tung Unrehearsed, Talks and Lectures*, 1956–1971, Harmondsworth: Penguin Books.
Schram, S., ed. (1917–18), Mao Zedong, 'Marginal Notes to Friedrich Paulsen, *A System of Ethics*'.
Schram, S. (1992), *Mao's Road to Power, Revolutionary Writings*, 1912–1949, Vol. I, *The Pre-Marxist Period*, 1912–1920, Armonk, New York, London: M. E. Sharpe.
Schram, S. (1983), *Mao Zedong, A Preliminary Reassessment*, Hong Kong: Chinese University Press.
Schram, S. (1977), 'Some Reflections on the Pfeffer-Walder "Revolution: in China Studies"', *Modern China*, 3 (2): 169–84.
Schram, S. (1969), *The Political Thought of Mao Tse-tung*, New York: Praeger.
Schram, S. (1989), *The Thought of Mao Tse-tung*, Cambridge: Cambridge University Press.
Schwartz, B. (1952), *Chinese Communism and the Rise of Mao*, Cambridge: Harvard University Press.

Schwartz, B. (1955), 'On the "originality" of Mao Tse-Tung', *Foreign Affairs*, 34: 74.

Schwartz, B. (1970), 'The Maoist Image of World Order', *Communism and China: Ideology in Flux*, New York: Atheneum, 228–42.

Short, P. (1999), *Mao: A Life*, New York: Henry Holt and Co.

Shi, Z. (1992), 'A New Document for the Study of Mao Zedong's Philosophical Thought: Introducing *The Philosophical Annotations of Mao Zedong*,' *Chinese Studies in Philosophy*, 23 (3–4). *Cf., Hongqi (Red Flag)*, No. 17(1987), trans. Nick Knight.

Snow, E. (1968), *Red Star Over China*, New York: Grove Press.

Snow, E. (1972), *The Long Revolution*, New York: Random House.

Somerville, J. (1968), 'Ontology, Logic and Dialectical Materialism,' *International Philosophical Quarterly*, 8: 113–124.

Soo, F. Y. K. (1981), *Mao Tse-Tung's Theory of Dialectic*, Vol. 44, Dordrecht, Boston, London: D. Reidel Publishing Company.

Spence, J. (2010), *Mao Zedong*, London: Penguin Books.

Starr, J. B. (1986), '"Good Mao", "Bad Mao": Mao Studies and the Re-Evaluation of Mao's Political Thought,' *The Australian Journal of Chinese Affairs*, 16: 1–6.

Su, S. (1992), 'The Study of Mao Zedong Thought in Contemporary China,' *The Philosophical Thought of Mao Zedong, Studies from China, 1981–1989, Chinese Studies in Philosophy*, 23 (3–4): 60.

Szonyi, M., ed. (2017), *A Companion to Chinese History*, Oxford: John Wiley & Sons, Ltd.

Terrill, R. (1980), *Mao, A Biography*, New York: Harper & Row.

Thaxton, R, Jr. (2008), *Catastrophe and Contention in Rural China*, Cambridge: Cambridge University Press.

Tian, C. (2005), *Chinese Dialectics from Yijing to Marxism*, Lanham: Lexington Books, Rowman & Littlefield Publishers Group.

Ts' ao, I. J. H. (1977), 'Mao Tse-Tung and China's Fate,' *Asian Thought & Society*, 2 (1): 135–146.

Tu, Wei-ming, *Humanity and Self-Cultivation: Essays in Confucian Thought*, Boston: Cheng & Tsui Company, 1998.

Wakeman, F. (1977), 'A Reexamination of the "Voluntarism" in Mao's Strategy and Thought: A Response', *Modern China*, 3 (1–2): 161–168.

Wakeman, F. (1973), *History & Will: Philosophical Perspectives of Mao Tse Tung's Thought*, Berkeley, Los Angeles, London: University of California Press.

Walder, A. G. (2015), *China Under Mao, A Revolution Derailed*, Cambridge and London: Harvard University Press.

Walder, A. G. (1977), 'Marxism, Maoism and Social Change', *Modern China*, 3 (1–2): 110.

Walder, A. G. (1977), 'Marxism, Maoism and Social Change: A Reexamination of the "Voluntarism" in Mao's Strategy and Thought', *Modern China*, 3 (2): 125–160.

Wang, R. (2002), *Xin faxian de Mao Zedong: Puren yanzhong de weiren (A Newly Discovered Mao Zedong: The Great Man in the Eyes of His Servant)*, Hong Kong: Mingbao chubanshe.

Watson, B. (1968), *The Complete Works of Chuang Tzu*, New York: Columbia University Press.

Wilhelm, R. trans. (1967), *The I Ching* or *Book of Changes*, rendered into English by Carey F. Barnes, Foreword by C. G. Jung, Bollingen Series XIX, Princeton: Princeton University Press.

Wilson, D., ed. (1978), *Mao Tse-Tung in the Scales of History, A Preliminary Assessment Organized by the China Quarterly*, Cambridge: Cambridge University Press.

Wittfogel, K. A. (1963), 'Some Remarks on Mao's Handling of Concepts and Problems of Dialectics', *Studies in Soviet Thought*, III (4): 251–269.

Wu, N. K. (1993), *A Single Tear: A Family's Persecution, Love and Endurance in Communist China*, Canada: Little, Brown & Company.

Xu, Q. (1992), 'From the "Negation of the Negation" to "Affirmation and Negation" in Mao Zedong's Thought,' *Chinese Studies in Philosophy*, 23 (3–4).

Yang, C. (1978), *Lun Mao Chu-hsi che-hsüeh t'i-hsi* (*On Chairman Mao's philosophical system*), Hsi-yang ti-ch'ü yin-shua-so, 2 vols.

Yang, J. K., et al. (1973), *Chien-ming Chung-kuo che-hsüeh shih* (*A Brief History of Chinese Philosophy*), Peking: Jen-min ch'u-pan she.

Yang, C. N. (1985), *Dushu jiaoxue sishinian* (*Learning and teaching for four decades*), Hong Kong: Hong Kong Branch of Sanlian Press.

Zarrow, P. (1990), *Anarchism and Chinese Political Culture*, New York: Columbia University Press.

Zhang, Everett, Kleinman, Arthur and Tu, Weiming (2011), *Governance of Life in Chinese Moral Experience, the Quest for an Adequate Life*, New York: Routledge.

Zhang, W. (1992), 'Mao Zedong's Critical Continuation of China's Fine Philosophical Inheritance,' *Chinese Studies in Philosophy*, 23 (3–4): 117, 120.

Zhou, X. (2013), *Forgotten Voices of Mao's Famine, 1959–1962*, New Haven and London: Yale University Press.

Žižek, S. (2007), *On Practice and Contradiction, Mao tse-Tung*, London, New York: Verso.

Žižek, S. (2011), 'Revolutionary Terror from Robespierre to Mao,' *Positions*, 3 (19).

INDEX

All in One Self-Study Notes 32
Altruism 41–2, 45–7, 50, 57, 60–2, 77–8, 93, 99, 178
American Revolution 30, 32, 186
Analects 70–1, 75–6
Anti-Dühring 162
Aristippus 30
Aristotle 44–5, 49, 58, 65–70, 76, 88–9, 154
   On Noble actions 62
Aristotle and Confucius 44–5, 65–70, 76
Augustine 37, 62

Bentham 30, 44, 54
Benton, Gregor 2
Bethune, Norman 46
Bluntschli, Ike 28
Bohr, Niels 102
   on complementarity 102
Book of Changes. *See Yijing*
Bourgeoisie 129, 137, 173, 175
Bradley, F.H. 30
Buddhism 46–7, 133

Cai, Yuanpei 36
Capital 146, 162
Capitalism 101–2, 108–9, 115–17, 137–8, 171, 174, 177
Catherine the Great 30–2
CCP 7
Cheek, Timothy 7, 162, 176
Ch' en, Jerome 23
Chen, Yung-fa 178
Chinese Classics 22, 31, 95, 106, 111, 117, 164
Chong, Yinghong 158
Chuang-Tzu 152
Class Struggle 8

Cohen, Arthur 143–5, 169–70, 180
A Commentary on the Philosophical Thought of Mao Zedong 9
Communist Manifesto 8, 162
Confucianism 16, 19, 22–4, 26, 40, 51, 67–8, 71, 74–5, 97–8, 100–2, 111–18, 166, 175
   Book of Filial Piety 74–5
   Modern Revival of Confucianism 19, 114, 117
   Song Confucianism 26
   tension with Capitalism 101
Confucius 7, 11, 20, 22, 40–1, 44–5, 49, 65–77, 94, 114, 117–18, 151–2, 164, 178–80, 188
   Central Ethical Principle 73
   Extension of Love to Society 71–3
   The Great Learning 69–70
   Influence on Mao 70
   Self-Sincerity as Opposed to Self-Love 69–70, 76–7
   Separation of Happiness and Morality 45–6, 49, 66–7, 88
Confucius and Aristotle. *See* Aristotle and Confucius
Creel, Herlee 21
A Critique of the Gotha Program 162
Cultural Revolution 3–5, 13, 27, 48, 69, 88, 104–6, 108, 115–16, 119, 155, 178, 186
Cunning of Reason 103, 182

Daodejing 10, 18, 104–5, 135
Daoism 10, 104–6, 140
Darwin 30, 138
de Gaulle, Charles 166
Deng, Xiaoping 101, 112–13
Dewey, John 29

Dialectic 9–12, 100–3, 108–13, 121–7, 130–3, 142–5, 169–73, 180–1, 183, 185
   Hegelian Dialectic 101, 109–11, 113, 124, 126–7, 131–2, 139, 185
   Aufheben 109–10
   Mao's Dialectic 110–11
   Marxist Dialectic 108–9, 123, 128, 173
   Primary and Secondary Aspects 184
On Dialectical Materialism 143–4
Die List der Vernunft. *See* Cunning of Reason
Dikötter, Frank 4
Dream of the Red Chamber 163–4
Duke of Wellington 32
Dunayevskaya, Raya 161

Earl of Oxford 149
The Economic and Philosophic Manuscripts of 1844 145, 162
Engels 12, 122, 124–5, 130–1, 133, 145–6, 160, 172, 177–8
Epicurus 30, 87
Existentialism is a Humanism 53, 87, 90

Fairbank, John K. 1
Fann, K. T. 46
Fichte 30, 44, 54, 101
Filial Piety 72–5
Findlay, John 121
First Provincial Middle School 30
First Teachers Training School 25
Fitzgerald, C. P. 5
Five-Year Plan 5
Fourth Normal School in Changsha 25, 68
French Revolution 28
Freud 22, 54, 98

German Idealism 25, 31, 100
German Ideology 146
Ginsberg, Allen 116
Gladstone, William Ewart 30
Goethe 30
Great Leap Forward 3, 5, 115
Great Way 105

Green, T.H. 30, 98
Grundrisse der Kritik der Politischen Oekonomie 162

Hegel 14, 30, 31, 84, 101, 103, 109–14, 117–18, 121–8, 131–3, 136, 139, 141, 158, 162, 170–3, 176, 180–2, 185
Hegelianism 114
Heidegger 118–19
Heraclitus 185
Hexagram(s) 84, 100–2, 128, 134
Hillel 58, 73
Hindenburg, Marshal 27
History of Socialism 8
Hobbes 30, 37, 40, 50, 57, 60, 106–7
   Safeguard for Unbridled Egoism 106
Holtzendorff 28
Holubnychy 125, 145, 169
Homer 119
Huxley, T.H. 30

Infinity 125, 158, 160
   The problem with evaluating it 125

Kaminsky, Johannes 165
Kant 7, 26, 30–1, 37, 42, 44, 50, 52–5, 66, 98, 101, 154, 178
Karl, Rebecca 22
Kaufmann 91
Kautsky, Karl 8
Keynes, John Maynard 17
Kirkup, Thomas 8
Kissinger, Henry 166–7
Knight, Nick 1, 7, 9, 11–12, 122–3, 143–5, 148, 170
Koller, John M. 175
Kraus, Richard 163
Kropotkin, Peter 8

Lam, K. C. 163–4
Laozi 14, 18, 104–5, 118–19
   His influence on Mao's formulation of the Cultural Revolution 105–6
Lau, D.C. 67–8, 81

Lee, Feigon 2, 145
Lee, T. D. 158
Leibniz 30, 37, 63
Lenin 125–7, 130, 136, 144, 160, 162, 164, 174, 176–7, 182–3
Levine, Steven 8, 162
Li, Jiu 38
Lin, Chun 2
Lincoln, Abraham 30, 32
Liu, Kang 147–8
Liu, Rong 7–9
Liu, Shaoqi 7, 69, 162–3
Locke 107
Lord Acton 85

Machiavelli 30
Mao
    Application of Philosophy as Ideology 147
    Applying Philosophy to suit his purposes 49, 81
    As a bridge between Contemporary China and Confucianism 188
    Comparative Philosophical Tendencies 54–5
    Comparative Philosophical Training 29, 31
    Confucianism's Influence on Mao 70
    On Contradiction 9, 121–2, 124, 127, 138–9, 141, 143, 145, 148–9, 170
    Contradictions in Mao's Philosophy 135
    On the Correct Handling of Contradictions 129, 137
    Critique of Chinese Education 32
    Critique of Engel's Triplicity 124
    Critique of Paulsen's Altruism 41
    Critique of Schopenhauer's Ethics 45
    On Death 86–7
    Departure from the Classical Chinese Notion of Harmony 102
    Deviation from the Concept of The Great Harmony 84
    Distinction between Antagonistic and Non-Antagonistic Contradictions 130, 135
    Egoistic origins of Altruism 52
    Endorsement of Chinese Studies 69
    Idea of the Great Man 4, 20, 39–40, 80–2, 85, 166, 178, 186
    Intermediate Synthesis 101–2
    Love of Philosophy 17–20
    Mao's marginal notes 19, 29, 32, 35, 37–9, 43, 50–1, 56, 63, 84, 106, 111, 136, 151, 160, 166, 178, 180
    Mao's Metaphysics 82–4
    As a Marxist 108
    As a Monist 130
    On the necessary connection between the Natural World and Humanity 83
    On Objective Morality 42
    Philosophy of Egoism 16–17, 24, 35, 37, 39–40
    Poetic Abilities 32
    On Practice and Contradiction 9, 143, 145, 149, 169, 182–3
    Preference for Analytic and Systematic Thinking 33, 44
    Pre-Marxist Thought 7–8, 11–12, 15, 17, 19, 27, 37, 79, 108, 137, 149, 160
    Primacy of the Individual 39, 64, 99
    Primacy of the Will 39–40, 92, 98, 167, 176–7
    Principal and Secondary Aspects of Contradictions 138
    Rejection of The Great Harmony 84, 103–4, 118
    Rejection of Hegelian Synthesis 133
    Self-actualization as the foundation of Ethics 42, 44, 47–8, 89–91
    Self-studies 28, 35
    Similarities between his temperament and philosophical tendencies 98
    On Social Welfare 99
    Study of the Four Books and the Five Classics 22
    Synthesis of Chinese and Western Philosophy 14–15, 19, 26, 33, 47, 54–5, 97, 106, 141

On Universal Love 58, 71–3
Mao and Aristotle 66
   On the pursuit of happiness 88
Mao and Confucius 69–77
Mao and Hobbes 106–7
Mao and Marx 108–9
Mao and Mencius 68–9, 77–9
Mao and Nietzsche 88–92
Mao and Paulsen 35–44
Mao as an illiterate peasant 23, 25, 29
Maoism 146–7, 174–5
Maoist revolution 1
Mao's marginal notes. See under Mao
Market socialism 101, 108–9, 113, 117
Marx. See Marxism
Marxism 6–14, 16, 18–19, 24, 29, 39, 79, 102–3, 108–10, 112, 127, 136–7, 140, 142–3, 145–8, 164, 169, 171, 173–7
Maslow, Abraham 59
Meisner, Maurice 2, 9, 21, 26–7, 145, 166, 171, 174, 177
Mencius 14, 20, 40, 57, 67–8, 72, 74–5, 77–8, 80–2, 86, 98–100, 106, 166, 178, 187
   Exclusion of Egoism from Altruism 77–8
   Greater Emphasis on Filial Piety than Confucius 72–5
   Mao's adaptation of Mencius 80–2, 99
Mill J.S. 30, 44, 54
The Mirror of Government 162
Mohism 46–7
The Monkey 23
Montesquieu 30
Mozi 47, 71
   Doctrine of Universal Love 71

Napoleon 30–2, 55, 80, 141, 166
Napoleonic War 32
Needham, Joseph 29
Negation of Negation 103, 121–9, 131, 133, 136, 139
Neo-Confucianism 26, 54–5
The New Youth 26–7

Nichomachean Ethics 85
Nietzsche 14, 30, 32, 40, 52–3, 62, 83, 88–92, 98–9, 106
   The Overman 90–2, 99
   As the Reviser, rather than Abandoner, of all Values 89
   Three Metamorphoses 91
   Twilight of the Idols 32, 89
Nixon 166, 168

Orwell, George 179

Pantsov, Alexander 8
Paulsen, Friedrich 4, 14–15, 19, 25, 29, 31, 35–6, 37–41, 43, 45, 53–8, 60–3, 68, 78, 79, 80–3, 85, 86–8, 92, 97, 98, 103, 111–12, 122, 126–7, 136, 141, 144, 156, 160, 166, 176, 178, 180
   Paulsen's strong influence on Mao 14–16
Payne, Robert 21
People's Republic of China 13, 23, 108
Peter the Great 30, 32
The Phenomenology of Mind 176
Plato 30–1, 85, 100, 119
   The Philosopher King 100
Politburo Colleagues 165
Pre-Marxist 7–8, 11–2, 15, 17, 19, 27, 37–8, 79, 108, 136–7, 141, 149, 160
Principle of Self-Cultivation (*xuishen*) 68–70, 86
Proletariat 8, 108, 129, 137, 171, 173–5

Republic 100
The Romance of the Three Kingdoms 23, 163
Rousseau 26, 30, 57
Rue, John E. 173–4
Russell, Bertrand 29
Russia 32, 55, 108, 164, 170

Sakyamuni Buddha 46
Sartre 53, 87, 90, 116
Schopenhauer 14, 28, 30–1, 37, 45, 52, 83, 98, 101, 178

Schopenhauer's Concept of Will as an influential idea for Mao 98
Schram, Stuart 3, 4, 6, 8, 9, 24, 29, 49, 71, 110, 111, 114, 122, 123, 126, 127, 129, 131, 136, 142, 143, 144, 155, 161, 173, 175, 179
Schwartz, Benjamin 171, 177
Self-Actualization
   Unsuitability as an Ethical Foundation 48
Shakespeare 149
Shi, Zhongquan 170
The Short Course 3
Short, Philip 164
Similarities in Agent and Act Morality 67
Smith, Adam 17, 30
Snow, Edgar 29, 93, 116, 144, 163
Snyder, Gary 116
Socrates 87–8
Spencer, Herbert 26, 30
Spinoza 30, 31, 37, 44, 54, 63, 84, 88, 101, 140, 156
Stalin 2–3, 126–8, 130, 143–5, 174–6
Starr, John Bryan 2
State Capitalism 108
State of Nature 106–7
Stoicism 30, 54
Sun, Yat-sen 11, 25
Sun, Yixian. *See* Sun, Yat-sen
A System of Ethics 14–15, 19, 31, 35, 38–9, 43, 141, 166

Talk on Questions of Philosophy 134, 152
Tawney, R.H. 29
Teiwes, Frederick 4
Temporary end of Classical Chinese Thought 103
Terrill, Ross 26, 30–1, 92, 162–3, 168
Thilly, Frank 36
Tian, Chenshan 162
Tillich, Paul 59
Tolstoy 28
Trotsky 181
Ts' ao, Ignatius 148

United States of America 152, 164
Unity of the Opposites 123–4, 127–31, 134, 137–8

Voluntarism 79, 82, 95, 97–8, 127, 145–6, 179, 182

Wakeman, Frederick 8, 26, 30, 163–4
Walder, Andrew 3, 146–7, 177
Waldron, Arthur 1
Wang, Fu-chih 26
Wang, Ruoshui 162
Warring States Period 104
Washington, George 30–2, 80, 166, 186
The Water Margin 23
Wilde, Oscar 27, 31, 41, 165, 180
   The Ideal Husband 41
   The Importance of Being Earnest 180
   Influence on Mao 31, 41
   Lord Goring 41
Willmott, Bill 4
Wittfogel, Karl. A 143

Xiao, San 30
Xiao, Zisheng 32, 69
Xu, Quanxing 122

Yang, Changji 17, 25, 29, 68
   nicknamed "Confucius" 26
Yang, Zhu 24, 95
Yang, C. N. 158
Yang, Kaihui 17, 25
Yijing (*Book of Changes*) 10, 12, 84, 99–102, 109–14, 117, 121, 123–6, 127–8, 133–4, 139–40, 142, 144, 161, 171, 178, 181, 185–6
   Mao's adaptation of the *Yijing* 121
   Mao's dialectical adaptation of the *Yijing* 110
Yin-Yang 9–10, 12, 101, 113, 123, 128, 133, 139, 141, 154, 156, 161, 171, 186
   Yin-Yang Complementarity 102
York, Alvin, Prussian General 55

Yoshimaru, Kanie 36
Yuen, Chen Ming 5

Zarathustra 91
Zhang, Wenru 11
Zhou, Enlai 7, 159, 160
Zhou, Peiyuan 159–60

Zhuangzi 14, 49, 93–5, 104–6, 118, 149, 152–3, 157, 160, 164
   story of the Cicada Catcher 49, 93–5
Zhu, De 7
Zhu, Guangya 158
Žižek 115, 124–5